100 THINGS CANUCKS FANS SHOULD KNOW & DO BEFORE THEY DIE

100 THINGS CANUCKS FANS SHOULD KNOW & DO BEFORE THEY DIE

Thomas Drance
and Mike Halford

Library of Congress Cataloging-in-Publication Data

Names: Drance, Thomas, 1987– author. | Halford, Mike, 1979– author.
Title: 100 things Canucks fans should know and do before they die / Thomas Drance and Mike Halford.
Other titles: One hundred things Canucks fans should know and do before they die
Description: Chicago, Illinois : Triumph Books LLC, [2017]
Identifiers: LCCN 2017010953 | ISBN 9781629373454
Subjects: LCSH: Vancouver Canucks (Hockey team)—Miscellanea. | Hockey—British Columbia—Vancouver—Miscellanea. | Hockey—Canada—Miscellanea. | Hockey—United States—Miscellanea.
Classification: LCC GV848.V36 D73 2017 | DDC 796.962/640971133—dc23 LC record available at https://lccn.loc.gov/2017010953

This book is available in quantity at special discounts for your group or organization. For further information, contact:

Triumph Books LLC
814 North Franklin Street
Chicago, Illinois 60610
(312) 337-0747
www.triumphbooks.com

Printed in U.S.A.
ISBN: 978-1-62937-345-4
Design by Patricia Frey
Photos courtesy of AP Images

To my loving and supportive wife, Laura, whom I fell in love with during the 2010–11 Canucks season.
—Thomas Drance

To my mom, who is mad I wrote a book before she did. To Grayson, the unquestioned love of my life. And to my dad, who always reminded me to drive safely.
—Mike Halford

Contents

Foreword

Every NHL team has its stories. Unfortunately, the Canucks don't have a Stanley Cup story. Making it to the Finals is one thing, but every hockey player's ultimate goal is to hoist the Cup. That said, teams that *don't* win often tend to have the better stories. And that can certainly be said of Vancouver. From the very beginning, the Canucks have had a story; from the initial draft of 1970 to the riots of 1994 and 2011, this franchise has its own unique history.

I have been fortunate enough to be part of this history, both as a player and a broadcaster. I've watched my teammate, Tiger Williams, ride his stick down the ice in celebration. I've also seen Tiger, in an almost equally memorable moment, go after Randy Holt.

As a broadcaster, I've experienced a lot. I worked through the ill-fated Mike Keenan and Mark Messier era, and watched John Tortorella storm into the visitor's locker room during an intermission to get at Flames head coach Bob Hartley.

I also witnessed the rise of the Canucks as they captured back-to-back Presidents' Trophies; the skill and competitiveness of Trevor Linden, Markus Naslund, and future Hall of Famers Henrik and Daniel Sedin; and much more. The Canucks are the embodiment of great stories...and great entertainment.

100 Things Canucks Fans Should Know & Do Before They Die touches on all those stories, taking an in-depth look at the history and nuance of a truly unique market. I hope you're entertained by this book.

—John Garrett

1 Brace for the Pain

First, know this: it's not easy being a fan of the Canucks. Though the modern Canucks have shed the doormat status they toiled in for their first 20 years, it's fair to say that the greatest moments in franchise history remain near misses, marred by civic catastrophe. Oh, and there were the losses.

Throughout Vancouver's history, few teams in the National Hockey League have been defeated with such regularity. Among the league's 30 teams, only recent expansion outfits Florida, Columbus, and Tampa Bay have a lower regular-season winning percentage.

And then there's the heartbreak. The Canucks have been to Game 7 of the Stanley Cup Finals twice. And they've lost, twice. No other NHL team has done that.

There's something grim—yet appropriate—about those high-profile losses, and the higher-profile riots that followed. What makes being a Canucks fan so difficult, after all, isn't so much the losing or the scattered moments of public embarrassment. It's the repetition.

Some of the best Canucks stories involve patterns of hard luck and failure—patterns that often repeat, as history is wont to do. Like, say, trading a franchise icon to the Florida Panthers. Or, say, a gruff American head coach forcing a beloved player out the door. Often, bad things in Canucks history have happened in twos, so bracing for pain is inherently crucial to the experience. Longtime supporters not only know that things will go badly but also *when* they'll go badly. They can generally spot catastrophe from several kilometers out.

If there's one thing, then, that should be on every Canucks fan's bucket list, it's to make peace with the masochistic nature of fandom. It's an essential survival skill, necessary to preserve sanity.

So how does one achieve the Buddhist-style detachment required to root for the Canucks? It helps to have a support group.

Though we—the authors of this book—have both grown up into objective adult professionals (depending on whom you talk to) we have also been die-hard Canucks fans for the better part of our lives. And many of our lifelong friends—not to mention fans we interact with in the digital realm—talk regularly about the possibility of dying without seeing Vancouver win the Stanley Cup. It's a grim subject for sure, but it's also a shared experience. A singular connection that serious Canucks fans will always have with one another.

One can detect evident dark pleasure—gallows humor, if you will—when Canucks fans recall their darkest moments. Nathan LaFayette's shot ringing off the post. Jonathan Toews' game-tying shorthanded goal. The first five minutes of Game 6 of the 2011 Stanley Cup Finals. Whatever the case, there's a willingness to nurture a collective wound, if only for the way it binds Vancouver hockey fans together.

That social element, that shared experience, is what hockey fandom is all about. Professional sports are entertainment, the "toy department of life," as legendary NBA coach Pat Riley famously put it. And it should be noted that this most recent generation of Vancouver's hockey fans—you lucky, lucky souls—have now genuinely been treated to some quality hockey over the past two decades.

Quite truly, the Canucks have gone from being "the L.A. Clippers of the NHL" to being a model franchise. In terms of revenue, the organization consistently ranks in the top five and, on the ice, has enjoyed a tremendous run of success. This will play a major role in this book. We'll relive some great moments and hear from some of the characters and power players who keyed the franchise's maturation. And we hope our unique experiences growing up with the franchise will allow us to shed some new light on some familiar stories, and offer fresh perspective on some of the greatest and most memorable moments in Canucks history.

Despite the litany of disappointments, this team has forged a deep connection with the city of Vancouver. It's an idiosyncratic and unconventional hockey market in one of Canada's most idiosyncratic and unconventional cities. So perhaps the connection hasn't been forged in spite of, but *because of*, the unique spirit of fatalism so peculiar to local fans. Maybe bracing for pain is secretly part of the fun.

2 Vancouver Has Long Been a Center of Hockey Innovation

Not that you need a reminder this early in the book, but the Canucks have never won a Stanley Cup. That said, more than 100 years ago a Vancouver-based pro team *did* manage to win hockey's ultimate prize.

The Vancouver Millionaires won the first Stanley Cup contested by teams outside Canada in 1915. Founded by Frank Patrick, the Millionaires began playing in the Pacific Coast Hockey Association in 1911. Frank; his brother, Lester; and their father, Joseph, started the PCHA and ran it as a successful business for 15 years.

In 1907 Joseph—who had come to Nelson, BC, after running a general store in Drummondville, Quebec—sold his business, Patrick Lumber Company, for just shy of $500,000. Joseph's sons, Lester and Frank, were talented hockey players based in Montreal, with Frank playing at McGill University while Lester played for a Montreal Wanderers team that won the Stanley Cup. (During the Challenge Cup era, the Stanley Cup was contested several times per year. The Millionaires won the Stanley Cup in the first year it began to be awarded annually.)

In terms of raw purchasing power, the money from the sale of Patrick Lumber Company would be worth more than $11 million today, a relatively pedestrian amount, but it was enough for Joseph and his sons to embark on a grand project—the PCHA—that would change the trajectory of professional hockey. The inaugural season began in 1912, one year after the founding of the PCHA. Initially the league was comprised of three teams: the New Westminster Royals, the Victoria Senators, and the Vancouver Millionaires.

To facilitate games in Vancouver's mild climate, the Patricks built a "mechanically frozen" artificial ice surface at Denman and Georgia Streets. Back when Vancouver's picturesque Coal Harbour meant exactly that—a harbor of coal—the Denman Arena in Vancouver was a marvel of modern engineering and the first indoor, permanent hockey rink of its kind.

At the time of its construction, the Denman Arena had the capacity to seat 10,500 people, making it one of North America's largest coliseums. The Denman Arena quickly became an important meeting place in the city, hosting everything, including the opera, boxing, evangelist preachers, and public skating. In some ways, the arena helped drive the urban development of downtown Vancouver.

"It was a magnet for entertainment," hockey historian Craig Bowley told Joe Pelletier. "It was probably the most important cultural center in the city. If you look at the city at this time, you

Taking Wings

Jack Adams played one year for the Millionaires before moving to the Victoria-based PCHA franchise and winning the Stanley Cup in 1925. When the Patrick family folded their western-based hockey league—the PCHA had merged into the WCHL in 1924—and sold their players and teams east for $300,000, the Cougars relocated to Detroit and eventually were renamed the Red Wings.

Cyclone Taylor: The Man and the Myth

Though the PCHA and WCHL were both the Patricks' show—Frank was a player, coach, and owner—the Millionaires player whose name even still reverberates in Vancouver is Fred "Cyclone" Taylor. Taylor was the team's biggest star and is honored annually by the Canucks, who award the Cyclone Taylor Trophy to their team MVP. His name is also recognizable to Vancouver hockey fans for the eponymous hockey equipment retailer, Cyclone Taylor Sports, which has four locations across the lower mainland.

Taylor bridges Vancouver's ancient and contemporary hockey history, and lived to see the inauguration of the Canucks NHL franchise. At the first Canucks team's first home game on October 9, 1970, the 87-year-old Taylor was introduced during a pregame ceremony as "Vancouver's hockey man of the century."

The response to Taylor was in stark contrast to what the fans had given then–Vancouver mayor Tom Campbell, who Canucks fans booed "out of habit," according to *Vancouver Sun* reporter Denny Boyd. Taylor's introduction, meanwhile, was met with "tumultuous cheers."

see a big block of wood [and] you wonder what it's doing there. It was used for everything." (Though the arena was originally constructed of wood, it was retrofitted with brick in 1936 so it would better withstand the threat of fire. Ironically, the arena burned to the ground later that same year.)

Beyond the technical and cultural innovation of an indoor rink with a mechanically frozen surface, the Patricks—who were businessmen first and foremost—came up with the idea to put numbers on the backs of players' sweaters to make individuals more easily recognizable and marketable. In recent years we've seen Vancouver often—and incorrectly—portrayed as being somehow "outside" the traditional historical hockey sphere, but the fact is a lot of simple things regarding the appearance and facilitation of the contemporary game can be traced to the West Coast.

Of the Patrick boys, Lester was a more shrewd innovator. While Frank managed and played for Vancouver's franchise, Lester was the steward of the PCHA's Victoria-based club, which was first named the Senators, then the Aristocrats, and eventually the Cougars.

It was Lester who pioneered the forward pass and the blue line. Tactically, he was the first to allow his goaltenders to dive onto the ice to stop shots and cut off the bottom of the ice. In all, Lester advocated for several rule changes that were adopted internationally and are still reflected in the modern game.

During the Millionaires' run, 13 future Hall of Fame players dressed for the club, including legendary Montreal Canadiens forward Newsy Lalonde and Detroit Red Wings coach Jack Adams, for whom the NHL's Coach of the Year Award is named.

3 An Identity Forged in Obscurity

High-level professional hockey was absent from the Vancouver market for 44 years after the Maroons and the West Coast Hockey League departed. Somewhat ironically, it was during these lean years that a unique Canucks identity was forged.

A variety of minor league clubs populated the city throughout the 1930s and '40s, often playing in the Vancouver Forum, in mostly forgotten circuits such as the Northwest Hockey League or the Western Canadian Hockey League.

In 1945 Vancouver had a team named the Canucks. The club debuted in the Pacific Coast Hockey League and was owned and managed by a tough-talking hotelier named Coleman E. "Coley" Hall, who would eventually become a minority owner of the NHL Canucks.

The Name Game

Here is a list of the names of professional minor league or semiprofessional minor league teams that played in Vancouver in the 1930s and 1940s:

- The Lions
- The Maroons
- The Towers
- The Ex-King George
- The Amateurs
- The Maple Leafs
- The Cubs
- The Quakers
- The Young Liberals

The PCHL Canucks began recruiting players just 10 days before their first season started. Those players—12 in total—mostly comprised World War II veterans and working Joes playing for beer money. The most notable name on the roster was Bernie Bathgate, whose brother, Andy, ended up in the Hockey Hall of Fame.

The original Canucks traveled in beat-up limos, with the players taking turns as chauffeurs. Players were each given three dollars to spend on meals when the club was on the road, and all thought it was a grand deal. It was professional hockey but minor league professional hockey, a massive step down from the grandeur of the NHL.

The Canucks won the PCHL championship that first year, and again in 1948. In 1952 the Canucks joined the Western Hockey League, adding four more titles before joining the NHL in 1970.

In many ways, the early identity of the Canucks was forged during these seasons. The PCHL team used the iconic Johnny Canuck logo on one of their sweaters, and another included the word Canucks emblazoned on the chest—in similar fashion to the club's contemporary blue Vancouver sweater. Yet another Canucks jersey used by the PCHL club included a flying *V*, albeit with a significantly toned-down blue-and-red color scheme.

After transitioning to the WHL, Vancouver was able to attract a variety of future NHL stars and Canucks executives. Orland Kurtenbach, who went on to captain Vancouver's inaugural teams and coach the club in the late 1970s, played a season in 1958. Phil Maloney, who eventually became the Canucks' general manager and guided the team to its first-ever playoff berth, starred on the teams that regularly won WHL championships.

There was also an abundance of talent in-net. Johnny Bower, Gump Worsley, Tony Esposito, and Bruce Gamble spent time with the WHL Canucks, as did future New York Rangers coach Emile Francis.

In addition, Jim Robson, who took over as the play-by-play announcer for the WHL teams in the 1950s, went on to become the voice of the NHL Canucks for generations of fans.

It wasn't big-league hockey, but at the time Vancouver didn't really view itself as a big-league city. Even after *Hockey Night in Canada* debuted on television in 1952, Vancouverites didn't exactly harbor mature ambitions of competing against the likes of the Montreal Canadiens and the Toronto Maple Leafs. It wasn't long before that all changed.

4 The Canucks Got a Franchise Over Smythe's Dead Body

In August 1964 Toronto Maple Leafs president Stafford Smythe, the heir to Maple Leaf Gardens, touched down in Vancouver with a plan. Smythe wanted the city to grant him an attractive two-block piece of downtown real estate that included the old bus depot at

Seymour and Dunsmuir Streets. The property was valued at $2.5 million, but he only wanted to pay a token $1 amount. In return, Smythe promised he'd build an $8 million 20,000-seat arena within two years. He'd also throw in, as part of the deal, the goodwill of Toronto's voting block when it came time for the NHL to discuss expansion.

There was little disagreement about the city's need for a new arena. The Vancouver Forum was dingy, even in comparison to some of the other WHL rinks. When legendary comedian Bob Hope described the old Forum as "one of the nicest garages I've ever played in," most Vancouverites just nodded. If Vancouver was ever to attract an NHL team, the city needed a more suitable barn.

The arena proposal exposed nerves in Vancouver's psyche. The attention from a major NHL figure, as Denny Boyd put it, "inflamed the hockey passions" of the dormant West Coast market. When Smythe landed with his plan and architectural model of Vancouver Gardens, he brought with him the "realization that perhaps Vancouver had been too long in the hockey boondocks, that perhaps the city had big-league potential and that perhaps the NHL might some day open the golden gates to another Canadian team."

Talk of a new arena, though, was complicated. Everyone agreed the Forum was insufficient, and most agreed it would be a thrill to host regular NHL hockey in Vancouver. But nobody could agree on where the new arena should be located—much less how to pay for its construction.

Even before Smythe arrived, the debate pitted powerful interests against one another. The Pacific National Exhibition, unsurprisingly, wanted a new stadium to be built on its grounds, like the Forum was. The Downtown Business Association, as its name might imply, wanted a multipurpose downtown arena and had a proposal at the ready.

The debate became quite vocal, with politicians and hockey dignitaries of all stripes chiming in publicly. Showing genuine foresight, then–Vancouver mayor William Rathje thought the plan to give away $2 million of prime downtown land to "anyone" was something he couldn't do. Instead, Rathje proposed the city offer Smythe an extended 125-year lease. BC premier W.A.C. Bennett, meanwhile, backed Smythe by offering generous tax incentives.

The matter was to be settled by plebiscite in the 1964 mayoral election. If Smythe's plan were to be approved, it would require "more than three-fifths" support from voters. The "bylaw sale of land as a site for a sports coliseum" ultimately "failed to receive assent" from voters, and by a wide 27-point margin.

Why did Smythe's plan fail so spectacularly to appeal to the Vancouver electorate? Well, for a variety of reasons. It certainly hadn't helped Smythe's case when NHL president Clarence Campbell stated, on the record, that a new rink in Vancouver didn't necessarily guarantee an expansion franchise. Vancouver's voters may have also been moved by a general sense of western skepticism—a sense inflamed by loose talk of Smythe's other plans for the property.

"Smythe and his assistant, Harold Ballard, came west to promote their plan, but turned off many with their brash approach," wrote hockey historian Joe Pelletier. "Westerners were always weary of Easterners' exploiting intentions. Some rumors had Smythe building a hotel and racing track on the property, too."

The result of the vote infuriated Smythe, who lashed out at the denizens of Vancouver. Calling it a "bush town," Smythe vowed to the media and the heavens that the city would never get an NHL franchise "in [his] lifetime."

Smythe was unable to make good on his threat. When the NHL officially confirmed the Canucks would be awarded an expansion franchise in January 1970, Smythe had been deposed as president of the Maple Leafs, but he was still alive and kicking.

5 The Big Fumble

"It is too bad the Vancouver group fumbled the ball so badly when they had it in the first place. It would have been in the best interest of the NHL to have another Canadian franchise."

—NHL president Clarence Campbell

When, in 1965, the NHL announced plans to double its six-team league beginning with the 1967–68 season, it had been four decades since Vancouver had had top-level professional hockey. The time seemed ripe for the city and a variety of moneyed interests to make moves for a team.

Frederick Hume led the way. Nicknamed Friendly Fred, Hume was a self-made man, a colorful personality, a passionate sportsman, and a talented lacrosse player. Born in New Westminster, Hume was an effective businessman who became the largest electrical contractor in western Canada in the early part of the 20th century. At heart, though, Hume was a politician, and at 29 was elected alderman in New Westminster. Less than a decade later, he'd serve as mayor.

Hume moved to West Vancouver and became a staple of the community. He began a tradition of decorating his British Properties home with a massive Christmas lights display, a practice continued by the house's current owner, business magnate Jim Pattison. And despite living in a neighboring community, Hume was elected mayor of Vancouver proper in 1950.

A true believer in the civic power of athletics, Hume cherished a long-held dream that Vancouver could be home to a major professional sports team. And beginning in the 1950s, he put his focus on hockey. In 1962, when the WHL Canucks were struggling with financing, the aging and affable career politician purchased the team. When a deal to purchase and finance half the team, with the New York Rangers covering the other half, fell apart—fortunately, as it turns out, because it may have complicated Vancouver's NHL expansion bid—Hume bought the team outright and financed it himself. It wasn't a perfect outcome, but from Hume's perspective, it was better than seeing the sport leave Vancouver once again.

Vancouverites were parched for high-level professional hockey, and the NHL's announcement of a plan to expand to six teams for the 1967–68 season only deepened the city's thirst. Hume, who saw an opportunity to realize his lifelong dream of bringing a big-league team to Vancouver, was first to act.

The offer was generous. Hume would construct a 22,000-seat rink on the Pacific National Exhibition grounds, and would do so with no guarantee that an NHL team might, in short order, be awarded to Vancouver. The idea was that a state-of-the-art barn might serve to entice the NHL to choose Vancouver over the many other expansion bidders.

Ultimately all three levels of government ended up providing a combined $5 million of the $6 million in funds to construct the Pacific Coliseum, which opened in January 1968 with the Ice Capades. Hume's gesture, and ownership of the WHL Canucks, made it plain that any credible expansion bid would go through him.

Hume's legacy of sports-related philanthropy in Vancouver was unmatched in his time, but he turned 72 in 1965, and his health was failing. He had the team and he had the money, but he needed someone to carry the torch across the finish line.

So he began looking for a suitable group to which he might sell his team and associated hockey interests. The one that initially stepped up was led by an oil baron named Frank McMahon, who headed a cabal of well-heeled investors that included former

Vancouver Sun owner Max Bell and legendary hockey broadcaster Foster Hewitt.

Hume and McMahon completed a handshake agreement, on the condition that the strictest secrecy regarding the sale be maintained. And it was all but done until a reporter, chasing down a scoop about the pending sale, approached McMahon for a quote, which he fatefully provided.

Hume was furious. Reversing course, Hume sold the WHL club to Cyrus H. McLean—a silver-haired board member of the British Columbia Telephone Company (later BC Tel). There were now two competing groups interested in landing Vancouver's first NHL franchise, but McLean's group owned the team and held the cards. Hewitt defected from the McMahon group, joining McLean for their expansion pitch to the NHL governors.

The pitch itself was an unmitigated disaster. According to Denny Boyd, the McLean group was "virtually laughed out of the meeting room." Why were the NHL's governors so unmoved by the presentation from McLean's group? For one thing, it wasn't nearly as well financed as McMahon's. In fact, McLean and Hewitt were initially greeted with a telling remark of "Where's my friend Frank McMahon?" from Blackhawks governor Jim Norris.

McLean certainly believed the die was cast before he and Hewitt even made their presentation. He later remarked that he'd been "set up as a patsy." Though it's clear the NHL preferred McMahon, it was reluctant to have three teams based on the West Coast, preferring to go with two instead. The McLean group was likely competing with other bidders for one of two open expansion slots, rather than for six. What's more, the Oakland and Los Angeles groups were able to offer the league a significantly more attractive television market, which surely worked in their favor.

Denny Boyd also suggests—though he admits nothing was said on the record—that the NHL wasn't eager to jump into bed with Hall. He was notorious for his short temper and pushiness, which Boyd suggests may have made the NHL somewhat squeamish. The McLean group minimized Hall's standing on paper, giving him an advisory title, but "Hall was never for a minute out of the picture."

Whatever the NHL's ultimate motivation, they declined to award Vancouver an expansion team at that time. The league instead expanded—with varying levels of success—into Philadelphia, Pittsburgh, Los Angeles, Oakland, St. Louis, and Minnesota, with each of the six new ownership groups paying a quaint $2 million expansion fee. Vancouver's NHL dream would have to wait.

6 The Purchase

Western alienation has, over time, comingled with repeated disappointments among Vancouver hockey fans and produced a unique character and outlook. Vancouverites harbor suspicions that their team and city aren't always respected or done right by the rest of the hockey world. Sensitive to real and imagined slights and suspicious of the intentions of the East Coast—NHL executives and sports media personalities alike—this sense of grievance can be traced almost directly to the founding of Vancouver's NHL franchise.

In the aftermath of Smythe's rejected arena plan, Smythe's vengeful comments after the fact—particularly his description of Vancouver as a "bush town"—fueled notions that the NHL was hostile to Vancouver's hockey interests. Clarence Campbell's comments, which referred to the Cyrus McLean bid during the initial round of NHL expansion in 1966 as a "fumble," comprised yet another round of humiliation.

As hockey became increasingly central to the Canadian national identity through the latter half of the 20th century, the stakes of landing an NHL franchise were raised. For many Vancouverites in the 1960s, it began to feel as if the NHL was—to paraphrase Boyd—denying them their national heritage. Outraged locals even organized boycotts of brands that were closely associated with the league, including Molson Breweries and Imperial Oil.

The lingering sense of grievance was real, but it wasn't persistent. Relative to the power of hope—hope that high-level professional hockey might soon return to Vancouver—boycotts and the like didn't stand a chance.

In December 1967 the groups led by McLean and Frank McMahon joined forces, releasing an overly dramatic statement that promised that an NHL team would soon come to Vancouver. "We will push forward in a united front in what continues to be everyone's prime objective," McLean said. "That is, to bring the NHL to Vancouver at the earliest possible date."

While construction of the Pacific Coliseum neared completion and the NHL prepared to play its first season as a 12-team league, another possible avenue for entry into the hallowed halls of NHL competition presented itself.

It didn't take long for some of the NHL's six newest markets to begin to struggle. Attendance was modest and money was tight for the Pittsburgh Penguins, but even more pressingly, the California Golden Seals were unable to draw fans, and their owner, Barend Van Gerbig, was already experiencing buyer's remorse.

Van Gerbig asked the NHL if he might move the team, but the league wasn't prepared to allow that. So he sold the team to Labatt Brewing Company, contingent on their ability to "move the club to Vancouver." The iconic Canadian brewer "made three separate offers to place the franchise in Vancouver," wrote Denny Boyd, "but the proposition never got as far as the NHL because there were no takers in Vancouver." For Vancouver, it was Canucks or bust.

In the summer of 1968, it became apparent the NHL was again considering expansion, and this time the league was making positive noises about Vancouver's chances. McLean, McMahon, and the Canucks' founding fathers sent a $25,000 bond to the league to secure their place at the presentation table.

It was at this point the Canucks group brazenly pushed their chips into the middle. The club purchased the entire roster—31 players, including a knuckle-dragging defenseman named Don Cherry—and head coach Joe Crozier of the American Hockey League's Rochester Americans in August 1968, for a sum of nearly $1 million.

Vancouver didn't have an NHL team yet, but the Canucks had acquired an expensive roster and one of the most highly regarded young head coaches in the world. The enthusiasm was real. As Crozier said boastfully at his introduction, "We're going to the NHL, so let's all get on the bandwagon and go."

7 Sticker Shock

Today, the National Hockey League is a multibillion-dollar business. Contemporary teams—even those that consistently operate at a loss—are valued in the hundreds of millions, and no one bats an eyelash when a star player signs for an annual salary of $5 million or more. But before arena sponsorship, dynamic ticket pricing, inflationary pressure on broadcast rights, collective-bargaining agreements, and corporate boxes were the norm, the business of hockey was relatively quaint.

There's an anecdote in Dan Robson's biography of Pat Quinn, *Quinn: The Life of a Hockey Legend*, about a heated exchange between a die-hard Canucks fan and team owner Frank Griffiths in the 1970s. On one evening as the Canucks were being soundly beaten at home, a fan spotted Griffiths, recognized him, and hurled an insult in his general direction. "I'm sick and tired of wasting $18 on this crap!" he yelled. "Well, I'm sick and tired of wasting $50,000 a night on this crap!" was Griffiths' reply.

The money and stakes involved in professional hockey have increased enormously, clearly. An $18 ticket in 1976, even when adjusted for inflation, is a massive bargain in today's climate. And $50,000 a night to ice an NHL-caliber lineup seems like a pittance compared to the 2015–16 Canucks, who cost ownership an estimated $950,000 in salary on a per-game basis.

But contemporary sports fans (or sportswriters) are so used to throwing around mind-bending figures when discussing the business side of the sport, that any discussion of sticker shock in the 1960s and '70s seems rather adorable. The fan who verbally accosted Griffiths didn't have the benefit of our hindsight; $18 then, which is more like $75 today, *was* a lot to pay for a ticket, and $50,000—more like $225,000 today—*was* a lot to spend on the players. Especially when the players were dogging it nightly on a losing team.

By the time of the 1968 NHL expansion, Vancouver's bid was virtually a foregone conclusion. The Pacific Coliseum opened during the 1968–69 WHL season, just in time to spotlight the new-look Canucks, armed with an AHL-caliber roster, as they ransacked their way to a championship.

"The league is committed to Vancouver," said David Molson, president of the Montreal Canadiens, titillating the city's hopeful hockey fans. "If we expand again, it will have to be by two cities to facilitate scheduling, but when you have two weak sisters, you have to be a little hesitant about going out and adding two unknowns."

The troubled clubs Molson was referring to were the Pittsburgh Penguins and California Golden Seals, teams that were losing money and struggling to draw fans. That loomed over the process in a way that will seem familiar to any contemporary NHL fans who have followed the efforts of Quebecor to secure a return of the Quebec Nordiques in recent years.

And indeed, there was another round of efforts to move the Golden Seals north and into Vancouver, which the NHL again rebuffed.

In September 1969 the NHL came to Vancouver and announced their plan to expand by two teams—the Buffalo Sabres and the Vancouver Canucks—for the start of the 1970–71 season. But instead of the long-anticipated sounds of unrelenting joy, the announcement landed with a thud. The NHL was demanding the two new expansion franchises pay $6 million each, which was basically what the six teams from the 1966 round of expansion had paid combined. Considering two of the six were openly described as financial failures, the Canucks found the terms obscene. "I wouldn't be interested at that price," Frank McMahon said. "Two years from now, you'll be able to go out and buy almost any expansion club you want for less." Coleman Hall, meanwhile, called the price "ridiculous."

For Coach Joe Crozier, the problem wasn't so much the total cost—it wasn't his money, after all—but rather the protected lists, which would govern the expansion draft. The rules allowed NHL teams to protect 17 skaters, 2 goaltenders, and all first-year players. Basically, Buffalo and Vancouver would be able to select a minor league goaltender or—in theory—the worst player on any particular team's roster. "At $6 million, it means we have to pay $300,000 each for players who wouldn't have been able to make our last year's WHL team!" exclaimed Crozier.

After a half-decade-long crusade to land an NHL team, one had been granted to the unified Canucks ownership group. An NHL team was on offer, but none of the many Canucks owners were willing to foot the $6 million bill.

8 The Problem with Carpetbaggers

Over the past 25 years the Vancouver Canucks have developed into a model NHL organization. That's not to say there aren't some problems, but in a macro sense, the Canucks are "haves" and not "have-nots." They spend to the upper limit of the salary cap, and ownership consistently allows management to sign relatively expensive minor league deals, ensuring solid depth. The club employs an above-average number of scouts, and the team's digital team and public relations department are among the best in hockey.

Canucks players are treated to excellent facilities that will be bolstered further with the construction of a practice facility in the next few years. Vancouver also hosts a preseason Young Stars tournament and regularly finishes in the top five teams in the league in generating revenue, per *Forbes*.

Despite the club's vast on-ice and financial improvements, owner Francesco Aquilini and the Aquilini Investment Group routinely faces criticism in Vancouver. Credible sources claim the current Canucks ownership group may have a penchant for micromanagement, but in no industry outside hockey is it seen as "beyond the pale" for owners to take an active role in the management of their property. And it's a simple, unavoidable truth that the Canucks have enjoyed their golden era under the stewardship of the Aquilini Investment Group.

Now, we don't mean to say contemporary Canucks fans are spoiled. Nor do we intend this as a defense of some of the odder things that have occurred during the Aquilini era. We present this as context, because we're about to discuss the Canucks' first owner, Thomas K. Scallen.

With the then-exorbitant $6 million expansion fee staring them in the face, the Canucks' founding fathers—Coleman Hall, Cyrus MacLean, Frank McMahon, and the like—found themselves without the means to actually secure the team they'd been granted. They made desperate pitches to the league, even suggesting the NHL should expand by four teams rather than two, to reduce the expansion burden.

The league wasn't having it. Denny Boyd later wrote:

> The NHL told the principals of the Vancouver hockey operation that if they were not ready to put their money where their pleading mouths had been for so many years, then the NHL, itself, would take the money initiative.
>
> And furthermore, the Vancouver people were told, if you don't like the way we do things and try to interfere, we will call a press conference in your town and we will tell the public that only your waffling and stubbornness are keeping the NHL away.

Then the NHL went money hunting on Vancouver's behalf.

In searching for a partner who would foot the bill, several NHL governors agreed Minnesota's Medical Investment Corporation, known as Medicor, was a promising potential partner. Scallen, Mecdicor's president, was a sharp financial operator—though not sharp enough, as it would turn out—who through a series of clever maneuvers diversified a small private medical equipment leasing firm into a genuine, publicly traded entertainment company. Scallen owned the Ice Follies and had champion figure skater Peggy Fleming signed to an exclusive deal. As such, Scallen was seen as a natural fit by the NHL. He already knew how to put on a show on ice.

So Scallen, along with Medicor vice president Lyman Walters, essentially took over from the men who had campaigned so long and so hard for an NHL franchise in Vancouver. On December 22,

1969, the deal was done: Scallen had purchased four dozen players, two minor league professional franchises, and head coach Joe Crozier—with whom he would clash incessantly. In short order, the NHL officially granted Vancouver an expansion franchise.

Though Scallen struggled to properly pronounce the name of the city in which he owned an NHL team, Vancouver welcomed him warmly. Most of the city's residents were just desperate, at long last, to have a team to call their own. No fans or local print media "were so cavalier as to suggest that Minneapolis ownership of a Vancouver hockey club amounted to a genteel form of carpetbagging," wrote Boyd. But in Canucks history, things have often been dysfunctional when businessmen hailing from south of the 49th parallel have owned the club. John McCaw and Orca Bay would, in due time, get an undeservedly bad rap for their ownership tenure, leaving the Scallen era as the most egregious example.

Walters was the first of the Medicor people to really step in it when he, perhaps under the influence of a strong cocktail or two, was quoted casting aspersions on the Canucks moniker. "I'm not completely sold on the team name," Walters said. "The word *Canucks* strikes me as a slang expression that I don't particularly like. If there are no serious objections, we are going to consider a change."

The locals didn't like that, and the new Canucks owners were forced to promptly walk it back. Scallen released a statement saying he'd been briefed on the history of "the Canadian fighting man" Johnny Canuck and was now "happy to let the name stand." It went mostly downhill from there.

Only two years had passed since the previous Canucks ownership regime paid $1 million to Rochester for Crozier's services when Scallen fired him amid charges of "rank insubordination."

In truth, some of the drama surrounding Crozier predated Scallen. An excellent tactician, well-liked by fans and respected by players, Crozier was prideful and jealous of his autonomy and not nearly as good at managing up as he was at managing his skaters.

Crozier and Hall had already butted heads when Hall suggested—publicly—that he wasn't sure if Crozier had the experience to be the team's first NHL bench boss (which Boyd has insisted prompted an inebriated call from Crozier to McLean, who was in Victoria at the Government House, dressed to the nines, at an "elite government reception").

Finally, in February 1969, things came to a head. There had been a bit of a dustup in the press about Punch Imlach, a Crozier pal, who had been on the payroll at $25,000 a year without ownership's direct knowledge. Hall and Crozier had a public back-and-forth on the matter, with McLean ultimately siding with Hall.

Scallen arrived at the Pacific Coliseum shortly before a game, determined to clear the air. He told team PR man Greg Douglas to go get Crozier, because he wanted to talk to him. Douglas called down to the locker room, but the team trainers refused to get Crozier on the phone. Scallen sent Douglas running down to fetch him directly. "Tell him to go stuff himself," was Crozier's reply to Douglas. "I got a hockey game."

You might imagine Crozier's response wasn't well received in the president's suite, but Douglas—a Crozier loyalist—smoothed things over, promising to produce the coach at the first intermission. When he went to do so, however, Crozier resumed his militant stance. "Stuff that guy," Crozier repeated, according to Denny Boyd. "You go back and tell him I've been writing to him and trying to phone him for weeks and he's never answered me, and there's no goddamned way I'm crawling to him now. And tell him I said he can stuff himself." And that was the end of that, really.

Crozier considered crashing the press conference the next morning when it was announced he'd been fired, even showing up at the rink, where Hall refused to shake his hand, calling him a "lying bastard."

"When Joe refused to meet with us, he put himself ahead of the club," Scallen explained to the press. "Crozier has many fine qualities, but no man can come ahead of the club. He is fired for rank insubordination."

Lawyers got involved—Crozier sued the team for $35,000—and the dispute was eventually settled. Money aside, this was a brutal look for a nascent NHL franchise. Crozier was supposed to be the Canucks' first coach and general manager, yet now the team looked dysfunctional—and had just seven months to build a management structure ahead of its inaugural campaign, set to begin in October 1970.

9 The Ballad of Bud Poile

"I'm more embarrassed than anyone else. I've had success everywhere else except here, the place I want to live."

—Bud Poile

In the immediate lead-up to the launch of the NHL experiment in Vancouver, the Canucks found themselves without a general manager or a head coach, and with a lawsuit pending from the man they'd just relieved of both duties. Good start.

Amid the chaos, the Canucks chose to turn to Norman "Bud" Poile, a loyal hockey lifer—and yes, the father of current Nashville Predators GM David Poile. At the time of the Crozier dismissal, the elder Poile had only recently joined the Canucks front office in the nebulous role of assistant to President Tom Scallen.

Poile was an ultimate hockey vagabond. He served his country in World War II and played for five of the six original six teams before leaving the NHL for good at the age of 27 for a career in coaching. While building a résumé as a coach and manager, Poile worked in Tulsa, San Francisco, Glace Bay, and Edmonton, learning the game from the ground up.

When Poile finally landed an NHL gig—he had been passed over by the Detroit Red Wings organization, despite being Jack Adams' handpicked successor—it was with the expansion Philadelphia Flyers. His time working for Ed Snider in Philadelphia was short-lived and tumultuous. Though Poile played a big part in acquiring Bobby Clarke and Bernie Parent, his two seasons in Philadelphia were difficult. The experience left a sour taste in Poile's mouth, and he wasn't exactly looking to jump headlong into the mix with another fledgling expansion franchise.

But when the Crozier situation exploded, Poile seemed a suitable enough man for the job. And what's more, he was already there. Overnight, Poile went from an advisory position, in which he was expected to help plan for the expansion draft, to the general manager of an organization with an expansive portfolio. Poile had to do it all: staff the team with players and coaches, build the business side, and manage an expansion and amateur draft—all while massaging the expectations of an ill-defined and chaotic ownership group. "I was really in a bind," Poile recalled to Denny Boyd.

Coleman Hall had hired Poile for the advisory position, and the two knew each other from some of Poile's minor league stops. The brash hotelier, who spent much of his time in Hawaii, promised Poile and his family an all-expenses-paid trip to the volcanic islands the day Poile brought the Stanley Cup to Vancouver for the first time. "Crissakes, Coley," Poile responded. "By the time we do that they'll have built a bridge to Hawaii!"

At least Poile had a sense of the challenges that lay ahead of him. He had very little staff, very little time, and very little luck.

Poile made a variety of mistakes along the way, and his tenure in Vancouver was ultimately cut short due to illness, but it's tough not to feel for him. He was thrown headfirst into a difficult situation, and while the on-ice product he produced was iffy, Poile was an excellent marketer and showman. Even as the losses piled up throughout his Canucks tenure, the team always sold tickets.

In fact, Poile's tenure was marked by innovation on the business side. The Canucks became one of the first NHL teams to sell a program with a different cover on the front for every home game, which proved a profitable initiative. And despite 50 losses in that inaugural 1970–71 season, Poile managed to oversee an expansion of season ticket packages from about 6,500 in year one to more than 15,000 in year two.

He also deserves tremendous credit for the grace and good humor with which he handled even the worst news or situations. "When I played for the Canucks, I was never really in GM Bud Poile's office," Pat Quinn—who was claimed by Vancouver in the 1970 NHL Expansion Draft—recalled to author Jason Farris following Poile's death in 2005. "I learned about Mr. Poile later on, first when he was running the Central League and then the International League, and I found out what a good man he was and how he cared about the players."

In *The Vancouver Canucks Story*, Boyd relates a story that seems a perfect metaphor for Poile's time in Vancouver. As Boyd tells it, one night Poile treated Vancouver's traveling media members to dinner and drinks at a high-end establishment in Calgary. Among the broadcasters, journalists, and other luminaries in attendance was Jim Robson, who was seated beside Poile. During the dinner Poile finished a glass of red wine, and Robson reached into a nearby wine bucket and produced a bottle that he was certain was nearly empty.

What Robson didn't realize was the waitstaff had replaced the previously empty bottle with a fresh one. So Robson turned a completely full bottle upside down over Poile's glass, causing the wine to rush out and cover the Canucks GM "throat to knees" with Beaujolais. Poile examined his stained attire for a while before telling Robson patiently, "Uh, no more for me. Thanks, Jim."

The ability to joke was a skill that, by the end of his Vancouver tenure, Poile had seemed to perfect. When news broke that Canucks owner Tom Scallen was facing charges of having stolen $3 million in club funds in 1972, Poile was hosting a variety of local and visiting Boston media for a luncheon. "I've got some good news and some bad news," Poile said to the media in attendance, clearing his throat. "The good news is that our owners have been charged with swiping $3 million. The bad news is that we have to play the Bruins tonight."

10 Black Tuesday

In the long history of the Canucks' tough breaks, the legend of Black Tuesday stands out. Though popular retelling has warped the story, Canucks fans still talk about Black Tuesday in hushed, pained tones 45 years later.

"Vancouver Canucks [fans] will always remember June 9, 1970, as 'Black Tuesday'" wrote *Vancouver Province* reporter Tom Watt (not to be confused with the future Canucks coach of the same name). "It's a day they would sooner forget—the day their number did not come up. No one who was part of the large audience in the Grand Salon of the Queen Elizabeth Hotel Tuesday will ever forget the snub the Canucks took from Lady Luck."

The NHL didn't have a draft lottery until 1995. As such, it wasn't often in those days a team's fortunes were so heavily altered by pure luck. Black Tuesday was a rare exception. On that fateful Tuesday in 1970, all 14 NHL clubs gathered in a conference room at the Queen Elizabeth Hotel in Montreal for the expansion draft. Before it took place, though, there was a pressing matter to determine: which of the two new expansion teams—the Canucks or the Buffalo Sabres—would get the No. 1 pick at the 1970 amateur draft.

The stakes were tremendous. Several prospects were available—well-regarded defenseman Dale Tallon and forward Darryl Sittler to name two—but there was one major prize up for grabs: Gilbert Perreault.

First, the league held a coin flip to determine which expansion franchise would have first dibs on any player placed on waivers by the other 12 NHL clubs. Sabres general manager Punch Imlach won the coin toss.

There would then be two spins of a big red-and-white prize wheel, numbered 1 through 12. These spins would determine whether the Sabres or the Canucks would pick first in the expansion draft. This would be followed by a subsequent spin, which would determine the order of the 1970 amateur draft and who'd win the chance to pick Perreault.

Imlach, because he'd won the coin toss, got to choose between the high numbers or the low numbers, and he picked the high numbers, meaning any spin that landed on a number from 7 to 12 would give the Sabres the first pick in the expansion draft, and any spin that landed on a number from 1 to 6 would result in the Canucks selecting first.

NHL president Clarence Campbell spun the prize wheel, which landed on 8. In the expansion draft, which was to take place that day, the Sabres would select first. Then it was time for the most important and impactful spin. The Sabres once again had the high numbers, and the Canucks had the low. Randomness would determine the future trajectory of the two newest NHL franchises over the next decade.

1970 Expansion Draft Comparison

Canucks

Positional breakdown: 8 centermen, 3 wingers, 7 defensemen, 2 goalies
Average Age: 27.6
Total games played: 1,857
Total Goals: 255
Total Assists: 437
Total Points: 693

Sabres

Positional breakdown: 2 centermen, 3 wingers, 10 defensemen, 2 goalies
Average Age: 27.1
Total Games Played: 1,637
Total Goals: 168
Total Assists: 401
Total Points: 569

"Remember it's Buffalo high, Vancouver low!" Campbell helpfully and ironically reminded the room as he removed his glasses and put his right arm on the prize wheel, mugging for television cameras in the smoke-filled room.

The wheel whirled, the clapper jittering loudly as it smacked the pins. As the wheel slowed, the clapper clicked narrowly past the final few numbers: 5, 9, 3. It looked for a second like it was going to stop, but didn't, jumping over one last pin to land on 11.

Now, this is where things get interesting. There are numerous fantastical iterations of the story that exaggerate the Canucks' bad luck. An older Canucks fan, perhaps after a few pregame drinks, might tell you that the indicator of the prize wheel jammed, making it look like Vancouver had won the spin. Nope. Any version of the Black Tuesday story that includes something spectacular like equipment malfunction is false.

There are other, toned-down variations of the story in which Campbell thinks the number is a 2 in roman numerals (i.e. II instead of 11), causing him to mistakenly announce the Canucks had won the right to pick first overall. That's closer to the real story but also not what happened.

Here's the real story: The wheel was poorly designed from a visual standpoint. The two-digit numbers were arranged in a strange and confusing manner. Instead of the number 11 being displayed with the numbers appearing side by side, the prize wheel displayed the number 11 with two ones on top of one another.

"The number is one!" Campbell announced in the room, to roars of celebration. Then, to the chagrin of the Canucks, he quickly changed his ruling, admitting, "I miscalled it."

The Sabres table stood, applauded, and cheered. They'd won waiver priority, the first pick in the expansion draft, and the first pick in the amateur draft. It was a coup.

Almost 50 years have passed since Black Tuesday, and the Canucks have yet to pick first overall in the draft.

This incident is often cited as the start of some curse, a bad omen of things to come for the Canucks. Losing out of Perreault was a tough blow, but it wasn't robbery and it wasn't all that unlikely. A 65-year-old man removed his glasses before the crucial moment when he'd have to read a number off a poorly designed prize wheel. When literally the single-most-unreadable number on that wheel came up, he flubbed the announcement. It was as simple as that.

11 The Canucks Got the Best of the 1970 Expansion Draft—and It Didn't Matter

The 1970 NHL expansion draft was stacked against the Vancouver Canucks and the Buffalo Sabres, and rival NHL general managers knew it. Though both paid hefty expansion fees by the standards of the day, the league's 12 existing members were permitted to protect scores of their players—17 skaters plus two goaltenders per team—making it nearly impossible for the Canucks and the Sabres to build a team that could compete quickly. So when both teams lost boatloads of games in their first two seasons, it was no real surprise.

Arriving at the NHL's annual meetings in Montreal in mid-June, executives such as Emile Francis of the New York Rangers were all but boasting publicly to reporters about how well they'd planned for the expansion draft, and how they weren't going to lose anything of substance.

The Canucks picked second, but there's no doubt Bud Poile and the Canucks mined more talent from the expansion draft than the Sabres did. They found a future captain in Orland Kurtenbach; some quality offensive contributors such as winger Wayne Maki and productive forward Rosaire Paiement; some reliable stay-at-home defensemen—including Pat Quinn—and solid young blueliners who would contribute for several years, such as Barry Wilkins.

Overall, players selected by the Canucks at the 1970 expansion draft played more games for the franchise, scored more goals, and recorded more assists and points than the players selected by the Sabres.

Climbing Uphill

Vancouver's picks may have produced at a better clip, but it's fair to suggest Buffalo took a more thoughtful approach. The Sabres built from the net out, dealing their first overall pick—future WHA scoring stud Tom Webster—for a young goaltender, Roger Crozier, who would play six seasons in Buffalo, including three as a workhorse-type starter. Buffalo's draft picks were also younger on average by more than half a year.

We should also mention that the single-most-productive skater selected in the 1970 expansion draft—winger and future Sabres general manager Gerry Meehan—went to Buffalo.

Punch Imlach, the Buffalo GM, also selected 10 defensemen in the expansion draft, six of them younger than 25. In comparison, Vancouver took seven defensemen, only three of whom were younger than 25.

While Buffalo focused on building their blue line, the Canucks were preoccupied with adding center depth. Poile selected eight centermen, including Kurtenbach and Paiement. "The mistake at the expansion draft of 1967 was that the new teams didn't take enough centers," Poile went on to explain.

Whatever one thinks of the relative merits of Buffalo's and Vancouver's work at the expansion draft, the fact is it didn't really matter. There just wasn't enough talent made available for Imlach and Poile to do anything but ice a team destined to be overmatched. The Sabres and Canucks would be cannon fodder for the Montreals, Torontos, New Yorks, and Bostons of the hockey world.

"Would you pay $333,333.33...for a not-so-youthful belter who was slowed down by a spinal fusion operation?" *New York Times* columnist Gerald Eskenazi wrote, referring to Orland Kurtenbach. The way Eskenazi saw it, Vancouver wasn't just giving the Rangers a couple extra notches in the win column. No, in addition to the Blueshirts' share of the expansion fees (a cool $1 million), all the team lost in terms of players was Kurtenbach, young defenseman Alan Hamilton—"who flunked out in each of three chances"—and forward Don Marshall, "a 37-year-old...who sat out the last two months of the season with a separated shoulder."

"Thus," Eskenazi wrote, "the Rangers lost three players who weren't expected to be with the club next season and wound up richer for it."

As for the Canucks, well, their absentee ownership group had invested a lot of time and money into realizing their dream of bringing NHL hockey to Vancouver. Now the time had arrived, and it was clear they were going to face an uphill climb.

Poile would joke to Hal Laycoe, the man he'd hire to be Vancouver's first head coach, "There's $6 million worth of talent; now don't screw it up." Laycoe, though, quickly realized $6 million didn't buy him much. And a year after expansion process, he was killing it.

"They tell me, 'Be patient,'" Laycoe said following a 6–1 loss to the Rangers. "They tell us, 'We were losers for 10 years before we got moving.' But should be you be patient if you've paid $6 million for a club? Or should the 15,000 fans who come to all of our home games be patient?...I commended my players after the game, but isn't it a hell of a statement on expansion when a coach commends his players after they were outshot 52–16?"

12 How the Canucks Failed Dale Tallon

Vancouver and the NHL's 13 other member clubs reconvened on June 10, 1970, at the Queen Elizabeth Hotel for the amateur draft. Black Tuesday kept the Canucks from the chance to land a true franchise player in Gilbert Perreault. He, of course, would go on to record more than 1,300 points and make the Hockey Hall of Fame, and is still widely considered one of the game's great puck handlers.

With the second overall pick, the Canucks trained their sights on a consolation prize: Dale Tallon, a gifted young offensive defenseman who was coming off a nearly 80-point season for the Toronto Marlboros.

Possessing an NHL-ready frame, excellent mobility, a high-end skill set, a pro-level golf game, and a thick shock of hair, Tallon looked the part of a franchise cornerstone. But his potential was never realized, and he was traded after his third season with the club.

One might argue the Canucks would've been better off selecting Darryl Sittler or Rick MacLeish or Reggie Leach at No. 2, but there are two reasons why we won't do just that. The first is that Tallon was the best defenseman in the 1970 draft class, and had the best career out of all the blueliners drafted that day. He was mostly an effective NHL defender for a decade, which is all you can really expect—even with the second pick.

The second thing to remember? He joined a Canucks team that was a total mess. Might Tallon have developed into something more than he was in a more stable situation? That's a big what-if, but evidence suggests those early Canucks put a cocky teenager into a lousy developmental environment. No matter whom the Canucks had selected, that player was likely in for a rough ride.

Tallon, 19, was overhyped—and he was about to be, by the standards of the time, overpaid. Back in 1970 there was no standardized entry-level system in place for contracts, and players were only just beginning to be paid like stars. Gordie Howe, for example, made only $100,000 in 1970–71.

Tallon's lawyer was Alan Eagleson, one of the most famous talent representatives at the time. What's more, Tallon had been a Canadian amateur golf champion. Vancouver's first-ever draft pick was good enough on the links that he could dangle the possibility of joining the professional golf tour as leverage in negotiations. Not for the last time, Eagleson had Poile over a barrel, and the Canucks signed Tallon to a $60,000 contract.

The deal had far-reaching implications, even directly contributing to the standoff between All-Star defenseman Brad Park and the Rangers in the summer of 1970. Park, we might mention, settled for a deal worth much less than the Canucks paid Tallon.

Poile would later admit that he pretty much caved. "Eagleson told me if we didn't come up with *X* number of dollars, Dale would just give up hockey for pro golf," Poile told journalist Denny Boyd.

The teenage Tallon was welcomed to Vancouver in grand style, the future of the franchise. The club held a press conference to introduce him to the local media, and he showed up wearing "a forest-fire red blazer, white flares, Gucci boots, and an optic-numbing tie."

Those early Canucks teams weren't entirely deficient in leadership—Orland Kurtenbach was a fine captain by all accounts, and the team had Pat Quinn—but Tallon was the team's highest-paid player, which made the task of mentorship daunting.

The young defenseman had a productive first season, totaling 14 goals and 56 points. There were nights when he looked like a star, but there were more nights when Tallon looked like a converted forward. Even on a team that permitted nearly 300 goals against, Tallon's minus-25 rating was the worst on the team.

His boyish immaturity, contract status, and the lack of structure surrounding him made for a brutal situation. It wasn't made any easier when two Canucks coaches during Tallon's tenure—Hal Laycoe and Vic Stasiuk—insisted on playing him as a swingman, lining him up alternatively at both forward and defense with little rhyme or reason.

Tallon's next contract proved difficult as well. Following another arduous round of negotiations—this time Eagleson threatened to have Tallon jump to the WHA and again got Poile to cave—Tallon returned to a club that was as dysfunctional as ever. Things reached a fever pitch in Tallon's third season, when the players staged an all-out revolt against Coach Stasiuk.

At a November practice in Pittsburgh, the Canucks began to leave practice early. Only Rich Lemieux and Kurtenbach remained on the ice, and they were jeered by their teammates. When the media came to the locker room, the players didn't bite their tongues.

In another incident sometime later, Stasiuk assigned his players a drill and told them that he was leaving—but he wanted them to finish the drill in his absence. He then watched from an exit and took names as the players unenthusiastically sleepwalked through the drill and began to leave the ice. When Stasiuk went into the locker room to confront his charges, only a handful of players returned, and two of those who did—Dunc Wilson and Jocelyn Guevremont—did so in their street clothes.

These days, the subject of whether a coach "lost the room" is thrown about with an almost reckless abandon. But Stasiuk truly had. The players weren't just tuning him out—they were insurrectional. Though no one has ever explained precisely why, at some point during this whole kerfuffle, Stasiuk stripped Tallon of his assistant captaincy.

It was a surprise to no one when Tallon demanded a trade, and he got his wish that summer. The Canucks sent their first-ever draft pick to the Chicago Blackhawks for goaltender Gary Smith and forward Jerry Korab. Happily, it was an exchange that proved fruitful for Vancouver.

In later years Tallon came to be referred to as a "bust," but a close reading of history suggests the truth is more complicated. Tallon may have failed to live up to his immense potential in Vancouver, but by a greater measure, a dysfunctional Canucks organization failed him.

13 Quinn Had a Smart Trick for Making Vets Look Good at Training Camp

Pat Quinn changed the cultural fabric and historical trajectory of the Canucks franchise. But that was Quinn as president, general manager, and head coach. As a player, his impact was limited.

A plodding depth defenseman, Quinn was most famous during his playing days for a play in which he Kronwalled Bobby Orr along the boards during a playoff series between the Boston Bruins and the Toronto Maple Leafs. The hit caused Quinn's likeness to be burned in effigy at the Boston Garden.

In Vancouver, Quinn was essentially a tough guy. In the team's first-ever NHL game, he was assessed 14 penalty minutes. He played that first year with Gary Doak on a matchup pair and fared decently well, finishing the year with a plus-2 rating on a porous defensive team.

Quinn's teammates called him Clancy, and he served as something of a de facto social captain for the team. He once raised an elbow to brace for an Orland Kurtenbach hit in practice, and the two heavyweights fought it out on Pacific Coliseum ice.

These sorts of anecdotes are few and far between, though, as Quinn's playing days in Vancouver aren't altogether well-documented. We know he fought often and played big minutes in year one. We know he fell out of favor with Laycoe and management in year two. We know he was exposed in the 1972 NHL expansion draft. And that's about it.

Quinn isn't mentioned once in Denny Boyd's essential early history of the team and is only mentioned fleetingly in the historical "12 Years and Nothing" section of Tony Gallagher's book *Towels, Triumph and Tears*. Most of the good anecdotes and details concerning Quinn's playing tenure come from Dan Robson's biography, *Quinn: The Life of a Hockey Legend.*

The best is a story that David Poile, Bud's son, told Robson about how Quinn made sure veterans looked good at the Canucks' first-ever training camp. The younger Poile had just graduated from college, and though he'd played collegiate hockey, he didn't have any realistic NHL aspirations. He would play a small handful of games for Vancouver's AHL affiliate that season, but mostly he attended the camp to get a feel for the business side of the game.

It was early on in training camp, as the story goes, and the team was out for a big group dinner when Quinn started to work the young guys, rallying everybody to go for drinks at a local beer hall where pints cost 25 cents.

"He was larger than life to a young guy like me," Poile recalled to Robson. "You could just feel his presence. I've never met somebody that you just wanted to be around as much as him. There was a combination of comfort and knowing that you're going to have fun."

So the Canucks were drinking into the night, and obviously the younger players couldn't exactly keep up with the grizzled vets. As those rookies and younger players tried to leave, though, Quinn forbade it. "Oh no, you're not going anywhere," Quinn would say.

So everyone kept drinking, and the next morning the veteran players—also veteran drinkers—were feeling fine, but the young players were feeling it. Which, of course, allowed the veterans to skate circles around their younger counterparts with relative ease. It was the consummate veteran move.

"There was a method in his kindness—or madness—to be inclusive, if you will," Poile said of Quinn's gambit. "He was indoctrinating us into pro hockey."

14 The Canucks' First Franchise Victory Was Over the Maple Leafs

After years of backroom dealing—the last six of which often felt like an endless series of rejection, politicking, humiliation, and struggle—the Vancouver Canucks were finally set to make their NHL debut. It had been nearly 45 years since Vancouver had played host to top-level professional hockey. The lengthy drought, at long last, would come to an end on October 9, 1970, in a game against the Los Angeles Kings at the Pacific Coliseum.

The mayor of Vancouver, Tom Campbell, had proclaimed the days leading up to the game to be National Hockey League Week in the city. Parades, receptions, and a well-attended Canucks open practice had stoked the sense of fanfare. Vancouver was a big-league city.

As you might imagine, the first NHL game in Canucks history didn't exactly go off hitch-free. An early computer system relied upon to sell tickets had malfunctioned. Though the computer said the game was sold out—which the Canucks spent weeks relaying to inquisitive fans—it turned out 1,500 tickets were unsold. The Canucks didn't even realize it until the next day. "Needless to say," manager Bud Poile recalled, "we got ourselves a new ticket manager."

The game was broadcast coast-to-coast on *Hockey Night in Canada*, but therein lay another issue: the lights at the Pacific Coliseum were insufficiently powerful to properly support a color broadcast.

And of course there was the team itself, which was outshot 37–25, falling 3–1 to the Los Angeles Kings. Both Quinn and Orland Kurtenbach were assessed major penalties in the opening frame.

But at least it wasn't a shutout. Defenseman Barry Wilkins ensured that a little more than two minutes into the third period by skating into the Los Angeles end, holding the puck...and holding it a little bit longer...and making one last extra move...and then another, before scoring the first goal in Canucks history.

Fittingly, the first goal was accompanied by the first great call by Jim "Voice of the Vancouver Canucks" Robson. Wilkins had made so many moves in the lead-up to his shot that Robson had time to cry out, "Is he ever going to shoot the thing?" He did eventually shoot the thing, and the result was a historic, unforgettable marker in Canucks history.

Vancouver's opening night loss to the Kings did nothing to dispel the enthusiasm in the market for NHL hockey. Just two days later more than 15,000 fans again filled Pacific Coliseum—and this time, the game was sold out—to watch the team defeat the Toronto Maple Leafs 5–3 and record their first win against NHL competition.

Kurtenbach opened the scoring in the first, and the club poured it on with Wayne Maki contributing two tallies as Vancouver built a five-goal lead. Even though Toronto stormed back to make it somewhat interesting, it was a dominant performance for the fledgling NHL club, and a historic win.

15 The Early Teams Were Unbelievably Dysfunctional

The early Canucks had it all, really: goaltending controversies, player-led insurrections against a multitude of head coaches, public infighting among key management figures, and losing. Lots and lots of losing. If Canucks fandom was to become a painful experience down the road, at least the franchise established those expectations early on.

Not all failings can be laid at the feet of management. The expansion process hadn't provided the club with a solid enough pool of players to be competitive right off the bat—neither the Canucks nor the Buffalo Sabres won their 40th game in franchise history until year three. But still it's hard to argue Poile, Laycoe, and company maximized the limited assets available to them.

One of the biggest early mistakes the club made—one that foreshadowed decades of instability and drama—was to carry three goaltenders on their roster for the first two seasons: 37-year-old Charlie Hodge, hotheaded hippie Dunc Wilson, and eccentric veteran George Gardner.

The three-goaltender setup never works in hockey. There are only two nets on the practice sheet, after all, but the Vancouver setup had an additional wrinkle—the players' eccentricities made the situation untenable. Wilson, for example, was quick to anger and loved to fight. He once scrapped with Dale Tallon at a December practice at the North Shore Winter Club, and in March of the first season he was reprimanded by NHL president Clarence Campbell after he left his crease to fight…for the eighth time that season!

As for Gardner, he had rather significant vision issues, but for years he refused to wear glasses or contact lenses. He survived by tricking team doctors. He'd memorize the team's Snellen chart—the most common type of chart used to test vision, with letters that decline in size the further down you go.

Finally, a Canucks doctor wise to Gardner's ruse swapped the chart out for one with different, less familiar numbers. Gardner—too blind to see even the bigger numbers on the chart—rattled off all the wrong numbers with relative confidence. "You can't trust those doctors," Gardner said of the incident. "I've had that bloody eye chart memorized for years, but this damn guy sprung a new chart on me in there. Hell, I couldn't tell a capital *A* from a small *X*."

Gardner was also in the habit of answering every question with a cryptic response when he was on the road and being interviewed by a writer he didn't know: "I am a self-educated man."

These signs of the team's lack of seriousness weren't limited to the crease. Players, as mentioned, openly defied various head coaches—often over petty grievances—and were occasionally abrasive even toward their own fans. Denny Boyd recounted one occasion where inconsistent winger Mike Corrigan, hearing it from critical fans as he often did, skated to center ice and gave the Pacific Coliseum faithful the middle finger.

Coach Laycoe was apoplectic.

The Canucks may have struggled, but they still managed to get the puck in the goal once in a while.

16 From Laycoe to Stasiuk to McCreary, and All the Dysfunction in Between

The studious, statistics-obsessed Hal Laycoe had good reason to be upset in his second season as coach—and he was, frequently. His team was overmatched, and his complex breakout system, which relied on defensemen making smart decisions while skating the puck up ice, was a poor fit for a club composed of blueliners who were either too inexperienced or too slow to execute.

As the season progressed, Laycoe was increasingly under siege. After a critical article in the *Vancouver Sun*, Laycoe barred a young reporter named Bob Dunn from entering the dressing room for a time. It was an overreaction and Laycoe relented, but it's a testament to the pressure he was under.

It didn't help that the club's goodwill ambassador, Babe Pratt, reamed Laycoe—an analytic thinker and progressive, who collected and obsessed over data—in a very public manner.

"He's a 'don't' coach—don't do this, don't do that," Pratt said of Laycoe in a later radio appearance. "I'm a 'do' person. Teach them what to do, what not to do."

Turning to the subject of Laycoe's data sheets, Pratt continued, "Statistics are for losers. All this business of who to play against who is a bunch of bullshit.... Plus-minus is crap.... There's a lot of things wrong here, and you won't fix them staring at a bunch of reports."

Amazingly Bud Poile sidestepped the public and made no comment on the matter. Poile's silence served to cast further aspersions on the suitability of Vancouver's first head coach, but he did even more damage when he went about chiming in. "It isn't a case of whether I'll fire Hal," Poile said at a late-season luncheon. "It's a case of whether we'll rehire him."

Poile later admitted the comment was "stupid" and had served to make a bad situation worse. To Laycoe's credit, he took the high road. He didn't explicitly fire back at Poile or at Pratt in public, though he did tell Vancouver radioman Jim Taylor there were ugly cultural undercurrents sabotaging the club. "Things have been done and said to undermine the hockey club. Continually," Laycoe said matter-of-factly. "And nothing has been done about it. Lack of unity, lack of loyalty, it's a cancer."

On May 2, 1972, the Canucks fired Laycoe and replaced him with Vic Stasiuk, who had worked with Poile in Philadelphia. (Laycoe's magnanimous handling of a rough season later paid off for him when he took over from Poile as the club's general manager

A Picture of Failure

One image would come to symbolize the sense of chaos and disorder that marked Vancouver's first half decade in the NHL.

At the 1973 amateur draft the Canucks selected Dennis Ververgaert, a big, physical winger who was heralded as the next great NHL power forward. Ververgaert was a dominant winger with the London Knights and would show occasional flashes of brilliance in his Canucks tenure. Like many early Vancouver draft picks, though, Ververgaert never lived up to his potential, and unfortunately for the team, some of his most notable fights happened off of the ice.

That was later, though. On this day the new hottest thing in Canucks hockey was being introduced to the press, and it was suggested by Hall—a fitness buff who was the most visible of the Canucks chairmen while Scallen dealt with his legal issues—that Ververgaert should remove his shirt to show off his chiseled physique to the assembled media. The press then goaded Hall into doing the same, imagining an image featuring the Canucks' two new strongmen in full flex, and Hall obliged.

Unfortunately just before the photos were snapped, Hall decided to suck in his stomach and his pants fell to his knees. Both Vancouver newspapers ran the photo of the wardrobe malfunction the next day.

when Poile took a health-related leave of absence from the team in the winter of 1973.)

Stasiuk was a hard-charging type, which didn't work with a group of players that frankly didn't seem all that committed to the cause of winning hockey games. He clashed with first-line center, Andre Boudrias, early in the season and once scheduled a 7:30 AM practice on the road, nearly prompting a player mutiny.

Things deteriorated further as the season went along, as did Stasiuk's grip on the situation. The coach suspended center Bobby Lalonde for not participating in a drill during a road practice, only to be overruled by Lalonde's agent and Laycoe later that day. The embattled coach nearly fought on the bench with Dunc Wilson at the Los Angeles Forum as the entire arena observed them yelling at one another.

After one particularly rough altercation with the players, Stasiuk was observed with his head in his hands as the players engaged in a bawdy sing-along at the back of the team bus.

"Like every other important decision the Canucks ownership ever faced, they waffled on this one too," wrote Denny Boyd of the sacking of Stasiuk. "Coley Hall fired Stasiuk by innuendo in the press before he fired him officially."

That summer, the summer of 1973, was a real opportunity for the Canucks to change direction. And they pursued some of the brightest names in hockey to fill their head-coaching vacancy.

Vancouver was, in fact, one of two finalists for the services of legendary New York Islanders bench boss Al Arbour. Arbour may have even elected to come west had it not been for the sense of dysfunction that radiated from the early Canucks franchise. "The Canucks offered me the job, but I was a little bit worried about the management of the club at the time," Arbour later recalled. Less than a decade later he'd celebrate the second of four consecutive Stanley Cup victories on Vancouver ice.

Vancouver's interview process also put them in touch with Scotty Bowman and Roger Neilson, who impressed Canucks brass but who was ultimately deemed too inexperienced. So the Canucks turned to Bill McCreary, an odd choice if experience was a factor, since he'd only coached 24 regular-season games at the NHL level prior to landing the Canucks job.

McCreary was a disaster, and lasted only 41 games in Vancouver. Shortly after he was fired Laycoe took a leave of absence ("from which he has yet to return," Tony Gallagher observed wryly a decade later) while Poile resigned his post for good.

In three and a half seasons the Canucks had worked their way through three coaches, all of whom had failed to instill a sense of structure or even basic work ethic in a series of moribund Canucks teams. Patrick family biographer and *Vancouver Province* columnist Eric Whitehead took aim at the players themselves when he observed of McCreary's tenure that he wasn't magical enough to "coddle, coax, or otherwise cunningly inveigle maximum effort out of the local broody mix of hirelings who have to date held three coaches out for ransom."

And we would be remiss if we didn't mention that while all this was going on, Canucks owner Tom Scallen was facing highly publicized charges for stealing $3 million from the hockey team (and for drawing up a false stock). It was a righteous mess.

17 Orland Kurtenbach Was a Stone-Cold Badass

New York Rangers center Orland Kurtenbach was 34—and only two years removed from becoming essentially immobile due to severe back problems—when Bud Poile selected him fourth overall at the 1970 expansion draft. Poile saw a prideful, committed, dignified, tough-as-nails forward who could lead his fledgling team. And Hal Laycoe saw a player who, if not necessarily a star, was a rock in a sea of dysfunction. "Maybe we didn't draft the best hockey player in the league when we got Kurt," Laycoe said, "but we certainly drafted the best team captain."

Up and down the lineup, Vancouver lacked what Kurtenbach had the most of—a level of dignity and professionalism that connected with fans. As bad as things were in the early years, the Canucks would've been much worse off without the captain.

Through most of his career, Kurtenbach was a third-line center, renowned for his toughness and defensive reliability. In Vancouver, though, he had an opportunity to be more—an opportunity he seized, going from 14 points in his last season with the Rangers to 21 goals and 53 points in Vancouver.

"It's true that now that I'm the team captain, I'm in a slightly different role," Kurtenbach said of his newfound scoring touch. "Before, I was always the third center, specializing in checking assignments. Now I'm getting a chance to spend more time on the ice and to work on power plays. That's made a difference, simply because I'm getting more opportunities. Shots are going in for me. My passes are getting to where I want them to go. It's just the way it is in sports."

That aw-shucks demeanor was standard for Kurtenbach. Self-effacing, modest, and committed, he was famous among his teammates for his steady gaze and his ability to keep an even keel.

Kurtenbach's ability to handle the emotional aspect of the game and to manage tough circumstances had been crucial in overcoming a back issue that, throughout his career, had caused him unbearable discomfort and nearly led to early retirement. He described himself at Rangers training camp as "near crippled." He couldn't bend over to take a draw, much less skate quickly enough to compete in the NHL. Despite excruciating pain, though, he tried.

Orland Kurtenbach (25) looks on as teammate Dunc Wilson blocks a shot against the Rangers in 1972.

Today, just like back then, there are only two options for a herniated disc: manage the pain or opt for a risky surgical procedure. In 1968, when still with the Rangers, Kurtenbach went with No. 2. In a last-ditch effort to prolong his career, Kurtenbach opted to undergo the surgery, in which part of his hip bone—the length of three vertebrae—was removed and inserted over three lumbar (the third, fourth, and fifth) in his spinal column.

Dr. Kazuo Yanagisawa, the cigar-smoking resident physician at Madison Square Garden (and a former sumo wrestler, if Denny Boyd is to be believed), performed the operation. The good doctor is famous in hockey history for stitching up a gruesome Jacque Plante facial laceration—the infamous cut that led directly to the birth of the goalie mask. Yanagisawa saved a lot of careers in those days, performing successful spinal fusion procedures on NHL players such as Harry Howell, Jean Ratelle, and Rod Gilbert—oh, and legendary NBA player and coach Phil Jackson, who underwent the procedure while playing for the Knicks.

Recovery from the surgery wiped out nearly all of Kurtenbach's 1968–69 campaign, most of which he spent wearing an aluminum brace. Considering the level of pain involved and his advancing age, Kurtenbach would've been justified had he opted for retirement. Not his style, though.

"Even when I was in traction, I kept my hopes up," Kurtenbach told Denny Boyd. "I never let myself consider that I might be washed up. Being indifferent to the bad things that happen to you is a very big part of being a professional athlete. You have to take the bad things with the same objective reaction that you receive the good things."

Kurtenbach was also a well-respected and feared fighter. Though he never notched more than 100 penalties in minutes in a single season—he took pride in not being considered just a brawler—the carbon dating on that particular statistical fossil may tell us more about his impact as a deterrent than it does about his willingness to drop the gloves. "Kurtenbach was such a good fighter that he is actually beyond fighting now; he just doesn't have to do it anymore because he has made his reputation," explained veteran NHL referee Lloyd Gilmour in the early 1970s. "Anyone who challenges him is out of his mind."

Perhaps the highest compliment paid to Kurtenbach from those early years is that the Canucks weren't a total doormat when he was in the lineup. This was especially true that first season, according to Denny Boyd, who wrote, "With Kurtenbach in the lineup, the Canucks had a .413 winning percentage. Without him (Kurtenbach sustained a knee injury on a Bobby Baun hit), they fell off to a dismal .208 percentage. That was the difference between Leadership and Leadership Lost."

Amid regular player revolts, the coaching carousel spinning wildly, infighting with management, and an owner under indictment, Kurtenbach was a steadying presence for the Canucks, and one who played some fine hockey. In doing so, he built a reputation as an inspirational leader who conducted himself with class. Kurtenbach was the first among those who managed to represent the franchise with dignity.

18 The Original Owner of the Canucks Stole $3 Million from the Team

The *Vancouver Sun* headline about Canucks owner Tom Scallen was damning: $3 Million Theft Alleged. Scallen was a lawyer by training, a smooth-talking showman. The *New York Times* once wrote that P.T. Barnum would've liked him.

Before owning the Canucks, Scallen had built a career as a fitful sort of financial whiz and entrepreneur. Hustling all the way, he turned a medical equipment firm into an entertainment property, a leap that is as telling a comment on his personality as you'll find. He'd purchased the Ice Follies and, not content to let his newest property gather cobwebs, he invested heavily in championship-quality skating talent. Later on in his life—after spending nine months in a Canadian jail over the debacle from his time with the Vancouver Canucks—he purchased the Harlem Globetrotters.

In this particular context, facing charges of misrepresentation and theft in a city that only a few years earlier had welcomed him as a savior, Scallen was an outsider. The Minnesota-based businessman had parachuted into a strange situation when the NHL demanded an exorbitant expansion fee that the Canucks' founding fathers—most of whom became minority shareholders in the club—couldn't pay on their own. He'd brought liquidity, but he wasn't a particularly hands-on owner, and issues between him and the likes of Cyrus McLean, Max Bell, Coley Hall, and Frank McMahon were whispered about well before these serious charges were filed.

The four Canadian chairmen, in fact, had announced a plan to step down and dissociate themselves from Northwest Sports—the company that owned, operated, and financed the Canucks—in June 1971, shortly after the BC superintendent of brokers announced an investigation into two dubious money transfers from Canada to the United States totaling $3.5 million.

More than half of Northwest Sports had been placed into escrow in June 1971, but despite clear signs of trouble, the theft charges landed like a bombshell in February 1972. "I'd have to say it was the most embarrassing day in my entire hockey career," Bud Poile later recalled. "There was nothing we could do but try to laugh our way through."

The trial itself commenced in April 1973 and was conducted in Vancouver, which was likely to be bad news for Scallen—though he didn't seem to realize it. Denny Boyd wrote that Scallen was "optimistically making social and business appointments" virtually right up until his conviction. NHL president Campbell and a pair of league governors testified in the splashy trial, which was covered breathlessly by the Vancouver dailies.

On April 11, 1973, a jury found Scallen guilty of both theft and of making a false stock prospectus. "You used the $3 million in funds for your own selfish ends, placing in jeopardy the money entrusted to you by the public," said Justice Harry McKay, who presided over the trial. Scallen was sentenced to four years in prison, though he would only serve nine months and receive a full pardon in 1982.

Scallen's lawyers appealed the verdict, and he was released on bail for $25,000. In an interesting side note, it was prominent Vancouver businessman Jim Pattison who put up the bail money. As a younger man, Pattison had made some general inquiries about purchasing Northwest Sports, though in short order he would move the WHA Blazers into Vancouver instead.

So what had actually occurred? Had Scallen really stolen $3 million from the hockey club? The short answer is yes, but it was complicated. It's likely the first owner of the Canucks franchise had bad advice and, in walking a tightrope to secure the necessary financing to bring the NHL to Vancouver, had misjudged a crucial step. And so he fell.

Here are the key details: Before putting up the expansion fee, Scallen first had to buy Northwest Sports, which owned the Vancouver Hockey Club Ltd.—owned by founding fathers Hall, Bell, McLean, and McMahon. This was the entity that held the lease to the Pacific Coliseum and owned and operated the WHL Canucks, the Rochester Americans, and various other affiliated hockey interests. Scallen arranged to buy Vancouver Hockey Club Ltd. for $2.8 million.

Scallen's company Medicor was regarded as being flush with cash at the time. But as it turned out, Scallen was working constantly—and in shady fashion—to avoid being short. Confident in his financial wizardry, he took out a $3 million loan from a Chicago-based firm called the Walter Heller Company and, as one witness suggested, flew to Vancouver in a small private plane to deliver the requisite $2.8 million to the group at the last second.

In order to offset that loan, Scallen began to investigate the possibility of underwriting a public offering of Northwest Sports to raise some capital. At no time was it suggested—either publically or more formally in the official stock prospectus—that this capital would be used to pay off his debts. Often corporate entities will leave themselves more flexibility in these sorts of situations. Critically, Scallen failed to do so.

So when Scallen made a series of transfers availing him of the money raised in the public offering to pay his Heller debt, he committed theft and fraud. He did so even though the $3 million was effectively returned to the club—which he continued to own, operate, and finance.

And so it was that an NHL franchise, bad on the ice and criminally mismanaged off it—both literally and figuratively—took a massive public relations hit. Within 13 months, Scallen and Medicor's shares in Northwest Sports, and by extension the Canucks, would be purchased by Frank Griffiths through Western Broadcast Sales, the media company he operated, for $8.5 million. Twenty years would pass before a controlling interest of the club would again be owned by an American-based corporate entity.

What's remarkable about all this is that for all that had gone on—for all of the losing, the grift, and the dysfunction—the Vancouver Canucks franchise had *appreciated* in value as an entertainment property. Then again, why not? Results aside, the club was still reliably drawing 15,000 fans to the Pacific Coliseum for home dates.

19 Vancouver's Hockey Fans: A Rambunctious History

In the early 1970s two singular events—one that directly involved a Canucks game, and one that did not—stand out for how they foreshadowed the emergence of the Vancouver hockey market's, *ahem*, peculiar characteristics.

First, the incident that didn't involve a Canucks game: The character of the local hockey fan, oft commented on in uncharitable terms by those outside the lower mainland, has been criticized harshly in recent years—most notably in the days and weeks following the 2011 Stanley Cup riot. And in examining the particular breed of boisterousness that Vancouver hockey fans are known for, one must concede this rowdiness has been on display too often.

We would contend, though, that there's nothing *necessarily* malevolent at play. As a psychoanalyst in Toronto once said of group behavior and sports fandom: "If you can root, you can riot."

The nature of the "Vancouver hockey fan" bends toward the disorderly, but it's less a defining trait than that same fan's relative intolerance of failure and a penchant for fatalistic wallowing. This is subjective, of course, but whatever traits you find in Vancouver hockey fans, it's difficult to know where they came from. *Toronto Star* columnist Bruce Arthur wrote: "When I was growing up in Vancouver, my mother used to say that there was something about the unearthly, dreamscape beauty of this edge of the world that—well, it wasn't so much that it drove people to madness so much as it unmoored certain minds from reality, a little or a lot."

Whatever forces are at play, what's beyond argument is that Vancouver hockey fans are a different sort. Lacking the weary devotion of Toronto fans, the full-throated snobbery of Montreal fans, or the single-minded "hockey as sole civic identifier" preoccupation of hockey fans in Canada's cold prairie towns, there's something distinct about the way fans in Vancouver interact with the sport.

If it wasn't clear before Game 4 of the 1972 Summit Series, then it was so declared on that fateful September 8 night at the Pacific Coliseum.

For a generation of baby boomers who missed the Second World War but lived through the Cold War era and the Cuban Missile Crisis, the Summit Series took on a mammoth level of cultural importance. There was more on the line than a jingoistic defense of "Canada's game."

It was supposed to be a cakewalk for a Canadian side coached by Harry Sinden and composed of the best NHL players. The Soviet team, though, proved to be far sturdier competition than first thought. They were in better shape, more familiar with one another, and played a brand of skilled, possession-forward hockey that, over the course of the next 40 years, would fundamentally change the game.

The series opened in Montreal, where Canada jumped out to an early lead, before the Soviet side turned it on and crushed the NHL's best in a decisive 7–3 victory. Two days later, the seasoned NHL professionals rebounded in Toronto, winning Game 2 convincingly by a 4–1 score. It appeared that order had been restored. But in Game 3 in Winnipeg, the Soviets managed another shocking result, erasing a pair of two-goal leads to manage a hard-fought 4–4 tie.

Game 4 was to be played on September 8, 1972, at the Pacific Coliseum. It represented the final Canadian stop of the eight-game series. Dignitaries and fans filled the stadium, which buzzed with nervous energy. The fans in attendance that night were genuinely disappointed in how Team Canada had performed. There was a feeling that this series really mattered, and that the NHL's superstars weren't approaching it with due gravity.

Right from puck drop, the Canadians were out of sorts. They took two early penalties, and the Soviets capitalized on the ensuing opportunities, building an early lead.

In Toronto, Canada had triumphed. In Winnipeg and Montreal, perhaps the fans were too shocked. In Vancouver, though, the shock turned to anger and recrimination. The Canadian national ice hockey team—more prized in Canada than apple pie to our southern neighbors—was booed throughout the game, and ultimately off the ice at the end of a 5–3 loss.

Vancouver fans supported the Canucks through an initial decade of awfulness before attendance began to slip but in that same time period had no patience for lousy play from NHL superstars. (Perhaps in that gap between high expectations and harsh reproach, we might hear echoes of the criticism Roberto Luongo would later endure during his stellar but controversial time with the club.)

As boos poured down, the players were caught off guard and shaken by the reaction. Prompted by this—and a small group of fans chanting "Communism is better, communism is supreme"—Phil Esposito decided to give an emotionally charged speech after the game. On TV, no less.

"For the people who booed us, jeez," Esposito said. "All of us guys are really disheartened and disillusioned, and we're disappointed in some of the people. We cannot believe the bad press we've got. The booing we've got in our own buildings!

"We came [to play] because we love Canada, and even though we play in the United States and we earn money in the United States, Canada is still our home, and that's the only reason we come. And I don't think we should be booed."

It was a great speech, one that media and fans have spent nearly 50 years pointing to as a seminal turning point. And if that were true, it could be argued Vancouver's hockey fans had actually served the national good. Which is fun to think about. But unfortunately

Esposito's speech as a "turning point" in the series is more myth than fact. In reality, there was no television in the Canadian locker room, so Esposito's teammates missed the interview.

Regardless of the impact the speech had on the team's performance, the impact on the psyche and reputation of Vancouver hockey fans was significant. The episode illustrates something elemental about Vancouver hockey fans, which remains true today. Unlike more masochistic fans in other markets, Vancouver hockey fans don't have a whole lot of patience for supporting a losing side. If the effort isn't there, if the results aren't there, Vancouver hockey fans will make their dissatisfaction known. They will boo, or worse, they'll stay away. It doesn't matter if it's the Canadian National Team, a cute puppy, or the Queen Mother; if they're observed to be dogging it against the Soviets or the Chicago Blackhawks, they're going to hear about it.

One other episode deserves mention here: In December 1972 the Canucks were hosting the Philadelphia Flyers when a pair of fights broke out in front of the benches. During a scrum in which Philly's Don Saleski had Vancouver's Barry Wilcox of the Canucks pinned to the ground, a fan leaned over and began pulling Saleski's hair.

What occurred next was a Malice in the Palace–style scene, as a variety of Flyers went into the stands. They "waded into the spectators, lashing out with their sticks as spectators from the first six rows, including many children, cowered or scattered," Denny Boyd recalled. During the melee, a Vancouver police corporal was shoved to the ground by Flyers backup goaltender Bob Taylor.

The NHL investigated, but before NHL president Clarence Campbell could render his judgment, the seven Flyers players involved were charged with causing a disturbance, while Taylor faced charges for assaulting a police office. Fines were levied and Taylor had to appeal a 30-day jail sentence (successfully, much to his relief).

"It was," Boyd explained, "the first time in the history of the NHL that a skirmish between players and fans had come before a court of law."

20 All It Took for the Canucks to Make the Playoffs Was a Division Change...and a Grenade

In Phil Maloney, the Vancouver Canucks found a head coach who, for the first time in franchise history, successfully instilled a sense of structure, discipline, and work ethic. Well-read, tough, and intelligent, Maloney took over from Bill McCreary as head coach midway through the 1973–74 campaign, and fared well in the second half. So much so that following the departures of Bud Poile (who had been on leave anyway) and Hal Laycoe (with whom Maloney served as co–general manager for a time), Maloney was named general manager.

Maloney, who was more interested in coaching, didn't love the idea of wearing two hats but accepted the appointment out of a practical sense of self-preservation. "I had to take it," Maloney later recalled. "Otherwise it might have been my ass!"

As a player, Maloney might've had an extended NHL career in a league with more than six teams. As it was, he was effectively a journeyman. As a coach, the Silver Fox (so named because of his shock of white hair) proved an able, if unorthodox, communicator.

One time, following a disappointing performance in the first period by his team, Maloney conspired to get the full attention of his charges by pulling the pin of a grenade and throwing it into the dressing room. The grenade wasn't an active explosive, just a prop Maloney had been saving for the right moment.

However it was accomplished, Maloney's greatest success in Vancouver was that he managed to infuse a team-first mentality into a roster with an unruly history. "These guys have got to get their heads out of their butt and their shoulders up," Maloney said at the time. "I'd like to instill some pride in these people if it's possible."

While some of the sort of silly, destructive off-ice hijinks that characterized the club's first few seasons still permeated—for example, during one game Canucks forward Mike Walton took to skating behind the Zamboni in between periods as a way of protesting his lack of ice time—they were reduced. Forwards such as team captain Andre Boudrias, a solid player who wasn't exactly famous for his level of effort on defense, turned in their best seasons under Maloney. The Canucks began to play as a team, and began to hold their own.

Though the improvement in both tactics and demeanor under Maloney is an important part of the story of the Canucks' first Stanley Cup playoff berth, there were more practical reasons for the success. Divisional realignment put the Canucks in the Smythe, with a variety of weaker teams—including the St. Louis Blues, Kansas City Scouts, Minnesota North Stars, and Chicago Blackhawks. The "sweathog division," as it was often called, gave Vancouver an easier path to the playoffs than its previous one, which had five of the Original Six powerhouses.

The Canucks also, for the first time in franchise history, had a reliable starting goaltender. Gary Smith had been acquired in 1973 in the Tallon trade, and the lanky 6'4" goaltender—a former Vezina Trophy winner—quickly became a fan favorite.

Smith was a character off the ice, a flashy dresser with an outspoken temperament, and a battler on it. After allowing the most goals in the NHL in his first year with Vancouver, Smith's second campaign went much better. He led all goaltenders in appearances, with 72, and recorded a team-record six shutouts. That led to a handful of Hart Trophy votes in recognition of his play.

The club also had some promising young blueliners. A 20-year-old named Harold Snepsts, who conducted himself well in a 27-game cup of coffee, while 6'5" behemoth Bob Dailey managed 48 points that season. Up front, there was a group of high-effort forwards led by Boudrias and Don Lever. Presto! The 1974–75 Canucks won the sweathog division crown with a 38–32–10 record. For the first time in history, Vancouver would host an NHL playoff game.

First, though, they had to play two games in Montreal against one of the most formidable dynasties in hockey history. The Canadiens of the 1970s were ludicrous. Led by Guy Lafleur, Larry Robinson, Ken Dryden, and a Hall of Fame supporting cast, the Canadiens won five Stanley Cups that decade. It was widely expected that the Canucks would get swept. And they nearly were as the Canadiens blasted through the Canucks in five games—though Maloney's scrappy crew did shock Montreal with a 2–1 victory in Game 2.

Even so, for a city and an NHL franchise that wasn't quite ready for their Sally Field moment ("You like me! You really like me!"), the 1974–75 season was seen as a major step forward, which it was. With the same basic core the Maloney-led Canucks would qualify for the postseason again the following year, losing in straight games in a best-of-three preliminary-round series against the New York Islanders.

"It's like being a steelworker on the 49th floor," Maloney said of his club's performance in the 1976 playoffs, "and someone on the 50th floor is throwing banana peels at you."

21 The Good Times, They Never Last

The short blip of respectability the franchise enjoyed in the mid-1970s ultimately proved fleeting, as a series of questionable trades came to sabotage the Maloney era. Bob Dailey, the big young defenseman, was dealt to the Philadelphia Flyers for an inferior defenseman named Larry Goodenough ("[He] was very poorly named," Tony Gallagher joked in the 1980s) and enforcer Jack McIlhargey, a limited enforcer who would later join the Canucks front office.

The club also parted ways with Gary Smith, their popular goaltender, following the 1975–76 season. Smith had seemed to wear out his welcome with Maloney and was traded late in the summer of 1976 in a deal shrouded by speculation and conjecture.

Smith was suspended during his final season with the club when—after being replaced in a game by rookie Ken Lockett—he opted to leave the arena before the end of the contest. "He drove home in his equipment [that night]," recalled longtime Canucks PR man Greg Douglas to Vancouver author Justin Beddall. In his book *Towels, Triumph and Tears*, Tony Gallagher passes along the theory that Smith "got into a shouting match at a Christmas party with the wife of a senior club executive" as an explanation for how Smith finally wore out his welcome with the Canucks. Smith was traded to the Minnesota North Stars in August 1976.

From there the gravity of mediocrity pulled Vancouver back to Earth and Maloney resigned as head coach midway through the next season following a gruesome 9–23–3 start. "I can no longer tolerate the situation," Maloney said of his decision to relinquish his head coaching title.

Though he'd given up the job he really wanted, Maloney remained the club's general manager and enlisted Orland Kurtenbach as his replacement behind the bench. Better suited to the daily subtleties of coaching than the blunt ruthlessness of talent evaluation and management, Maloney would hold the record for best winning percentage all-time among Canucks head coaches for 15 more years, or until Pat Quinn was through in 1996.

As for Kurtenbach, his time behind Vancouver's bench lasted one and a half seasons with a record of 36–62–27, an ugly .396 winning percentage. The team, quite obviously, missed the playoffs in both his seasons at the helm.

Following the 1977–78 campaign, Kurtenbach was fired by new general manager Jake Milford and replaced by Harry Neale. He'd never coach in the NHL again, and barely coach at all, save a couple stints at the American League and junior level.

His dismissal by the Canucks appeared to cut deep. "Following [Kurtenbach's] final game, fate sealed, [he] closed himself in his office and wept," Gallagher recalled. "If a man who had distinguished himself as a great leader during his playing career could be reduced to this, a great chore was certainly ahead for his successor."

There was one highlight from the Kurtenbach era, though use of the word *highlight* is up for debate. During the 1976–77 season, Maloney—desperate to add talent to a team largely bereft of it—took a flyer on legendary playboy Derek Sanderson. Sanderson, who shot to prominence in Boston in the early 1970s, was as close to a rock star as hockey had. Talented on the ice—he and Bobby Orr won back-to-back Calder Trophies for the Bruins, as well as the 1972 Stanley Cup—he was incredibly flashy off it, cruising around town in his Rolls-Royce, often with an attractive female companion.

Sanderson was named by *Cosmopolitan* magazine as one of the sexiest men in America, and at one point—thanks to signing a $2.6

million deal with WHA Philadelphia—he was the highest-paid athlete in the world.

But that wasn't the Derek Sanderson who arrived in Vancouver. No, the Derek Sanderson who showed up was 30 years old, in woeful shape from years of hard living, and only played 16 games—though he did score 16 points! It would be the second-to-last stop of his NHL career.

Maloney had been the most successful Canucks coach and executive in franchise history, but in June 1977—after only four seasons at the helm of the club—the Silver Fox was dismissed.

22 Shaky Jake and the European Invasion

Vancouver is an unconventional hockey market, and the Canucks have often required unconventional ideas and tactics to be successful. Enter Jake Milford.

Milford was a hockey lifer, remembered fondly for his warmth and his ability to spin a good yarn. He was also a different sort of cat, and when he arrived in Vancouver, he brought a radically different approach to roster construction with him.

Born in Prince Edward Island and heeled in Manitoba, Milford was a typical hockey man in many respects. Though he'd never made the NHL, Milford cut his teeth in a variety of professional minor leagues before shifting to management. He liked to tell a story about how Eddie Shore traded him for a pair of Art Ross nets, a wake-up call that convinced him he should probably get into management.

The story of the trade for two nets was retold whenever Milford was mentioned in the East Coast media, particularly in the lead-up to Milford's Hockey Hall of Fame induction in 1984. (Milford, in failing health at the time, was unable to attend.) In the early 1980s Milford admitted to Tony Gallagher that there was a player named John Baby who was also a part of the trade. "But it makes for a better story without him," he added.

By the time Milford became Vancouver's GM in 1977—arriving from Los Angeles, where he had served in the same capacity—he'd built a hockey résumé the hard way. A hardworking talent evaluator, Milford spent two decades running major junior teams and professional minor league teams in places such as Omaha, Brandon, and St. Paul.

But don't be fooled by what looks like a less-than-stellar résumé. This was a man who danced to the rhythm of his own music, and was worldlier than most NHL executives of the era. In the late 1930s Milford went to Europe to play professional hockey and became, it seems, rather enchanted by its culture, art, and dancing. His Wembley Monarchs teammates dubbed him Shaky Jake, a nickname that followed him as a hockey executive. Some thought the moniker referenced his jabberwocky skating stride, which was false. Milford earned his nickname because, as a young man, he liked to kick it at the snootiest local dance halls. "The full title was Shaky Jake, the Ballroom Fake," explained *Vancouver Sun* columnist Jim Kearney in the late 1970s. "During his three prewar seasons in the English National League, [Milford] spent as much time dancing up a storm in the Hammersmith Palais as he did on the ice at the Wembley Pool.... His teammates made him pay for his obsession with ballroom dancing. They imposed that title on him."

Milford went on to serve with the Canadian Royal Air Force, navigating bombers during the Second World War, but he considered himself a Europhile. It tells you everything you need to know that this Manitoba prairie boy kept mini versions of the Swedish and Czech flags on his desk in his Pacific Coliseum office.

Ultimately, Milford's affection for and familiarity with Europe would serve him well as in Vancouver.

In the mid-'70s, Europeans were only just beginning to make inroads into the NHL. The 1972 Summit Series actually proved to be a decisive flash point. The Soviets proved their possession-based, bandy-informed game stacked up against the Canadian version. And while training in Sweden prior to the Russian leg of the series, Canadian hockey scouts noticed a skilled defenseman named Borje Salming. Salming would come over to play in the NHL the next season, and his star shone brightly for the Toronto Maple Leafs.

The rush to scour Europe for talent was on. Milford, with his knowledge of Europe and no bias toward its players, was well suited to this evolutionary moment in talent acquisition. Until 1978 the Vancouver Canucks had never drafted a player trained outside North America. That changed under Milford, who at the 1978 amateur draft used a third-round pick on a Swedish Elite League forward named Harald Lückner. Over the next four years Milford targeted and drafted Europeans on a number of occasions, including Swedish forward Patrik Sundstrom and quick-skating Finnish forward Petri Skriko.

Milford's focus on acquiring Europeans extended beyond the draft and into all avenues. The club traded a conditional second-round pick to the Chicago Blackhawks for Thomas Gradin in 1978, dealt for Per-Olov Brasar in 1979, and signed a multitude of Swedish free agents such as Lars Zetterstrom, Lars Lindgren, and Lars Molin, of the epic Jofa helmet.

Integrating Swedish players into a North American professional team was one thing. There was occasional friction between the Scandinavian-trained players and their North American teammates, certainly, but this practice was widespread across the NHL by the late 1970s and early '80s. Where Milford really broke the mold was in prying professional players out of communist nations.

At the World Championships in 1981, Milford went over to Gothenburg in Sweden and watched with rapt attention as the team from what was then Czechoslovakia took home the bronze medal by defeating a Canadian team that featured Larry Robinson. On that Czech team was a forward named Ivan Hlinka, and Milford had designs on signing him as well as another Czech player, defenseman Jiri Bubla.

"They were communists," remembered Mike Penny, then part of Vancouver's four-person scouting team. "Czechoslovakia was part of the Warsaw Pact, and Milford worked diligently on it and secured Bubla and Hlinka's release."

For Milford, the situation was complicated by Czechoslovakia's political status. There was also no active transfer agreement between Czechoslovakia, Russia, and the NHL. Then–NHL president John Ziegler was working on a remedy, but Milford had other ideas. The story goes that at the 1981 World Championships, Milford, while operating in total secrecy, signed Hlinka and Bubla to contracts he smuggled out in his coat pocket. At least that's the story Milford told the *Toronto Star* the next spring.

Milford returned to North America with two veteran players hailing from a communist country under contract, but he kept the agreements totally secret. He wanted the moves to be a grand, splashy surprise for his NHL colleagues.

As it turned out, Milford's contemporaries weren't impressed. "We were in a pretty serious GM meeting at the draft somewhere, and Jake had been out of the room," Boston's Harry Sinden recalled to author Jason Farris. "[Milford came] running in [and] there was a stage there, and he got up on the stage and he said he had an announcement to make. It looked very serious, and everybody thought there was going to be a big trade or something.

"He announced that he had signed these two Czech players that nobody ever heard of. Everybody looked at each other," Sinden continued. "It was funny. They were good players, but to come in during the middle of the meeting, everybody thought it was going to be this big trade announcement. The GMs never let up on that one. Those players turned out to be good players. [Jake] knew that, and he felt he was really getting something for Vancouver and he had to tell the world."

The skepticism of rival coaches and managers proved unfounded. Immediately, Bubla and Hlinka were impact players. Bubla sustained a significant injury midway through his first season, missing out on the club's miracle run to the 1982 Stanley Cup Final. Hlinka, however, played a big role on that playoff team and for good measure notched 60 points in the regular season.

Though he was older than 30 at the time, Hlinka's 60-point performance set a record for points by a Canucks rookie that wasn't broken until the launch of the Russian Rocket.

23 Reasonably Good Players but a Bad Team

Jake Milford would come to be known as the architect of the Vancouver Canucks' 1982 Stanley Cup Finals team, but first he had to tear down a crumbling, often dysfunctional edifice and build anew. It was a process that the veteran hockey man, armed with his new ideas and progressive attitudes, undertook in a methodical and deliberate fashion.

In his first year on the job, Milford made few major changes. He even made noises in the press about being philosophically opposed to a large-scale teardown of the organization. He retained Orland Kurtenbach as coach and didn't make his first trade as GM for eight months (at which point he sold Claire Alexander to the Toronto Maple Leafs).

With the Canucks limping meekly through the 1977–78 campaign—the club only won 20 games that season and finished the year with just 57 points—Milford's impatience grew. It wasn't a question of *if* Milford would hold a fire sale. It was a matter of *when.*

As longtime Minnesota North Stars general manager Lou Nanne recalled to author Jason Farris: "I called [Milford] one day when he was GM in Vancouver and I said, 'How are you doing?' He said, 'How am I doing? Oh, I'll tell you how I'm doing. If I was the manager of the Canadian Olympic bicycle-riding team, I'd be doing great, because all that our guys do is ride bikes.

"'They can't play worth a goddamn, but they're great on the bikes. We've got bikes in the locker room now, and the players are hanging from the ceiling from ropes and everything else.' He says, 'I can have trapeze artists and I can have bike riders, but I've got a horseshit hockey team.'"

In May 1978 Milford hit the detonate button. That month, the club introduced Harry Neale as head coach at an extravagant luncheon in a pricey conference room at the Bayshore. "It was as if the Vancouver team knew that Neale would become more significant than any of its previous coaches," wrote Tony Gallagher.

At this point, it's worth mentioning Milford's progressiveness extended beyond the realm of player acquisition and into tactics and coaching. He was fond of having a diverse set of coaches, and his teams often empowered assistants beyond what was typical at the time (a practice that is now standard across the NHL).

Milford also didn't believe playing experience was a prerequisite for an NHL head coach. Neale hadn't played at the highest level. After winning the Memorial Cup as a major junior player, he attended teacher's college. Future Canucks assistant coaches Roger Neilson and Ron Smith fit a similar mold. It seems quaint from today's vantage point, but Milford's rejection of professional experience as a requisite for a bench boss was quite radical in the late 1970s.

As for Neale, he—like Milford—promised to be deliberate in how he approached his new charges. He would get to know them, figure out how to motivate them, and demand plenty. "My first important task is to get to know the players and to tell them what kind of contribution they're going to get from me as a coach," Neale said at his first availability. "Once that's established, I'll expect the same contribution from them."

It wasn't long before Neale and Milford, together, found a variety of players lacking, and went about offloading them. In

Could Have Been Bowman

Before settling on Milford as GM, Bill Hughes—who was the Canucks CEO for nine years during the early Frank Griffiths years and the vice president of Western Broadcasting limited—targeted legendary Montreal Canadiens bench boss Scotty Bowman for the role.

Yeah. *Scotty Bowman.*

Bowman, who would leave the Canadiens two years later to join the Buffalo Sabres organization, was apparently very serious about the possibility. But the deal fell apart because the Canucks weren't looking for someone to be both a manager and a head coach. They wanted Bowman's executive skills. "He felt that he could not make a decision on his future because of one overriding factor—that he still wanted to be...a coach," Hughes told the *Canadian Press* mere hours before the news of Milford's hiring broke.

"We had further discussions on the phone when [Bowman] said he still hadn't made up his mind, that he really felt he wanted to coach, but he would like to come to Vancouver, all things being equal," Hughes continued. "I said, 'I'm sorry Scott. You'll have to make the decision in light of what you see in Montreal because we aren't negotiating for a general manager and a coach.'"

With the Canucks and Bowman unable to agree on what his new role would look like, the two sides terminated their discussions.

Oh, what could have been.

June 1978—the same month Milford would complete a lopsided trade for Thomas Gradin—the Canucks traded leading scorer and occasional malcontent Mike Walton to the St. Louis Blues for a fourth-round pick. Before the season started, Garry Monahan and Ralph Stewart were sold for cash.

Though Milford's reconstruction of the Canucks roster was far-reaching and aggressive—by the time the Canucks made the '82 Cup Finals, only Harold Snepsts remained from the 1977–78 team—initially it didn't go far enough or fast enough for Neale's liking. In his very first season with the club, Neale came into Milford's office and started demanding a list of players be dealt. Milford had to calm his coach down, asking, "Do you realize you've just asked me to move 10 players?"

"I found out by Christmas [of my first season] that we had some reasonably good players but a bad team," Neale recalled of his first year with the team in 1982. "It was a collection of what three coaches and four general managers had left behind.... The players were totally motivated as individuals, not as a team. There was jealousy, envy. Players bragging about their own success, laughing at other players."

So the remodel continued. Gradin and Stan Smyl were providing a level of work ethic and skill previously unseen in Canucks history, and the team was showing signs of internal improvement by qualifying for the postseason in each of Neale's first seasons. But the fire sale went on. In December of Neale's first year, Dennis Ververgaert, once a promising power forward, was sent to Philadelphia for puck-moving defenseman and future Canucks captain Kevin McCarthy. It was a big deal, but Milford's most impactful, culture-shifting trades were still two years out.

24 Why You Couldn't Help but Admire Stan Smyl

There were plenty of quotes, from both players and the front office, deriding the culture that surrounded the Canucks in the late 1970s and early 1980s.

For much of its turbulent first decade, the team was afflicted by selfishness in the dressing room and mismanagement in the GM's suite. Whether that selfishness was the product of off-ice mismanagement or a partial cause of it is a chicken-or-the-egg type of thing. It's hard to tell. What's clear, though, is that players credited by early chroniclers as ones who "brought it" consistently on a game-by-game basis—Don Lever, Harold Snepsts, Orland Kurtenbach—made for a pretty short list.

In the fall of 1978, the Canucks debuted two new players who broke that mold in Thomas Gradin and Stan "Steamer" Smyl. Speaking of debuts, the club also broke out unsightly new jerseys depicting a black flying *V* (*V* for *Vancouver*, or for *Victory*) and a rather ridiculous new black, mustard yellow (or gold), and red color scheme.

The look became known across the NHL as the "Halloween suit" and was met with widespread derision. That derision didn't matter to Smyl, though. He always took pride in wearing the sweater. "I loved that jersey," Smyl told Iain MacIntyre in February 2016. "It was my first year in the NHL. That was my jersey, and I was going to do everything to wear it proudly. To this day, that's how I feel about it."

It's a telling quote. Smyl was a fan favorite in Vancouver throughout his playing career, and his No. 12 hangs retired from the Rogers Arena rafters (as it previously did at the Pacific Coliseum). Though he was a top-of-the-lineup-caliber winger through the first half of the 1980s, it was his level of pride and the night-in, night-out effort that endeared him to fans and distinguished Smyl from other early stars.

"You can be sure about Smyl," Dave "Tiger" Williams wrote in his autobiography, *Tiger: A Hockey Story*. "He will give it everything he has and if things don't go right, he isn't going to put his head on his chest. He's going to keep plowing away."

Though Smyl was undersized—and some will wrongly describe him as an underskilled overachiever, a ridiculous notion—he did the little things that endear players to savvy fans. From killing penalties to winning battles to fighting bigger men to hitting hard, one couldn't help but admire the tenacity with which Smyl played.

Those emotional leadership qualities made Smyl a rather obvious choice for captain. When his predecessor, Kevin McCarthy, went down with a preposterously ill-timed injury prior to the 1982 postseason, interim coach Roger Neilson named Smyl—then only 24 years old—the club's interim captain. Smyl wore the *C* all the way to the Stanley Cup Finals and didn't relinquish it until the 1990s.

But back to McCarthy for a moment. After being acquired via trade, he was named Canucks captain at the tender age of 22. Though he put in a number of excellent and productive seasons as an offensive defenseman in Vancouver, by the age of 25 he'd been stripped of that captaincy, and by the age of 28 he was out of the league.

In 1982—and in a classic Canucks incident—McCarthy attended an optional practice at Britannia Rink. He only took the skate because he was going to be rested in the final game of the season. During the practice, McCarthy got tangled up with Curt Fraser and took an awkward spill. He didn't think it was too serious, but then he couldn't get up off the ice. Like a bad joke—as the news got around town, McCarthy's Canucks teammates literally couldn't believe it—McCarthy had injured himself and would miss the entirety of the postseason.

And so it was that the Canucks entered the 1982 playoffs with three of their better defensemen—Jiri Bubla, Rick Lanz, and Kevin McCarthy—in leg casts and unable to play.

"Captain Kevin McCarthy was the Canucks' John F. Kennedy," Gallagher memorably wrote. "He was a leader, Catholic, and everyone remembers where they were when he went down."

McCarthy's injury didn't just cost him an opportunity to compete in the Stanley Cup Finals, it also cost him his captaincy. As mentioned earlier, the club had so much success in the 1982 playoffs under interim captain Stan Smyl that they made Smyl's captaincy permanent at the start of the 1982–83 season.

In his biography, Williams claims McCarthy was stripped of the captaincy because he laughed a bit too hard at a Bobby Schmautz joke about Jake Milford at the golf club during the summer of 1982. It's possible, but surely the logic behind retaining Smyl as captain after he led the team to the Stanley Cup Finals is compelling enough on its own.

However the decision occurred, McCarthy publicly requested to be traded at training camp the next season. "It will be better for me and the team if I get a fresh start somewhere else," McCarthy said. "It was a kick in the head. I can't see myself staying. I don't feel comfortable about it. I have asked Harry [Neale] to trade me."

Neale didn't exactly rush to accommodate McCarthy's request, and he spent the better part of two more seasons in Vancouver with Smyl wearing the *C*.

25 Milford Gave Away the Refrigerator but "Had Lots of Ice"

On paper, the trade that brought Tiger Williams to Vancouver is among the worst, most lopsided trades in the history of the franchise. In late February 1980 the Canucks were—once again—spinning their wheels. A promising young core of players, a group that included Thomas Gradin, Stan Smyl, Rick Vaive, and Bill Derlago, had worked their way onto the roster. Under Coach Harry Neale, the team got off to a respectable first few months of the season, and looked very much like a playoff team. Then the wheels fell off.

Over a 21-game stretch from December 15 through February 3, the Canucks went 3–17–1 and failed to win consecutive games. With another season seemingly waylaid, the club overreacted and made a win-now move.

Derlago was 21 years old at the time, while Vaive was 20. Neither was performing up to expectations, and the club was particularly concerned because they'd come to believe "[Derlago and Vaive's] finest displays were being staged in Vancouver's nightspots."

Jake Milford openly stated Derlago was as good as gone, and on February 18, 1980, the GM made good on his promise. Derlago and Vaive were dealt to Toronto, where—after a stern talking-to from Darryl Sittler—they developed into offensive stars.

For their part in the deal, Vancouver acquired Williams and 29-year-old farmhand Jerry Butler. "Maybe the guys we're getting aren't as talented as the two we gave up," Harry Neale admitted at the time, "but their work habits are a lot better."

Tiger would, fortunately for Milford, help the Canucks sneak into the postseason in 1980 and go on to score 35 goals in his first full season. It was nice production, but Vaive would transform into a 30-goal scorer the next year in Toronto, at which point the deal started to look like a poor swap from Vancouver's perspective. Over the course of the next decade, Vaive and Derlago combined to produce 892 points in Toronto. Butler and Williams produced just 204 in their seven combined seasons in Vancouver.

Taking a Knee

It isn't often mentioned in the same breath as the Cam Neely trade, or Joel Otto's kicked-in overtime winner, or the decision to waive Igor Larionov, but Denis Potvin's hip check that tore up Derlago's knee was a seminal moment—creating one of the greatest what-ifs in franchise history.

Derlago, the fourth overall pick at the 1978 NHL Entry Draft, was a ridiculous offensive player. He twice recorded more than 150 points with the Brandon Wheat Kings in the WHL and once scored 50 goals in the span of just 27 games.

Though Derlago was overweight when he reported to camp for his rookie season, he was still a dynamo. Those who watched his first nine games with the Canucks—particularly the two games in which he thoroughly dominated after playing himself back into shape in the minor leagues—swear he was an unstoppable offensive force, as creative and threatening with the puck as any player the Canucks had ever employed.

Nine games into his rookie season, though, just as Derlago was beginning to find his groove, he was dancing around the soon-to-be-dynastic New York Islanders when he took a brutal, injurious low-bridge hit from Potvin. It ruined his knee, though the ensuing surgery did allow Derlago to return. He had multiple 30-goal seasons and carved out a respectable niche as an offensive player with the Leafs, but physically and mentally, he was never the same.

"After that, the game just wasn't fun for him in the same way," longtime *Vancouver Province* beat writer Tony Gallagher said.

Derlago's Canucks career began with so much flash and promise. But it was over after only 63 games.

Though the deal looks lopsided on the back of a hockey card—heck, Milford himself called it the worst of his career a few months before the miracle run to the 1982 Stanley Cup Finals—one could argue that Tiger was precisely the sort of personality the franchise needed. And he did play a crucial part on the 1982 Stanley Cup Finals team, on their memorable Cinderella run through the playoffs. Vaive and Derlago's prime offensive years, meanwhile, saw the Maple Leafs hold court in the cellar of the NHL's standings.

"He is a mighty shrewd judge of talent, and he has made some fine trades for the Canucks," Canucks goodwill ambassador Babe Pratt once said of Milford, in front of a gaggle of Toronto media, including hockey writer Trent Frayne of the *Globe and Mail.*

"Didn't he trade Vaive and Bill Derlago to Toronto for Tiger Williams and Jerry Butler?" was the retort.

"Yes, he did," Pratt answered quickly. "And the Tiger did a good job out here. We've been in the playoffs every year since Jake made the trade and were in the Stanley Cup Finals in '82. Meantime, Vaive and Derlago have helped Toronto become a big loser. You'll never catch Jake giving away the refrigerator unless he has lots of ice."

26 "Fight Like a Bastard"

The acquisition cost of bringing Tiger Williams to Vancouver was exorbitant, and his on-ice contributions were—frankly—meager when compared with the gaudy point totals Rick Vaive and Bill Derlago managed. In Williams, though, the Canucks had acquired the type of player who, despite his worst impulses, habitual hot-headedness, and condescending attitude toward Europeans, took being a professional hockey player seriously. Very seriously. And in the first decade of the Canucks' existence, that was a rare thing.

Williams was a business-minded player with a flair for marketing himself and managing the media. He had a detailed understanding of how tax laws affected his earnings, and he worked hard to supplement those earnings with a variety of local sponsorships and appearance agreements. It's telling that he always sat at the front of the bus or the plane, crunching numbers near Harry Neale or Jake Milford and team management, which inevitably resulted in some grumbling and derision from his teammates.

"He knows the needs of the television industry and he meets those needs," Tony Gallagher wrote of Williams. "Though seldom in the starting lineup, he will often remain on the ice during the national anthem so the cameraman will pick him out, singing lustily."

Williams' penchant for self-promotion and his friendly posture toward management bothered teammates, and their laissez-faire attitude toward leadership and winning games bothered him. Right from the start, it seems, the attitude among some of the players—the lack of effort, the lack of tradition, the lack of culture—stood out as a major problem for Tiger, like it previously had for Milford. "There were some talented players on the Canucks," Williams remembered in his autobiography, *Tiger: A Hockey Story*. "But the team's attitude was bad. In fact you could say it was horseshit."

Williams clashed with teammates early and often, including defensemen Dennis Kearns and Bobby Schmautz. Snepsts, according to Williams, once told him the trade that brought him to Vancouver was one of the worst in club history. "I at least respected Snepsts for making those comments up front, even though I had to tell him he was talking horseshit," Williams recalled.

It was an incident with Kearns, though, that perhaps set the tone for how Williams would influence the Canucks. After sitting out a game for poor performance during that dysfunctional 1979–80 season, Kearns admitted he'd been hoping the team would lose so he could get back onto the ice. Those comments bothered Williams enormously, and he lashed out. "I said to my teammates, 'I can't change the management's attitude; I can't change trades, can't turn the clock back. All I can do is fight like a bastard to get some success, and if we all do that, we'll all benefit.'"

If that level of what we'd now consider basic professionalism seemed simple to Williams, it wasn't for his teammates. And he began to wonder if even the great leaders in the sport—in his autobiography he specifically name-checks Darryl Sittler and Bryan Trottier as examples—would've developed their flair for inspiring teammates in a situation like the one in Vancouver.

Williams put together a career year in 1980–81. He scored 35 goals, was named an All-Star and, in an iconic moment, rode his stick like a horse after scoring a goal in his return to Maple Leaf Gardens. But the Canucks team was thick with tension. At a team meeting late in the year, Williams led a small cabal in defending management against a dissatisfied group led, in Williams' account, by Schmautz.

After the season, Vancouver management sided with the hard-nosed forward at the front of the bus (though Williams denies he had anything to do with management's decision-making). Following another first-round playoff loss, Kearns and Schmautz were shepherded into retirement.

If Williams had helped to bring a new sense of competitiveness to the Canucks locker room, then that competitiveness was—at times—a double-edged sword. For all the off-ice dysfunction, the Canucks got hot late in 1980 and managed to qualify for the postseason. For their first-round series, Vancouver drew Gilbert Perreault and (who else?) the Buffalo Sabres.

Scotty Bowman, with Roger Neilson as his overqualified assistant, coached the Sabres, and the Canucks were rather convincingly dispensed of by their expansion cousin. What's best remembered from that series, though, is the hack Williams took at Bowman's head. No footage or photographs exist of the incident, and a variety of newspaper articles and color profiles disagree on precisely how it went down. In some accounts, Bowman leaned over the bench to watch a fight, and Williams came at him with a blindside slash to the noggin. In some versions Bowman was felled by the slash; in others, blood was drawn.

Williams later remembered that Bowman, who was annoying him throughout the game by repeatedly telling Kevin McCarthy that he belonged in the minors, was yelling directly at him. Tiger thought to skate away but also to push his stick "right down into" Bowman's wagging mouth. Instead he took a swing at his head, catching him "with a glancing blow" at "25 percent force."

"Bowman had been behaving like a jerk, and I just thought, *Oh shit, let's give him the lumber*," Williams recalled.

Bowman later joked he still owed Williams a slash. Williams, meanwhile, received a ridiculously paltry one-game suspension and saw his club eliminated during his absence.

True to form, Tiger expressed no regret when writing about the incident in his autobiography years later. "One opponent skated [up] to me in an exhibition game [the next season]," Williams wrote. "[He said], 'I still hate you, you bastard, but it was great the way you got Bowman.'"

27 The Unlikely King

Standing 5'7" and lacking the chiseled physique typical of professional athletes (even by 1970s standards), Richard Brodeur had spent his hockey career as something of a perpetual afterthought. A seventh-round pick of the Islanders in 1972, Brodeur's name was misspelled in the official draft guide. The Islanders weren't offering him much to play for their minor league team, and Brodeur wanted to face stronger competition, so he opted to play for the WHA's Quebec Nordiques instead.

With a technically advanced playing style polished by the standards of the day, Brodeur spent his peak professional seasons with the Nordiques, six of them as the starting goaltender. He was the star during the Nordiques' championship run in 1977.

Brodeur performed ably and loyally for Quebec, but he fell out of favor just as the Nordiques were set to join the NHL for the start of the 1979–80 season. At the 1979 NHL expansion draft, which was really a formalized merger of the WHA and the NHL, the Islanders reclaimed their rights to Brodeur, and the Nordiques—who had loaded up on goaltenders at the expansion draft—agreed to release him to Long Island for another goalie, the immortal Goran Hogosta.

In rejoining the Islanders, Brodeur landed in another difficult situation. Nicknamed Kermit by his teammates—a reference to his stature and gravelly voice—Brodeur was stuck behind Billy Smith and Glenn "Chico" Resch on the depth chart. He spent his one season with Long Island making just two appearances, spending most of his time with the club's minor league affiliate in Indianapolis.

Though he'd put in yet another solid professional season and was named the Goalie of the Year in the Central League, Brodeur found himself even further down the pecking order when his second Islanders training camp opened. The Islanders had used a high draft pick at the 1979 NHL Entry Draft to select a hotshot goaltender—a fresh-faced kid from New Brunswick named Roland "Rollie" Melanson—and when Melanson turned pro the next summer, the Islanders didn't even have a third-string spot open for Brodeur.

"We knew [Brodeur] was a good goaltender or we wouldn't have drafted him," recalled Islanders executive Bill Torrey. To their credit, the Islanders tried to do right by Brodeur. Torrey started working the phones, knowing full well he was about to do a rival team a favor. Longtime Detroit Red Wings executive Jimmy Devellano, then running the Islanders scouting department, convinced Brodeur to report to Indianapolis, which was no small feat. "I was ready to quit," Brodeur told Tony Gallagher of his second Islanders training camp. "I was washed up."

Brodeur was 28 years old at the start of the 1980–81 campaign. He had waited nearly a decade for a serious NHL shot, and only now, at the lowest point in his career, did it emerge. And it emerged in the form of a groin injury to Canucks backup Gary Bromley. All of a sudden Vancouver needed a third goaltender, which made them receptive when Torrey called about Brodeur. After a bit of haggling, Jake Milford and Torrey agreed to swap fifth-round picks in the 1981 draft, and the Canucks had their backup.

"We picked him up just before the waiver draft when [Bromley] was hurt and we realized we needed a third goaltender," explained Neale.

Private, humble, and self-effacing, Brodeur arrived in Vancouver just hoping to get a game. And that game came on a grueling road trip at the Philadelphia Spectrum—easily the toughest building to play in in the league at the time. Brodeur had only made two career appearances in the NHL. He was unknown to his teammates, who weren't particularly impressed with what they saw of him in warm-ups. The future Canucks star stole the show and two points from the Flyers that night, stopping 36 of the 38 shots he faced in a 5–2 victory. "Now we can't decide whether to send Bromley or Brodeur down to our farm," Neale quipped after the contest.

If Neale's candid admission that Brodeur had impressed in his debut was an act of generosity, it was also a comment that served to tempt fate. In the Canucks' very next game in Montreal, projected starter Glen Hanlon sustained a knee injury when Guy Lapointe crashed into the crease.

Nine years removed from the NHL draft and three weeks removed from losing his CHL gig to a 21-year-old rookie, Brodeur had finally earned the right to start at the NHL level. And he cemented himself as Vancouver's go-to netminder in Hanlon's absence with a glorious follow-up performance at the Nassau Coliseum, in a 6–3 victory over his former team.

"It was a real satisfaction to beat a team like the Islanders," Brodeur said afterward. "But not because I held any bitterness toward them. I understand why they couldn't play me and had to send me to the minors. Actually, I should feel nothing but kindness toward them for trading me to Vancouver. I had been so anxious to play in the league."

Brodeur continued, "I know I can play in the NHL. All I needed was the chance. I had to go down to the minors last season and was never in the Islanders' plans. It's sad to know that I had to get my chance because of injuries to other guys, but that's the way this game works."

If Brodeur as a starter was supposed to be a short-term arrangement, he certainly didn't follow the script. Brodeur managed to take full advantage of his shot. He wouldn't relinquish the job for another seven years.

Milford would come to refer to the trade as the greatest of his career. Acquiring King Richard for a swap of fifth-round draft picks is a special thing indeed. "I told Jake [Milford] that if Brodeur worked out he would owe me a steak dinner," Torrey later revealed during the 1982 Stanley Cup Finals. "After what I've seen in the NHL playoffs, I want the dinner at Maxim's in Paris. Of course, Jake's not necessarily invited."

The man they called Kermit in Long Island would be known as King in Vancouver. When the similarity between his story and the fable of the frog that was kissed by a princess and turned into a prince was pointed out to Brodeur by *New York Times* writer George Vecsey during the 1982 Stanley Cup Finals, King Richard replied with regal wit, "I did even better."

28 The Battle of Quebec

Roger Neilson was one of hockey's great innovators. Nicknamed Captain Video for his early and innovative scouting techniques, Neilson was a hypercompetitive dog lover and a baseball enthusiast with a different way of looking at the game. His reputation as a hands-on tactician who relied heavily on video was well-earned.

"They called him Captain Video, and it was true: it was more video than I had ever watched in my entire career," Stan Smyl recalled to Stan Taylor. "But he knew what he was doing."

The popular image of Neilson in a lab coat, scientifically testing and challenging the popular approach to and rules of the game wasn't just an exaggeration. His logic was rigorous and his particular habit of playing with the rules of the game, stretching them to their most extreme logical endpoint so as to benefit his team, resulted in a variety of memorable incidents.

As the coach of the Peterborough Petes, for example, Neilson—realizing the rules gave him some creative latitude—once put a defenseman rather than a goaltender on the ice during a penalty shot situation. Rather than relying on a goalie to stop the penalty shot, Neilson's defensive skater would charge the puck carrier. After Neilson went back to the well successfully on four more occasions, the rule was clarified: a goaltender had to be on the ice for a penalty shot.

A genuine eccentric—in Peterborough, he had a loyal dog named Jacques, who he taught to forecheck and often spoke to at length on the team bus—Neilson broke into the NHL with the Toronto Maple Leafs. He was once very publicly fired by Maple Leafs owner Harold Ballard, who later asked Neilson to return to the bench when he couldn't find a replacement.

In the summer of 1981, Neilson left his post as coach of the Buffalo Sabres. It turned out that Neilson and general manager Scotty Bowman were too similar and too controlling to coexist. Bowman and Neilson had a "public falling out in a parking lot," which left Neilson looking for a new job.

The Canucks came calling and hired Neilson as part of a succession plan. General manager Jake Milford was set to turn 67 in the summer of 1981 and was looking to hand off his responsibilities to Harry Neale, who in turn would hand over head coaching duties to Neilson.

As any Canucks fan knows by now, the best-laid plans of Canucks management are often waylaid by unintended consequences. In this case, fate would intervene to prematurely place Neilson on the bench for the duration of the Canucks' unlikely run to the Stanley Cup Finals in 1982. Ah, yes, the Battle of Quebec.

On March 18, 1982, the Canucks arrived in La Belle Province for games against the Canadiens and Nordiques. In an effort to turn the tide, Neale bumped Darcy Rota to the Canucks' top line with Thomas Gradin and Stan Smyl. The line proved an instant success in a 4–2 victory over the Habs.

In the following tilt against the Nordiques, Vancouver was leading late in the game when Quebec tied it up. With time expiring, Tiger Williams—who else?—began to scrap with Nords star Peter Stastny. "I got into a wrestling match with Peter Stastny and a fan reached over the glass and took a poke at me," Williams recalled in his biography, *Tiger: A Hockey Story*. "Neale went after the fan and he was followed by Doug Halward and our backup goaltender, Rick Heinz."

As Neale and the fan went at it—at least one punch was thrown—a variety of Canucks skaters, including Curt Fraser and Marc Crawford, did what they could to maintain order. Kevin McCarthy, meanwhile, threw a glove at a fan from the ice surface.

The fan who "took a poke" at Tiger identified himself as Pierre Fournel after the game, and he seemed to enjoy his moment in the spotlight. He claimed he was an innocent in the entire interaction. "I didn't start anything," Fournel insisted while holding court with the media postgame. "I was simply talking to the players. Neale was the one who hit me. I didn't touch any player. I'm going to lay charges."

Those charges never came. Daps for Fournel from the Nordiques locker room, however, were more forthcoming. "I found the whole thing amusing," Stastny said of the altercation, which had to be defused by police. "The fan did a great job against the Canucks."

When the dust settled, NHL president John Ziegler flew out to Vancouver—for only the second time in his tenure—to discuss the punishment that would be levied. Though the penalties seem rather modest from our contemporary vantage point, they were seen as extreme at the time, according to Tony Gallagher: "Ziegler came out of [Milford's] office to meet the media, said he would have no idea what the penalties would be and announced them five hours later—after he had left town. Neale was gone 10 games, Halward seven, McCarthy one and the fines were high. Hockey clubs usually take fines lightly but this was a little much. Neale was nicked $7,500 and the rest $500, even trainer Larry Ashley, the former Nordiques medical man.… The penalties were perhaps fair in the public's eye but in terms of league precedent they were extremely harsh. It was just another contribution to Vancouver's persecution complex."

And so, with just a small handful of games remaining before the 1982 playoffs were set to begin, the reeling Canucks got a new head coach in Roger Neilson. And with him, a shot in the arm.

"An incident like that unified [the] team dramatically," Williams recalled later. "It meant that Neale was able to hand us over to a coach who knew exactly how to exploit the strengths of a team that was in the mood to play."

The stage was set for the first real moment of triumph in the 12-year history of the Canucks franchise.

29 The Miracle Run

"We're an average team playing above average"—Harry Neale

The 1982 Cup Finals run is remembered as an improbable event, a Cinderella run by a scrappy group of underdogs. "Should we have been in the Stanley Cup Final?" then–Canucks scout Mike Penny asked. "Maybe not. We lucked out, found a way to get there."

Tiger Williams echoed that sentiment when looking back at his days in Vancouver. In his autobiography, he describes how a group of Canucks players believed the Chicago Blackhawks—Vancouver's opponent in the conference finals—had the superior roster and that if the Canucks were going to win, they had to win the contest of wills.

"When we looked at the roster of both clubs, some of the guys felt that Chicago had better players. I said, 'Yes, maybe so, but there's no damned way they're going to beat us.' They might have good players…but when you looked around their club you didn't see too many players who would make the big sacrifices."

There is some truth undergirding that common interpretation. By the standards of an average Stanley Cup Finals team, the 1982 Canucks were certainly left wanting. They were a solid defensive team in a high-scoring era, but their offense was of the popgun variety, and over the course of the season they'd only outscored their opponents by two goals—ranked 10th in the NHL that season.

So how were the Canucks able to run roughshod over the Clarence Campbell conference and qualify for the big dance? The first and most important factor to keep in mind is that the talent in the league was unevenly distributed between the two conferences. In the Prince of Wales, seven of the nine teams managed a positive goal differential. In the Campbell, there were two powerhouse teams—the Bobby Smith, Dino Ciccarelli, Neal Broten–led Minnesota North Stars and the Wayne Gretzky, Mark Messier–led Edmonton Oilers—and one middling team (the Canucks). Every other club was outscored in aggregate.

Without a lot of data to rely on—there's no simple way to look up leaguewide shot differentials or anything of the like—we're left to use rather blunt tools such as goal differential to render an objective assessment of team quality. And goal differential implies the 1982 Canucks were the third-best team in their conference and *never faced a playoff opponent of superior quality until they met the Islanders* in the Stanley Cup Finals.

If we accept—and we should—that at no point during the run did the Canucks vanquish a superior team, then it stands to reason that the good fortune the '82 Canucks enjoyed that spring was *not* derived from the series in which they actually took part. The source of Lady Luck's long-overdue but welcome first act of Canucks-directed kindness can be found in a pair of first-round series upsets: the Blackhawks beat the North Stars, and the Kings beat the Oilers.

Though the Kings boasted the Three Crowns line centered by Marcel Dionne, the series between Edmonton and the Los Angeles Kings shouldn't have been close. Gretzky recorded 12 points over five games, and even still the Kings managed a stupendous series of upset victories, winning 10–8 in the series opener and closing out the series with a decisive 7–4 victory in Game 5. The most memorable Kings win in that series came in Game 3—the so-called Miracle on Manchester—in which Los Angeles fought back from a 5–0 deficit to win 6–5. That "miracle" Kings victory remains the largest comeback in NHL playoff history.

"So instead of playing the Oilers, one of the best teams in the history of hockey, we were now playing the Kings," Neale remembered to Chris Taylor 20 years later. "That was the first big break we got. It showed us that once you get a ticket to the lottery, anything can happen."

In the case of the North Stars, they boasted an imposing top-six forward group, but their defensive corps was only average and their goaltender, Gilles Meloche, was outplayed by Chicago's backup, Murray Bannerman. The mustachioed Bannerman, a future NHL All-Star, was actually a Canucks draft pick originally, and he made a relief appearance for Vancouver during the 1977–78 campaign. In an odd, fateful historical quirk, Vancouver traded Bannerman to Chicago for forward Pit Martin. Martin, who was 34 when the Canucks acquired him, was modestly effective over 137 games in Vancouver at the tail end of his lengthy career. Bannerman was the "player to be named later" in the deal, and moved to the Blackhawks organization in the summer of 1978.

Bannerman had never played in the Stanley Cup playoffs, but he was forced into action by a late-season injury to Tony Esposito. He made his playoff debut against the North Stars and stole Game 1 on the road, an overtime victory, by stopping 45 shots. He stole the second game in Minnesota too, as the Blackhawks took a commanding 2–0 lead in the best-of-five series. Minnesota solved Bannerman in Game 3 but succumbed in Game 4. Chicago eliminated the North Stars in a series in which both teams scored 14 goals in aggregate.

While a hot goaltender and an act of God served to clear the field for the Canucks in the Campbell conference, upsets were all the rage in the Prince of Wales as well. The Montreal Canadiens were eliminated in the first round that year, and the New York Islanders were less than 150 seconds away from losing their opening-round series to the Pittsburgh Penguins before a pair of clutch John Tonelli goals resuscitated their dynastic ambitions.

It was "the year of the upset," and a variety of outcomes in Chicago, Minnesota, Los Angeles, and Edmonton had set the stage for the first playoff run in Canucks franchise history.

30 The First Series Win

Though three of their top defensemen began the 1982 playoffs shelved with injuries, the Canucks were favored in their opening-round series against the Calgary Flames. In 1982 the Flames were a shadow of the teams that would spend the next decade tormenting the Canucks. Al MacInnis made his NHL debut that year with the Flames, but he was a teenager and didn't factor into the playoff series. Paul Reinhart played in the series, but at 22 he wasn't yet the elite offensive defenseman he would develop into. Joe Nieuwendyk and Theo Fleury were still in high school, as was the right foot of Joel Otto.

The Canucks were the better team and had plenty of motivation. When the Canucks and Flames were close in the standings late in the year, Flames general manager Cliff Fletcher made a big show of complaining openly about the NHL's tie-breaking format. Fletcher's complaints and threats were for naught, as the Canucks got hot following the Battle of Quebec and finished the year on a 5–0–1 tear to outpace Calgary in the standings by two points. "Over the last 10 games of the season, we actually became one of the hottest teams in the league," Stan Smyl remembered 30 years later. "We were extremely hardworking and we were getting great goaltending at the time from Richard Brodeur. Going into the playoffs, that's a very dangerous combination."

As Game 1 approached, Coach Roger Neilson had distributed folders breaking down the Flames' tendencies and reminding his club of some fundamentals. The ticket sales in Vancouver were slow, though. "[The game] was on television, so 'why pay money to see what you can get for free?' was the order the day," Tony Gallagher wrote—and only 11,000 filed into the Pacific Coliseum to watch the game live. Those willing to shell out for tickets were treated to a barnburner.

Vancouver's memorable run got off to an auspicious start. Right off the opening faceoff, Thomas Gradin and Stan Smyl took advantage of a poor touch by Flames defenseman Phil Russell. Russell flubbed a shallow Curtis Fraser dump pass, allowing Gradin to find Smyl all alone in front with a deft backhand tip pass. Skating quickly and unmolested into the low slot, Smyl smartly one-timed the rolling puck, tucking it under Flames netminder Pat Riggin for the early go-ahead goal.

Behind the play, meanwhile, two heavyweight toughs—Fraser for the Canucks and Willi Plett for the Flames—dropped the gloves and went at it. Plett appeared to be getting the best of it when Fraser coldcocked him with a heavy right-handed punch and scored the technical knockout.

It's amusing and telling that in discussing the team in later years, several of the players on the Canucks remembered the early fight more clearly than Smyl's early goal. "That fight showed the Flames that we weren't going to back down from anybody," Darcy Rota recalled.

It took the Canucks only eight seconds to build a Game 1 lead that they wouldn't relinquish in a convincing 5–3 victory. There wasn't much time for either team to breathe or for the Canucks to rest on their laurels, as the first-round series began with a set of back-to-back contests. Game 2 would prove to be a grueling 74-minute affair.

The popgun offense carried the day in Game 1, and Game 2 was King Richard's time to shine. The stalwart netminder made 39 saves on 40 shots, holding the fort as the uncharacteristically permissive Canucks defense surrendered 17 against in the third period. The only puck that got by Brodeur that night was scored shortly after the expiry of a two-man advantage for Calgary.

Down 1–0, the Canucks battled back. Future Canucks head coach Marc Crawford has been more successful behind the bench than he ever was on the ice, but his only career NHL playoff goal served to tie Game 2 before the end of the second frame. Crawford was positioned well in the low slot when he tipped home an excellent backhand feed from Ivan Boldirev, who was fighting off a Flames defender behind the net. The excited rookie forward raised his hands in elation, jumping up and down repeatedly.

"I didn't get a lot of shifts," Crawford later recalled of his lone career playoff goal, "but I was put on a line with the great Ivan Boldirev. He was behind the net, put it on my stick in the crease, and I got a huge goal. I was so thrilled that I banged heads with him in celebration.

"He said, 'Hey, I know you're excited, but watch my hair.'"

The game was tied at 1–1 as a memorable goalie duel played out over the course of regulation and into overtime. Rota beat Riggin once, but his shot hit the post. That's when Snepsts decided to carry the puck into the Calgary end.

Snepsts was a hardworking, honest sort, and also Vancouver's best defenseman. He was at his best when he let the game come to him, not when he was pushing the play and trying to make things happen with his feet. Neilson's system, which didn't call for much creativity from the back end, was a perfect fit for Snepsts.

In overtime of the second of back-to-back playoff games, though—and remember, Snepsts was playing huge minutes with Kevin McCarthy, Rick Lanz, and Jiri Bubla out of the lineup—the rugged Canucks defender carried the puck out of his own zone. He beat Lanny McDonald's neutral-zone forecheck by protecting the puck with his backhand and skated deep in the Calgary zone toward the corner of the ice. As Flames defenseman Pekka Rautakallio closed on him, Snepsts shook him and McDonald by abruptly stopping, moving the puck to his forehand, and sending a pass to a trailing Lars Molin.

Molin, by virtue of his positioning and his being a left-handed shooter, couldn't get a lot on the one-timer, but he snapped a weak shot at Riggin. The puck bounced slowly at the Flames goaltender, deflecting off a Calgary skater before bouncing weakly off his right pad. It was a juicy rebound, and Tiger Williams, locked in a battle at the side of the crease with veteran Flames defender Bob Murdoch, managed to poke at the puck with his backhand while being wrestled to the ground.

It was a goal, the overtime winner, and it gave the Canucks a 2–0 series lead. Williams, standing up and admiring his handiwork, proceeded to unleash an epic celebratory parade down to the middle of the ice that was only halted by his tackling teammates. During the 1982 run to the Finals, Arthur Griffiths—the assistant to the chairman of the board at the time—called it the biggest goal in Canucks history. He wasn't wrong.

In their 12-year history, the Canucks had never won a playoff series. They now had a commanding lead over Calgary and an opportunity to finish off the series. Brodeur's heroics ensured they did.

To the Flames' credit, they didn't fold up shop when facing elimination. They were dominant in Game 3 and outshot the Canucks 30–14 through the first two periods. With both clubs exchanging power-play goals, it was 1–1 heading into the third. Once again, it was Williams who scored the game-winner.

The burly forward, who'd harassed Calgary's top line throughout the series, took a rush pass from Gary Lupul and wired a hard wrist shot home. Vancouver would add a Gradin insurance marker before Calgary even had an opportunity to pull their goaltender.

It had taken 12 years for the Canucks to win a playoff round. On this evening in late April 1982, victory tasted sweet.

31 Clutch and Grab: Silencing the Three Crowns

The Canucks remained in Calgary following their first playoff series victory. Even though the Edmonton Oilers were down 2–1 to the Kings at the time, the Canucks assumed—as most did—that their next series would also be played in Alberta.

Vancouver didn't win a single game at Northlands Arena against the juggernaut Oilers that season, a huge problem given Edmonton would enjoy home-ice advantage in a potential series. That the Canucks were rather openly rooting for the Los Angeles Kings goes without saying.

Canucks players even broke with hockey tradition. They admitted to the press they'd prefer to face the Kings. "We would rather play Los Angeles because for sure a guy like Gretzky is going to win three games by himself," Thomas Gradin said. "We didn't really even come close to winning up there, and against a player like that it doesn't leave you much room for mistakes." As it so happened, the Kings shocked the hockey world and eliminated the Oilers on Northlands Arena ice. The series would open in Vancouver.

The Canucks were built on shutting down opponents, a sound strategy in the playoffs where a stingy defense often trumps dynamic skill. And Vancouver's checking line of Lars Molin, Tiger Williams, and Gary Lupul had been crucial to Vancouver's victory over the Flames. Shadowing Lanny McDonald with aggression, the Williams line had held the Flames superstar to just one point in three games.

"Tiger Williams was a guy who would do absolutely anything to win," Jim Robson recalled. "In the first round he was checking Lanny McDonald, who had been his linemate in Toronto with Darryl Sittler. But Tiger was a very rough guy with his stick, and in that series he chopped at Lanny every chance he got.... Lanny couldn't believe that his ex-buddy was being so aggressive. But that was Tiger."

Against the Kings, Tiger, Molin, and Lupul would draw an even more difficult assignment: the Triple Crown line of Marcel Dionne, Charlie Simmer, and Dave Taylor—a high-scoring trio that was sound defensively, and had just bested the Oilers.

Vancouver's tight checking and penchant for physical play became a calling card, and as the playoffs went along, it was commented on with derision by a variety of Eastern media members and opponents. "I don't blame the referee, but he should look a little more," complained Denis Savard, following a Blackhawks loss to Vancouver. "They missed lots of interference calls out there, and the guys were hooking me all night."

Added Savard's coach, Bob Pulford, "It's pretty hard to play hockey when you're carrying them on your back all night."

By the time the club was in the Stanley Cup Finals, Islanders coach Al Arbour described their game plan as "Irish football," and Bill Torrey fumed about Vancouver's ability to turn the game into a "rugby match." "It's the way Roger teaches," Torrey said, playing the media like a fiddle. "You know that when you play a team of his, the game is going to be dragged down."

Those schemes, combined with the Williams-led checking line and top defensive pair led by Harold Snepsts, managed to "drag down" a variety of opponents. Dionne and company were the next targets.

Game 1 of the series was played at the Pacific Coliseum where, once again, the local fans opted not to fill the building. The Kings jumped out to a first-period lead on an unassisted Steve Bozek tally, but the Canucks controlled the play throughout and managed to tie it up at the end of the second period, thanks to a pair of power-play goals by Ivan Hlinka.

In the third, the Canucks got the game winner thanks to a massive body check that Ron Delorme—an unlikely hero, who the Canucks had acquired in the waiver draft from the Colorado Rockies the previous fall—put on Taylor and Larry Murphy. Knocking both Kings skaters to the ground with one hit, Delorme pivoted and hit Lupul with an excellent feed for the deciding marker. It seemed like the Canucks had control of the series, but the playoffs are nothing if not unpredictable.

In Game 2, playing in front of a sellout crowd at the Coliseum, the Triple Crown line broke through. Darcy Rota opened the scoring, but the Canucks turned in a flat effort in the second period. Vancouver was outshot 13–7, and both Dionne and Taylor each scored goals to negate the Canucks' early advantage. Stan Smyl tied things up with his second goal of the playoffs before the second ended, but it was an uninspired performance by the home side.

The sense of lethargy permeated the third period and overtime, as the Canucks were outshot 10–5 over the final 24 minutes of the game. Bozek emerged the hero for the Kings, as a Rick Chartraw pass attempt bounced off Ivan Boldirev then off Bozek's thigh… and into the net. It wasn't pretty, but the Kings had stolen home-ice advantage.

As the series moved to Los Angeles, there was an incident at the Canucks' hotel in the wee hours of the morning. A fire alarm went off at close to 3:00 AM, and as all the players filed out and milled about on the Los Angeles street, they looked up and saw Williams on the roof of the building. Tiger was cheekily looking down at his teammates and snapping some photos. When the hotel asked what exactly he was doing on the roof, Williams replied that he was working for the *L.A. Times*.

In Game 3 another unlikely hero emerged for the Canucks. Colin Campbell—who would later go on to become the NHL's vice president of hockey ops—was a stay-at-home D-man. He was largely considered a depth player and hadn't scored a single goal all year. In the third game of the series he scored two, including the overtime winner. "I'm not Dionne or Taylor," Campbell said sheepishly after Game 3. "I'm the team joke!"

It's impossible for a team to go on a long playoff run without unlikely players contributing along the way. That night, Campbell got the accolades and the big media scrum, but the real star was Richard Brodeur. The Canucks were outshot 44–28 in the game, but Brodeur's 41 stops stole a crucial victory.

Brodeur's dominance continued in Game 4. Though Boldirev's two-goal performance captured headlines, again it was Brodeur's play that gave the Canucks a shot. Even as the Kings controlled the flow of play and recorded 37 shots to Vancouver's mere 15, the Canucks came away with a 5–4 victory. Playing possum with the lead for much of the contest worked for Vancouver, though, mostly because they had the superior goaltender.

By Game 5 the Kings were frustrated. The first period featured brawls aplenty, and the Canucks jumped out to a 2–1 lead. In the second period, with the score 3–1, Mike Murphy scored with just more than 30 seconds left to make things interesting. That level of interest would last for only 26 seconds, though, as Darcy Rota scored and dashed Los Angeles' comeback hopes in the process.

Brodeur and Vancouver's defensive scheme—or their clutching and grabbing, as the critics would have it—had held Dionne to just four points in the series. During the regular season, Dionne had 117.

32 White Towel: The Game God Couldn't Have Refereed

There's nothing more quintessentially Canucks than Roger Neilson's white towel moment. It's the most iconic image in franchise history, depicting a coach so upset at the referees that he opted for a defiant act of mock surrender. Neilson's flag-waving antics aren't just iconic in a figurative sense, either. Quite literally, the image has become iconic, forever immortalized with a statue in front of Rogers Arena and the phrase Towel Power.

Towel Power was born at the old Chicago Stadium, notorious for a smaller-than-usual playing surface and a terrifically unruly crowd. "The rink at the old Chicago Stadium was about as big as your living room," Curt Fraser recalled.

These days, the Blackhawks' home arena is seen as intimidating because of the volume with which Chicago fans sing along with the American national anthem. Back in the early 1980s, it was seen as intimidating because of the fights that would often break out in the stands. "The fights in the stands don't normally begin until the game does, but tonight they get started early with a scuffle in the upper deck," Tony Gallagher wrote prior to Game 1. "But no blood, so it hardly counts."

The stage for a vicious and controversial series was set. With wins over the Kings and Flames, the Canucks had advanced to the Campbell Conference final and were set to face a Blackhawks side led by Denis Savard, a future Hall of Famer. In the first game of the series, the Canucks won a double-overtime thriller with Jim Nill scoring off a rebound. "Roger [Neilson]'s biggest concern was that his video tape would run out before Nill scored," Harry Neale joked about Captain Video after the game.

Neale's comments probably weren't a stretch. Neilson was beginning to talk openly about how, with this group of players, he was confident every time the game went to overtime. Neilson's confidence was justified because of one guy: Richard Brodeur.

In Game 2, a particularly vicious contest, the game got away from referee Bob Myers. The Canucks killed three minor penalties in the opening frame and were down by two after 20 minutes. They mounted a territorial comeback in the second period but were stoned by Blackhawks goaltender Murray Bannerman. The 2–0 score was bothersome, but the penalty differential, heavily in favor of the home team, seemed particularly galling.

It was in the third period, though, when things really began to get out of hand. In a game that Frank Udvari, then the NHL's supervisor of officials, later described as one that "God couldn't have refereed," officials handed out six major penalties and nine misconducts over the final 20 minutes. One of those misconducts was to Harold Snepsts, who had fought Grant Mulvey, which enhanced the Canucks' growing sense of grievance. Earlier, Terry Ruskowski had avoided being similarly penalized despite beating

Decades after the team's improbable playoff run, Roger Neilson and Towel Power remain fresh in the minds of Canucks fans. This statue was erected in 2011, eight years after the coach's passing.

on Gerry Minor, a smaller Canucks forward who had just returned from injury.

Seven minutes later, Myers whistled Doug Halward for a phantom trip on Bill Gardner, which was lavishly embellished. "Off went Halward in the worst call of the playoffs," Gallagher wrote.

Then with less than five minutes remaining, Fraser appeared to score by capitalizing on a rebound. The score would've been 3–2, but that play was belatedly, incorrectly, and preposterously ruled offside, setting off yet another scuffle. In the ensuing melee, Bannerman viciously swung his stick at Fraser. But when the dust settled—Bannerman, Fraser, and Snepsts were all assessed minor penalties and Snepsts received his second misconduct of the period—Myers had granted the Blackhawks yet another power play.

"Myers had come to the rink with the idea that all the fans in the stadium, plus about 20 million people watching on TV, were most interested in seeing him referee than the players play," Tiger Williams recalled. "In the third period, Myers made some decisions that we thought were incredible. He was drawing attention to himself by making cheap calls."

When Savard scored to ice the game, Neilson decided to make a grand gesture. He knew he was going to make a scene but wasn't quite sure how. "Tiger Williams told me to throw some sticks on the ice," Neilson recalled some years later to Archie McDonald of the *Vancouver Sun*, "but I told him I had done that before."

Ever the innovator, Neilson reached for a white towel on the bench. In a fit of pique and inspiration, Neilson told Williams that he wasn't satisfied with merely making a scene. He wanted to surrender. Placing the white towel on a stick and holding it aloft, Neilson stood in protest for 40 seconds. Several players—Williams, Gerry Minor, and Lars Molin among them—joined in.

Even as the broadcasters marveled at Neilson's gesture, Myers still hadn't seen it. So the Canucks head coach resolved to send Lars Lindgren over the boards to make sure he noticed. Thoroughly provoked, Myers threw Neilson, Minor, and Williams out of the game but didn't punish Molin. "True to the pattern Myers kept all night, he missed somebody," Gallagher later joked.

The NHL wasn't impressed, opining that the Canucks had "disgraced the championship series." Neilson was fined $1,000 and the league levied an additional $10,000 fine against the team. Myers, who has been reluctant to comment on the incident for 30 years now, later said he thought Neilson's gesture was "bush league."

Canucks players and fans had a different opinion. The players were visibly moved by Neilson's gesture. As the Canucks coach crossed the ice following his ejection, he was mobbed by Stan Smyl, Richard Brodeur, and Williams. Tiger later described Neilson's protest as a "brilliant psychological move, one of the best I've ever seen in professional sports."

Fans in Vancouver agreed. Led by a local T-shirt entrepreneur Butts Giraud, merchants rushed to print white towels and bring them by the thousands to Game 3. It's true that the Terrible Towel phenomenon already existed in Pittsburgh by 1982, but Neilson had brought Towel Power to Vancouver and to the sport of hockey more widely.

"When we came back to Vancouver for Game 3, all you could see were 15,000 screaming fans waving their white towels," Neale recalled.

33 The First Canucks Fever

The city of Vancouver swooned as the Canucks, for the first time in their history, went on an extended run through the Stanley Cup playoffs. Richard Brodeur was the star as Vancouver stormed through the Clarence Campbell conference, providing the club with impenetrable goaltending. Thomas Gradin and Stan Smyl provided the bulk of the timely scoring, but it was Harold Snepsts and the Tiger Williams line that personified the Canucks' physical, clutch-and-grab, shutdown style.

On their path to the Finals, the Canucks only lost two games, and Neilson's smothering defensive tactics succeeded in frustrating some of the most dynamic offensive producers of their era. Denis Savard, Lanny McDonald, and Marcel Dionne—all currently enshrined in the Hall of Fame—combined for just nine points in 13 playoff games against the Canucks.

Shutting down Mike Bossy and the New York Islanders, though, proved a different story. Bossy is one of the best snipers in league history, and no one—even dating back to the late 19th century—has ever scored goals at a higher per-game clip. And Bossy was only part of what made the Islanders' dynasty so imposing.

The Cup Finals were, to put it bluntly, a mismatch. The Canucks hung tough in the first game and proved a tougher opponent than the Islanders expected, something head coach Al Arbor acknowledged after the fact. Even still, it was a sweep. Vancouver never really had a chance.

Unlike their subsequent Cup Finals losses in 1994 and 2011, this loss wasn't regarded as an epic missed opportunity. Even in the wake of a convincing sweep, the Canucks' playoff run was cause for celebration. A front-page headline in the *Vancouver*

Sun summarized the whiplash experience Vancouver enjoyed: Suddenly the Bums Are Gods.

Throughout the run, a dormant sense of civic pride boiled to the surface. During the Blackhawks series the Vancouver Symphony Orchestra, as a method of welcoming the well-heeled classical music fans back from intermission, began by playing the *Hockey Night in Canada* theme and announcing the score of the Canucks game—a 5–2 victory.

Politicians jockeyed to prove they knew more about hockey than their rivals. Premier Bill Bennett even landed in hot water when the Social Credit government spent nearly $15,000 on a newspaper advertisement celebrating the team. City hall got into the act too, as the council approved a resolution that would appropriate funds toward a celebratory parade in the Canucks' honor. The parade would go off, regardless of the result of the Stanley Cup Finals. "They've already won," explained then–Vancouver mayor Michael Harcourt.

After defeating the Blackhawks, the Canucks flew to Long Island and took up residence in brutal accommodations far from the Nassau Coliseum. When the club returned to Vancouver after dropping the first two games on the Hempstead Plains, thousands of fans mobbed the team at Vancouver International Airport. "Fire engines draped in our colors came racing along the runways," Williams remembered of landing in Vancouver before Game 3. "When I saw that I couldn't believe it for a few seconds."

On May 18, 1982—just a few days after the Islanders had hoisted the Stanley Cup at Pacific Coliseum—the Canucks reluctantly met downtown. A wide swath of the players weren't particularly looking forward to the parade, unconvinced that the city would show up after they failed to win even a single game in the Finals.

As the parade began to snake down Burrard Street, from Hastings to Pacific, the sight astonished the team. Children demanded autographs, thousands of towels were waved, and the club was cheered continuously as they made their way to Sunset Beach for a rally. Estimates by the Vancouver police suggested 50,000 Vancouverites took part in the festivities.

Roger Neilson and Harry Neale were offered horses to ride down the parade route. Though they were a pair of Toronto-born city boys with little experience on horseback, they gamely accepted the offer. "The guy running the parade asked Roger and [me] if we would ride a couple of horses. We both grew up in Toronto, and had never been on horses in our lives. But there we were, riding our horses through downtown Vancouver, the streets jammed with fans," Neale recalled. "At the end of the parade the guy in charge asked us how our horses were, and Roger said, 'My stallion was fine.'

"I said, 'Roger, how did you know it was a stallion?' He told me, 'Well, I heard a guy on the curb shout out, 'Look at the big prick on the white horse!'"

At Sunset Beach, a crowd of nearly 10,000—not including those who'd gathered to watch from the Burrard Street Bridge—prompted a variety of emotional responses from the Canucks players in attendance. "We honestly didn't think anybody was going to come to this parade," Stan Smyl said at the rally, as he choked back tears.

Vancouver fans spent more than a decade supporting a franchise that seemed perpetually stuck in the mud. The faint hint of playoff success resonated further than might've been anticipated. With their underdog persona and their workmanlike demeanor, the 1982 team accomplished something new for the franchise, something important. At long last, the Canucks franchise found itself connected in a meaningful way with the civic fabric of Vancouver.

34 Watt a Pity: How Vancouver Missed Out on Two Elite Power Forwards

The relative stability of Jake Milford's managerial tenure, which culminated in the stunning high of the 1982 Finals run, proved short-lived. It didn't take long for the Canucks to quickly revert back to the dysfunction that had previously characterized the franchise.

Milford stepped aside as general manager following the run to become senior VP, though he provided the Canucks with one last talented import player, Swedish center Patrik Sundstrom, before bidding farewell. Milford was replaced as GM by Harry Neale, who handed over the coaching reins to Roger Neilson.

Those early 1980s Canucks teams were still decent. They qualified for the postseason with regularity but just couldn't compete with the rising juggernauts in Alberta. Over the balance of the 1980s, the Canucks qualified for the Stanley Cup playoffs on four occasions. On all four occasions, either the Edmonton Oilers or the Calgary Flames promptly dispatched them.

"There were lots of good players on those Canucks teams," said former Canucks goaltender John Garrett. "But those two teams—the Calgary Flames and the Edmonton Oilers—they were 100-point teams, and that was when 100 points was 100 points; there weren't three-point games.... The NHL, in their infinite wisdom, would schedule those death valley games back-to-back, so you'd go get kicked by Calgary and then get beaten by Edmonton the next night. It was just like, 'Keep it under five!'"

Though the Canucks had a solid core of young talented players—Stan Smyl, Thomas Gradin, Tony Tanti, Cam Neely, Petri Skriko, Sundstrom, Doug Lidster, and Rick Lanz, for example—they were outgunned by two historically formidable teams, with whom they unfortunately shared the Smythe Division.

As a result, patience wore thin both off the ice and in the locker room. Several veterans grew bitter when management refused to renegotiate contracts for any players aside from Gradin. Adding to the frustration was the inability to recreate any of the magic from 1982. Neilson was fired midway through the 1983–84 season, replaced by Neale. Then Neale, after kicking the tires on potential replacements Tom Watt (then a coach with the Winnipeg Jets) and Mike Keenan, hired Bill LaForge.

The less said about LaForge's short and unsuccessful stint in Vancouver the better. He lasted just 20 games during the 1984–85 campaign, winning only four games. "LaForge comes in and is a total disaster," Mike Penny recalled. "God bless the man, but a brutal coach."

After firing LaForge, Neale took over one last time but was fired himself while at the 1985 Memorial Cup in Drummondville. It was at this point that chairman Arthur Griffiths, the son of majority owner Frank Griffiths and an increasingly active member of the ownership board, began to take on a more public-facing role.

Short in stature with a perpetually youthful appearance, the younger Griffiths had been the most hands-on member of the family in terms of managing the Canucks. With Neale deposed, Griffiths declared the Canucks would be embarking on a search for a "hockey czar."

In the fall of 1986, the search for said czar would result in the dawn of the Pat Quinn era, and a thorough reversal of fortunes. It's always darkest before the dawn, though, and that's the part of the story we've reached.

The Canucks cast a wide net in their search, prior to landing Quinn. They attempted to recruit the likes of Harry Sinden, Scotty Bowman, and legendary Montreal Canadiens executive Sam Pollock. But they struck out on all fronts and, needing someone to replace Neale ahead of the 1985 draft, promoted assistant general manager Jack Gordon to the post. "[The Canucks] tried to pretend that [Gordon] was the czar," Tony Gallagher later wrote. "But everyone knew Griffiths' shopping adventure had been a bust, and poor Gordon looked and behaved like a fish out of water."

Gordon was seldom heard from during his tenure, and Canucks reporters pejoratively referred to his office on Renfrew Street as Sleepy Hollow. The historical record should cast significant doubt on whether or not Gordon was even aware of the series of moves that eventually caused him to be labeled "the worst general manager in Canucks history."

At the same time Gordon replaced Neale, Watt was hired to replace Neale as Vancouver's head coach. Watt was also given the assistant GM gig, and it's fair to suggest Watt essentially held the cards in terms of personnel decisions. Watt had ties to Vancouver, having served as Neale's assistant prior to the 1982 Cup Finals run. Lured away by Winnipeg when Jake Milford decided to retain the general manager's chair (thus delaying Neale's ascension from the head coaching job, which prompted the Neilson hire), Watt was a solid tactician who had ingratiated himself with Canucks players, management, and ownership during his first stint with the club.

Watt's strength was an eye for talent (he's still employed as a scout with the Maple Leafs), and his scouting acumen earned the trust of Canucks management. Before he joined the club as an assistant coach, he'd recommended strongly to Neale and Milford that they consider drafting a player with roots in the Pacific Northwest—a raw, burly forward named Glenn Anderson, who had played for Watt on the Canadian national team. The Canucks ignored Watt's advice and later came to rue their decision, as Anderson racked up nearly 500 goals over a successful career.

Though Watt had his strengths as a bench boss, he demanded a lot from his players. A high level of tactical knowledge was a prerequisite, which filtered into the way his teams practiced. "He was used to older, more educated players," Garrett said of Watt's coaching style. "And Tom's practices were a study. You almost had to go to a class to understand the practices. You'd spend more time on the chalkboard than doing drills on the ice."

Watt's demanding approach proved a poor fit for Cam Neely, who the Canucks drafted with the ninth overall pick at the 1983 draft. In his three seasons with the Canucks, Neely was used as a mucker. He possessed a multitude of tools—speed, vision, and toughness—but was often tabbed for his pugilistic abilities. Neely led the Canucks in penalty minutes in his final two seasons with the team, fighting a combined 26 times, and was rarely placed in offensive situations. Watt, in particular, didn't see Neely's potential. "Watt said 'You better trade [Cam] before you end up getting nothing for him!'" Penny recalled. "Next thing I know Jack [Gordon] calls me and says we're going to trade Cam Neely. And I said, 'What are you doing? Don't do this.' That one boggled my mind."

Talk about irony. The Canucks ignored Watt's advice about Anderson—a burgeoning, BC-born power forward—but heeded his advice when it came to Neely...a burgeoning BC-born power forward. Only a franchise like Vancouver could manage such brutal timing.

35 From Neely to Lucic: The Butterfly Effect of a Historically Bad Move

The trade that sent Cam Neely and a conditional first-round pick to Boston for Barry Pederson wasn't, in fact, a pure player swap. It was actually a deal the two sides agreed to in lieu of compensation.

With Jack Gordon in place as general manager, but not really in control of the wheel, Canucks brass determined the club was in desperate need of help down the middle. The hunt for a center was on. Enter Pederson.

Though his name is now infamous in the annals of Canucks history, Pederson was, at the time, a 25-year-old pivot who'd managed better than a point per game over the course of his career. He'd also impressively come back from surgery to remove a tumor from his right shoulder—a procedure that nearly derailed his career. The year after surgery, Pederson scored 29 goals and 76 points.

Despite his successful comeback, the Bruins saw Pederson as damaged goods and a lengthy contract dispute ensued. Rather than grind out negotiations, the Bruins went out and signed Thomas Gradin as a free agent without compensation. In response, Vancouver approached Pederson about signing a deal.

Pederson was the equivalent of a modern-day restricted free agent. To sign him outright, the Canucks would have had to surrender two first-round picks or a first-round pick and a player off their roster (Vancouver would have been able to protect three players and all first-year professionals). Instead, the Canucks called Harry Sinden, who was only able to take the call because a planned golf outing had been rained out. After some haggling, Sinden and the Canucks worked out a swap that would become the Neely trade.

It's likely that Tom Watt and the Canucks were relieved to have only lost Neely, rather than a player they valued more, such as Doug Lidster, Rick Lanz, Tony Tanti, or Patrik Sundstrom, in the deal.

On draft day in 1986, the Bruins—who had the option of taking Vancouver's first-rounder in either 1986 *or* 1987—decided to push their pick back one season. That allowed the Canucks to take the immortal Dan Woodley at No. 7 overall. "I can't understand how Boston would pass up a talent like Woodley," Jack Gordon told reporters in a post-draft scrum. Tony Gallagher later called it Gordon's most memorable quote, qualifying, "although that was largely because he gave so few of them."

The next year, the Bruins selected D-man Glen Wesley third overall to complete the Neely swap.

A variety of details—some forgotten, some well remembered—make the Neely trade so difficult for Canucks fans to swallow. Neely, a local boy who played minor league hockey in Maple Ridge, was a lifelong Canucks fan. He wore the No. 21 in his three Canucks seasons because it was the inverse of 12, his junior number. And the reason he wore No. 12 in the first place was to emulate his favorite player, Stan Smyl. That's one layer of hurt.

The next layer? It literally took zero time for Neely to blossom into a dynamic offensive threat in Boston. In his first season, Neely scored 36 goals and was only narrowly out-pointed by Pederson. A big reason for Neely's breakthrough campaign was who he got to play with in Boston—Gradin. The two were teammates in Vancouver but never linemates, as Watt rarely skated Neely alongside the club's skill players. That part hurt too.

Pederson's sharp decline only added to the pain. After two decent seasons with the Canucks, a variety of back ailments derailed his career. Brief stops in Pittsburgh and Hartford followed, and a short return to Boston, before his playing days finished in 1992.

Through absolutely no fault of his own, he is remembered by Canucks fans in the most rueful terms. All told, Pederson played 233 games as a Canuck, recording 197 points. Neely alone managed 590 in 525 games with the Bruins while building a Hall of Fame résumé, but that's hardly where the benefits of this deal ended for Boston.

When you wade into the transactional fallout from the Neely trade, the butterfly effect is staggering. Though Neely retired with the Bruins and would later become the club's president, Wesley was dealt—after seven solid seasons in Boston—to the Hartford Whalers for an insane haul of *three* first-round picks.

One of those three picks was used to select Kyle McLaren, who would eventually be traded to the San Jose Sharks for Jeff Jillson. Jillson would eventually be traded back to San Jose for Brad Boyes, who a few years later would be shipped off to the St. Louis Blues for Dennis Wideman. In 2010, Wideman was the major piece—along with a couple draft picks—in a package that allowed Boston to acquire Nathan Horton and Greg Campbell from the Florida Panthers. Campbell and Horton would go on to play a significant role on the 2011 Bruins team that defeated Vancouver in the Stanley Cup Finals.

Another one of the picks acquired in the Wesley trade became Sergei Samsonov, a dynamic contributor in Boston for seven years. In 2006 Samsonov was dealt to the Edmonton Oilers for a meager return—Marty Reasoner, Yan Stastny, and a second-round pick. In 2007 the Bruins used that second-round pick to select another burgeoning BC-born power forward who had grown up a Canucks fan: Milan Lucic.

Losing Neely in a lopsided trade was painful enough. But the straight line that can be drawn across 25 years—from the Neely swap right through to the 2011 Cup Finals—is almost too cruel.

36 "Respectability for the Team"

While the Jack Gordon era limped from fiasco to catastrophe, Arthur Griffiths and the Canucks were still searching for their czar. Canucks ownership envisioned some sort of superboss, a guy who would stand up for the interests of the team and command respect within the hockey world. There was a sense Vancouver was a club to be taken advantage of, that the organization wasn't taken seriously. "We got bullied around a lot," remembered Griffiths. "We were polite Canadians, and we didn't really call anyone out. And if we did, we felt bad! [We had] a difficult time getting a break in those days."

Having struggled for nearly two years to land the aforementioned czar, Griffiths consulted with Coley Hall, an original Canucks minority owner. In an extended meeting, Hall put forth a name—former Canucks blueliner Pat Quinn, who was serving as the head coach in Los Angeles. "Look, there's nobody that's better qualified in the NHL today than Pat Quinn," Hall said, as Griffiths recalled. "I don't know what his status is contract-wise, whether he's available or not, but he's the guy."

Canucks ownership had previously reached out to Quinn in the summers of 1984 and 1985, but the recruitment was just one of many, and went nowhere. Following Hall's advice, the Griffiths family employed a new strategy. They picked a solitary target and focused all energy on him.

"We had three people on the list, and I can tell you who they were," Griffiths recalled. "Pat Quinn, Pat Quinn, and Pat Quinn."

There was only one problem with the master plan. Quinn was still employed by L.A., though he was in the last year of his contract. Poaching him might prove difficult.

"Okay, find out if he's available and go get him," Frank Griffiths told Arthur.

"Well, I'll do my best," Arthur replied, "but there's a thing called registered contracts and so on..."

"Well you just never know."

Frank Griffiths' sense of skepticism would prove fruitful, albeit controversial.

When the Canucks called Quinn's representative, Dick Babush, in the fall of 1986, Babush made it clear Quinn's future with the Kings was murky. His contract with Dr. Jerry Buss and the Kings stipulated L.A. had to either extend Quinn's deal or make him

GM for a three-year term. The deadline for this was October 1. When that date came and went without Quinn being provided that option, his contract was left unregistered at his own request.

Arthur Griffiths checked with the league office to see where things stood. When he found out the contract wasn't registered, the Canucks prepared their offer. The lengthy, frustrating search for a hockey czar seemed to be nearing the end. "[Pat] was legally in a position to sign a contract with his future employer if he so chose, or to negotiate with his current employer," Griffiths recalled.

After the winter league meetings in Florida, Griffiths made a "cloak-and-dagger" pit stop in Georgia, where he met with Babush to work out the finer points: terms, role, and money. The deal called for Quinn to become the president and general manager of the Canucks, not the club's head coach. The deal the two sides agreed to was lucrative and included a significant $100,000 signing bonus, which would ultimately cause headaches for Quinn, the club, and the league. "I'm pretty darn sure he would've been the highest-paid [team president] at the time, or pretty close to it," Griffiths said.

By early December the two sides had agreed in principle on a deal that would see Quinn jump ship from L.A. to Vancouver, but Frank told Arthur he wanted to meet with Quinn in person first. The Griffiths flew down to San Diego on the afternoon of December 15, 1986, and met with Quinn at the famous Hotel del Coronado.

The three men sat outside sipping scotch on a warm December night, while Quinn puffed his trademark cigar. As the sides engaged in a wide-ranging conversation about team-building philosophy and the business of hockey, Quinn turned to Frank—whom he always referred to as Mr. Griffiths—and asked the hockey executive equivalent of an existential question: "Well, Mr. Griffiths, what do you want from me?"

"Just respectability for the team," Frank replied.

Quinn considered this and then asked, as a means of clarification, "Not a Stanley Cup?"

"That will come; it will come together," said Frank. "Just build respect for the team on the ice."

If only it were that simple.

37 Quinngate

The Canucks thought they had their hockey czar. Pat Quinn had agreed to take over the club beginning June 1, 1987, but in the meantime, he had a small matter to attend to—coaching the Los Angeles Kings. Both the Canucks and Quinn believed they'd behaved appropriately, and that Quinn was effectively a free agent because his contract with the Kings hadn't been formally registered. As it would turn out, the NHL didn't agree.

On Christmas Eve in 1986, shortly after the Canucks beat the Kings in Vancouver, Quinn signed a formal contract to take over the Canucks beginning on June 1, 1987. Within this document, though, were a pair of provisions that led to a legal saga and Quinn's temporary expulsion from the league.

As mentioned, the contract called for a $100,000 signing bonus before January 23, 1987. This was a provision that the Griffiths family had demanded, as a means to ensuring they actually landed their man. "We had a previous experience in trying to sign a coach who was working for Hockey Canada," Arthur Griffiths recalled. "And in that process, we had a contract signed, sealed, and delivered. We were ready to make an announcement when we were bullied around by the league and Hockey Canada at the time. So my dad said that wouldn't happen again, [we were] going to have a different approach."

Signing on the dotted line was one thing, but the Canucks figured if their future superboss accepted money, it more forcibly consummated the agreement. "It was not Pat's idea," Dick Babush told Jim Robson of the signing bonus. "That's what the Griffiths wanted to do."

Then there was section 25 of the contract. According to the NHL's "Quinngate" investigation—which legal counsel Gil Stein completed for league president John Ziegler—section 25 claimed "this agreement or any notice thereof will not be filed with the NHL." The provision ensured the deal would be kept secret from the league's head office. Ziegler saw that as a smoking gun.

On January 2, 1987, when the Kings returned to Vancouver to play the Canucks, Arthur Griffiths had Quinn's signing bonus check at the ready. "It was a certified check delivered to his trainer by our trainer," Griffiths said. "The stories are true."

The deal, which was supposed to remain a secret through the balance of the regular season, was hidden for a grand total of five days. On January 7, 1987, Canucks color commentator Tom Larscheid caught wind of the deal and began pestering both Quinn and Kings GM Rogie Vachon for a comment. After being given a lengthy runaround, Larscheid went to press with the story.

Two days later, the NHL expelled Quinn—an unprecedented punishment that in the annals of league history had only been dealt to players who'd gambled on games they'd played in. The expulsion was pending a league investigation, which took nearly two weeks to complete, and even after that, Ziegler continued to conduct interviews regarding the situation.

On January 30, 1987, the NHL handed out stiff punishments to the Kings, Canucks, and Quinn. Vancouver was fined a whopping $310,000—$10,000 for every day each team knew about the deal but didn't inform the league office of it. Quinn was barred from taking part in any league activities until after the annual NHL meetings in June 1987, and banned from coaching an NHL game until 1990–91.

For the league, that Quinn accepted payment from a rival franchise while coaching another compromised competitive integrity. Though Buss and Vachon knew about the agreement between Quinn and the Canucks, they were unaware he'd accepted money from his new organization, and they were—understandably—upset.

"Quinn believes and believed that all of his actions and those of his representatives were legal and proper," Ziegler wrote in his formal decision. "However like Vancouver, Quinn forgot or neglected the most essential aspect of this business, the integrity of the competition." In his written decision, Ziegler also suggested that by keeping quiet, Quinn and the Canucks acknowledged the deal was of concerning legal validity.

The Canucks appealed the NHL's decision in BC provincial court, and the court ultimately decided to reduce the fine levied against the team from $310,000 to just $10,000 (finding the NHL didn't have grounds to determine a separate offense was committed every single day following the signing of Quinn's contract).

The court also noted Quinn had acted on professional-quality legal advice, and that NHL rules technically permitted him to negotiate a deal with a new employer, because his contract with the Kings wasn't registered. Quinn's coaching ban, however, was upheld. He used his time to finish up law school but was forbidden from properly preparing for the 1987 draft—one his first chances to make an impact as Vancouver's new hockey czar.

His reputation was also tarnished, at least in the short term. "A man works his whole life to establish a reputation for honesty," Quinn said. "This has been tough on me."

Looking back at Quinngate, it seems its namesake was technically correct about having the status of a free agent, but he clearly could've used some better legal advice (something Babush later came to admit). While it's unfair to say Quinn or the Canucks acted dishonorably in consummating their agreement, it sure was a murky start.

38 Burke the Bludgeon

During his lengthy exile, Pat Quinn took a break from his studies to attend a reunion for the 1978 Calder Cup champion Maine Mariners at the Sonesta Hotel in Portland, Maine. Quinn wasn't technically part of that team—he'd taken over behind the Mariners bench the next season—but he knew a variety of the players and coaches from his time with the Philadelphia Flyers organization, including future Canucks bench boss Bob McCammon.

That evening he had a fateful, lengthy, not entirely sober conversation with a 31-year-old player-agent named Brian Burke. This conversation would shape the next 20 years of Canucks hockey.

Burke and Quinn crossed paths at Flyers training camp in the 1970s, during Burke's one season of professional hockey. A fourth-line grinder, Burke played a depth role for the Mariners during their Calder Cup run, recording no points but racking up 25 PIM in the eight games he got into. Not long after, Burke gave up pro hockey to attend Harvard Law School. By the early summer of 1987, he was an associate at a Boston law firm and an established player agent with 33 NHL clients.

As Quinn and Burke drank and swapped stories into the early morning hours, they began to discuss the Canucks, and what was required to turn the struggling franchise around. It was 4:00 AM before Quinn turned to Burke and asked if he'd be interested in a job with the Canucks.

Burke, embarrassed initially, turned it down. Waking up the next morning, though, Burke reflected on the offer and picked up the telephone. "If you're serious, I'm interested," he told Quinn.

Quinn wanted a collaborative front office in Vancouver. His belief in collaborative dynamism formed during his time with the Flyers, who kept their departments separated from one another in a way that confounded Quinn. "I made up my mind at that time that if I ever ran my own organization, that's not what I would do," Quinn later recalled.

"Pat's approach was 'light hand,'" Burke said in Jason Farris' book *Behind the Moves*. "Hire good people, leave them alone."

Over the ensuing decade, Quinn's approach paid dividends for the Canucks and launched the careers of four future NHL GMs. One was Burke. Another was George McPhee, hired directly out of Rutgers Law School in the early 1990s. Another was Dave Nonis, promoted to the Canucks' sales and marketing department to hockey operations. Last was longtime PR man Steve Tambellini.

"I was really lucky to work with [Quinn] and learn from him, because he had a code of ethics and a level of integrity I think that was higher than most people," Burke recalled. "He certainly had a vision. He's a bright guy. He's an intimidating guy. You walk in that office and he's sitting there, with that big square jaw and the cigar. So you better be prepared and you better know what you're talking about when you walk into his office."

Burke would play a crucial role in the Canucks front office. He was a contract negotiator, an all-around fixer, and a high-profile spokesman for the team. When Quinn's portfolio expanded to include the head coaching job, Burke's services became indispensable. "I wanted to bring Brian Burke in [as assistant GM in Vancouver] in order to take some of the [organization building] off my plate on the management side," Quinn said. "I wanted input from a lot of people, and we didn't have a lot of people to start, but we started to build our organization. I always wanted inclusion of information, and I wanted discussion. So I would have Brian in on a lot of discussions, even though earlier on I wasn't sure in my own mind of his ability to know about the game of hockey.... He was a very good assistant and learned a lot because he's a doer."

Burke, of course, wasn't just a doer, he was also an unparalleled talker. Over the course of a lengthy executive career, he's earned a (well-deserved) reputation as one of hockey's most colorful and loquacious quotes. From "goalie graveyard" to "truculence," several memorable Burkisms have evolved into well-worn hockey clichés. For an organization that had long felt pushed around, Burke's bluster and belligerence—he would come to describe himself as "Pat Quinn's pit bull"—was a breath of fresh air.

"Pat brought an instant respect, and Burke was just the hammer," recalled Arthur Griffiths. "He was not afraid to say [what he thought], as we know. I would be driving into work and I'd listen to the radio or I'd read a paper and I'd think, *Oh my God, he said exactly what I wanted to say! Thank God, thank God somebody took that guy out!* It was wonderful. Suddenly we'd go into a fight and we'd have a big bruiser on our side."

In time, Quinn and Burke would lend the Canucks a sense of credibility that hadn't existed previously. But first there was a lot of work to do. As Quinn and his bludgeon settled into their new offices at the Pacific Coliseum on their very first day with the organization, Quinn glanced over at Burke and joked, "So what do we do now?"

39 Quinn Assembled an Elite Young Core, Mostly on the Trade Market

Those entertaining Pat Quinn–led teams of the early 1990s were built around two elite young players in Pavel Bure and Trevor Linden, both of whom were taken in the draft. But aside from those key stars, the complementary pieces were brought in through a series of savvy swaps.

In his first summer on the job, in 1987, Quinn was relatively quiet. He replaced Tom Watt as Canucks head coach with Bob McCammon, who he knew from his time in Philly. That was a significant move, but there wasn't much player personnel churn until right before training camp opened.

As camp approached, two first-year GMs were looking to shake things up. In New Jersey, Lou Lamoriello wanted to send his players a message. In Vancouver, Quinn was eyeing a guy he had coached at the 1986 World Championships—an underrated, BC-born forward named Greg Adams.

Trade talks developed, and it wasn't long before the trigger was pulled. Lamoriello and Quinn agreed to a deal that would send Patrik Sundstrom to the Devils in exchange for Adams and Kirk McLean, a 22-year-old goaltender who was coming off surgery. Canucks scout Jack McCartan, a former goaltender, really liked McLean's game, and Quinn—who was committed to managing in an inclusive fashion—trusted him.

Sundstrom would fare well in New Jersey over the next three seasons, even garnering some Selke Trophy votes, but Adams quickly became a mainstay in Vancouver's top-six forward group. On three occasions, he topped 30 goals in a campaign and—as we'll get to later—scored one of the biggest goals in franchise history during the 1994 Cup run.

McLean, meanwhile, would quickly build a résumé as the best Canucks goaltender of all time. Over a seven-year stretch from 1989 to 1996, McLean was an everyday starter who stopped an above-average rate of shots, and would occasionally turn in an elite season. In 1994 it was an elite run through the playoffs.

In the fall of 1988 Burke joined the NFL's New Orleans Saints for training camp and adopted a concept from Saints executive Jim Finks called the war room. The Canucks' version featured a giant whiteboard that displayed every NHL roster and organizational depth written down, so Quinn and Burke and other Canucks executives could better visualize trade possibilities, and focus on which minor league players might have value.

"So people would see Pat and me in the war room, and Pat would be standing there smoking a cigar, and we'd be staring at the walls," Burke said. "I know there were people who didn't know what that room was for, and they would walk by and think we were crazy."

Another of Quinn's gifts was finding diamonds in the rough. In particular, he had an enormous level of success dealing mid-round draft picks for castoff defensemen. Over a five-year span from 1987 to 1992, he acquired Jyrki Lumme, Gerald Diduck, Dave Babych, Paul Reinhart, and Dana Murzyn—all blueline mainstays—without surrendering a single consequential asset.

In changing over the roster, Quinn and company jettisoned a variety of veteran players who had spent much of the 1980s in Vancouver. Harold Snepsts was brought back but then traded to St. Louis for a bounty of draft picks. Tony Tanti and Barry Pederson were sent to Pittsburgh in exchange for Dan Quinn (and not much else). Petri Skriko was shipped off to Boston for a second-round pick, which the club would use to draft Mike Peca. Richard Brodeur was dealt to the Whalers. Then came the big one.

In a deadline day blockbuster in March 1991, the Canucks dealt Dan Quinn and blueliner Garth Butcher to St. Louis for Cliff

Ronning, Geoff Courtnall, Robert Dirk, Sergio Momesso, and an additional draft pick.

It was a coup for Pat Quinn and the Canucks. On multiple occasions Courtnall would record 70-point seasons and managed nearly a point per game in the playoffs. Perpetually underrated because of his 5'8" frame, Ronning was a hard-nosed and extremely skilled two-way center who emerged as a top-flight pivot. Momesso was productive in his three seasons in Vancouver and would play a third-line role during the best years of the Pat Quinn era, while Dirk provided tough, credible defensive depth.

So to recap: Pat Quinn basically built a blueline without surrendering anything but mid-round picks and depth players. The overall trade record from Quinn's first five years in Vancouver is enormously impressive. There were some losses at the margins, but they were few and of minor consequence.

Heck, even the deals that didn't turn out provided something—in the case of a player swap with Philly, a good chuckle. "Quinn and I made a deal once," longtime Flyers executive Bobby Clarke told author Jason Farris. "He sent me a [big, tough defenseman], and I sent him a forward who could really skate.

"Two weeks later, I said, 'Fuck, Pat. You sent me this defenseman with a bad knee.' He said, 'Yeah, well you sent me a forward who's had a fucking lobotomy.' I said, 'I guess we're even.'"

This, for accuracy's sake, was a deal at the 1988 trade deadline, when the Canucks sent 6'5" German-born defenseman Willie Huber to Philly in exchange for speedy forward Paul Lawless and a fifth-round pick.

Lawless quickly crashed out of the league, while Huber was productive in Philadelphia before sustaining a knee injury that effectively ended his career.

"We traded nothing for nothing," Quinn later recalled. "It was not a pretty deal."

40 Steers and Cheers: How Trevor Linden Knew He'd Be a Canuck

Vancouver wasn't better in Pat Quinn's first season than they had been the year previous. In fact, they were considerably worse. Outshot by a wide margin and beset by subaverage goaltending—Kirk McLean, still learning his craft at the pro level, led the team in starts and appearances—Vancouver managed the third-fewest points in the league. But because of a weird alignment quirk, Toronto, second fewest, made the playoffs in a weak Campbell Conference. That, in turn, gave the Canucks the No. 2 pick at the 1988 draft.

There was some speculation as to who would go No. 1—American scoring sensation Mike Modano or Trevor Lidnden, the WHL superstar. But to be fair, speculation was relatively modest. Modano was the consensus top pick, and while Linden was regarded as a potential cornerstone piece, he was a tier below Mikey Mo.

As such, Linden essentially knew he was Vancouver bound well before the Canucks took him second overall, then gave him a mustard-yellow sweater. "It was less dramatic [for me than it is for kids these days]," Linden recalled. "I was fairly certain that Minnesota was going to take Mike [Modano], and I was fairly certain that I was going to go to Vancouver."

Leading up to the draft, the Canucks asked Linden to visit Vancouver to meet with the team and go through a variety of psychological and physical tests. A few days before he was scheduled to fly out to the West Coast, Linden called Brian Burke and asked if he could meet with the club another time.

"Trevor gets embarrassed when I tell the story, but it's true," Burke recalled 25 years later. "He was supposed to come in

Saturday for testing, and he called me Thursday night and said he couldn't come in.

"I said, 'Why not?' and he said, 'Well, Saturday is branding day on my uncle's ranch [here in Medicine Hat], and my dad says I have to stay and help.' And I said, 'Well, what's your job?' and he said, 'Well, as the young cows come into the pen I grab them by the neck and hold them down as we brand them and turn them into steers.'

"I said, 'Kid, you can skip these tests.'"

Though he's a principled man, Burke is an epic myth builder, and some of his funnier stories need to be taken with a grain of salt. This one, though, is mostly true.

"[In Burke's version] I'm doing it all," Linden laughed. "I'm branding, castrating, I'm wrestling bulls and steers and all the rest.... But it's true. They asked if I could come out, and I did say, 'With all due respect, could I come the next weekend because my family is branding?'

"And we did. We'd grab the calf by the leg, drag him out, throw him down, [and] my grandpa would do the castration and the branding. So it is true, even if [Burke's] iteration of it gets better and better as the years go by."

Linden did eventually arrive in Vancouver to meet with Canucks brass. Former player and longtime assistant coach Jack McIlhargey picked him up at the airport and drove him across town to Quinn's house in the British Properties. He met with Quinn and Quinn's wife, Sandra; McIlhargey; and Burke. Though he was nervous, by the time the meeting was over, Linden was pretty confident the Canucks would be calling his name on draft day.

41 Even Linden Doesn't Fully Understand How He Forged Such a Deep Connection with Vancouver's Hockey Fans

Taking Trevor Linden with the second pick at the 1988 draft was a tap-in putt. The lanky power forward impressed with his off-ice demeanor and humility but was also the consensus second-best prospect in his class. He knew the Canucks were going to pick him—as did the rest of the hockey world.

Hindsight being 20/20, there were more dynamic forwards Vancouver could've taken with the pick, Teemu Selanne most notably. But even then, no self-respecting Vancouver hockey fan has ever looked back at the Linden selection with the same sort of retrospective hand-wringing over, you know, the Canucks taking Petr Nedved in 1990 while Jaromir Jagr was still on the board.

The primary reason for this is that Linden personified what locals wanted from their hockey team. Right from his first game, Linden proved himself a workmanlike player who raised his game when the stakes were highest. Personable, approachable, and respectful in his interactions with fans and the media, he forged a special bond with the fan base.

To this day, no other player in franchise history resonates with the crowd like Linden does. And the fact that he never achieved superstar status outside Vancouver almost makes him *more* endearing, as if Canucks understand Linden is "theirs" in a meaningful way.

"I totally appreciate people outside of this market just don't get it," Linden said of his relationship with Vancouver. "I don't totally get it! I'm not a Hall of Famer and I never will be. What resonated with people, I think, what people got, is that they saw this 18-year-old kid from Medicine Hat come in and be authentic and raw and likable. I think they got connected to him in a way.

"For the younger fans it was like, 'I was in high school and he's the same age!' so that was relatable. For the older people it was like, 'Boy, he's like a son to me.' And I had a great first year, I had 30 goals my first year. It was hope for people, this beacon of light for a franchise that had struggled."

In September 1988 Linden arrived on Vancouver Island for his first NHL training camp. Though it was unusual, he showed up without a contract. Committed to playing in the NHL as quickly as possible, Linden spent the summer bulking up. He weighed close to 200 pounds at camp, 15 pounds heavier than he was on draft day.

Trevor Linden has long been sweet 16 for Canucks fans.

Camp was a grueling experience for the young winger, with two-a-day practices for rookies. Linden was also surprised by the intensity of the competition for jobs. Fights were frequent, as aspiring enforcers auditioned for the role of resident tough guy. "[Brian Burke] had brought every thug he could find," Linden recalled, "so it was a total gong show."

Linden roomed with Harold Snepsts, learned defensive coverage nuances from Doug Lidster, and was treated to a meal by Garth Butcher. At one point, the team made the Alberta boy cook everybody steaks, an unnerving experience for Linden, who had little experience in the kitchen.

"You never forget the guys that were good to you," Linden said of the mentorship he received from a handful of Canucks veterans. "For me it was Richie Sutter and Garth Butcher and Doug Lidster and Stan Smyl. These were really guys that had my back."

As camp stretched on, Linden was playing well, even though his contract impasse persisted. There was a good deal of media speculation about whether he'd make the team, with internal discussions to match. "We weren't sure he was going to play that year," Griffiths recalled. "It was pretty unheard of in those days."

Ultimately the two sides ironed out a contract before the close of training camp. On the day of his NHL debut—October 6, 1988—an 18-year-old Linden walked into the locker room and saw that his jersey number had been altered. He'd worn No. 47 throughout camp, but now No. 16 adorned the jersey that hung in his stall. "That was kind of the first 'aha' moment for me," Linden recalled.

Linden started his rookie season tentatively but was soon scoring in bunches. Only six weeks into his NHL career, Linden recorded his first hat trick, against the Minnesota North Stars. By the end of December, he was leading the Canucks to upset victories—including some over the Edmonton and Calgary teams that'd terrorized the Canucks for so much of the decade. "That first year it was a little hard to slowly integrate him," Griffiths said. "Because he commanded more ice time."

By the end of Linden's rookie season, he tied Petri Skriko for a team-best 30 goals. With 59 points, Linden finished one short of matching Ivan Hlinka's team rookie scoring record. Remember though, Hlinka was 32 in his rookie campaign. Linden turned 19 during Vancouver's first-round playoff series that season.

Accolades continued to pour in. Linden won the Cyclone Taylor Trophy as Canucks MVP and finished second in Calder Trophy voting to Rangers D-man Brian Leetch. All of a sudden, the Canucks franchise had a hopeful, young face for fans to latch onto. One could see brighter days ahead.

42 Quinn and Uncle Cliff: The Negotiations for the KLM Line

As the Cold War thawed in the mid-1980s, NHL teams aggressively pursued Soviet players. The first ones were drafted in 1982, and what started out as a trickle soon became a flood. At the 1983 draft, a variety of teams—including Montreal, Calgary, and New Jersey—took a shot in the later rounds, selecting famed Soviets such as Vladislav Tretiak, Viacheslav Fetisov and Sergei Makarov. It took another six years before any of those gambles paid off.

For the rest of the decade, teams kept taking late-round fliers to secure the rights of top Soviets. Those same teams would then waste time and man hours in negotiations with Sovintersport—the Russian hockey federation—and notorious head coach Viktor Tikhonov in an attempt to secure the players' releases.

The Canucks dipped their toe in this pool in 1985, taking creative center Igor Larionov in the 11th round. The next year, the

Canucks drafted his teammate, Vladimir Krutov. The pair comprised two-thirds of the fabled KLM Line that, along with Sergei Makarov, had routinely dominated international competition.

Armed with the rights to Larionov and Krutov, Griffiths and the Canucks spent years engaging a variety of opaque Soviet institutions—the army, the national team, the hockey federation—in regular (and fruitless) rounds of negotiation. Beginning at the 1988 Olympics in Calgary, these talks were spearheaded by Pat Quinn, though both Frank and Arthur Griffiths remained heavily involved. "If we were able to bring those two to our team after the Olympics," Quinn said at the time, "they would make an immediate impact."

The Canucks had put in serious legwork to develop a cordial relationship with high-ranking Soviet officials. In the fall of 1986, for instance, the Canucks invited legendary coaches Anatoli Tarasov and Vladislav Tretiak to the club's training camp on Vancouver Island. The next year, the club arranged for Tarasov to have hip surgery in Vancouver.

Vancouver's goodwill gestures were wise but didn't really grease the skids all that much. Seemingly every off-season, Russian authorities would inform the Canucks they'd have to wait another year to secure Larionov and Krutov's services.

By 1989 the outspoken Larionov was taking full advantage of glasnost. He blasted the Russian hockey authorities openly in a conversation with the *Toronto Star*, and published a controversial letter criticizing Viktor Tikhonov, the practice of doping in Soviet hockey, and the undue control the federation exercised over his career.

That same year, the Soviet team ran roughshod over opponents at the World Championship. This despite Tikhonov and the team captain, Slava Fetisov, butting heads publicly before the tournament—causing a team-wide revolt and Larionov's resignation from the national team. Unfazed, they went 10–0 at the tournament, including a blowout victory over Sweden in the gold medal game.

The Soviet side had won the tournament, but they were about to lose their most promising young player—a rebellious 20-year-old forward named Alexander Mogilny. Mogilny was so talented that Tikhonov is said to have wept the first time he watched him play. He was also as westernized as any Russian player aside from Larionov, with a notable fondness for rock music and blue jeans and no love at all for Tikhonov's dictatorial style. "They take us out of the cage and let us sing," Mogilny said of his experience playing for the Soviet team. "And then they put us back in the cage again."

On May 4, 1989, Mogilny, having left his teammates in Stockholm with no warning (even his family wasn't aware of his plans), touched down in New York City. A new era for the National Hockey League had begun.

Mogilny's defection sent shock waves across the hockey world and created a sense of urgency. Some NHL teams, such as Lou Lamoriello's Devils, just went ahead and signed players whose rights belonged to them without dealing with Soviet authorities. Soviet hockey officials, meanwhile, realized if they didn't offer their younger players a realistic sense that their release might be granted in exchange for several years of loyal service, a flood of Mogilny-style defections could ensue.

In late June, Soviet hockey officials sent the Canucks a promising fax. Quinn remained skeptical, though. "I can't read the Soviets' minds," Quinn replied, when asked about Mogilny's defection and the impact it might have on Larionov and Krutov. "I've been dealing with them for over two years, and it's been awfully frustrating."

On June 27, 1989, Quinn and Calgary Flames general manager Cliff Fletcher flew to Moscow with the intention of negotiating the release of the entire KLM Line. Unsurprisingly, the negotiations proved difficult and tense. In the initial round of meetings, Quinn had no intention of giving in to what he thought were unreasonable cash demands by Sovintersport. When his hard-line stance caused negotiations to stall, Quinn had all but given up. "I had closed my book and was prepared to leave without Igor," Quinn later recalled.

In a subsequent and private round of negotiations, though, Fletcher decided to relent. He agreed to a deal that would pay Makarov $375,000 a year, with an equal amount going to the Soviet hockey federation. "Cliff and Pat were supposed to have a united front, but Cliff went in and agreed to it," Mike Penny recalled. "That's why we called him Uncle Cliff."

Quinn was meeting with Larionov when he caught wind of the Flames' agreement to secure Makarov's release. He was caught in a bind. How exactly could he fly home without Larionov, when a rival general manager had secured Makarov's services?

"[Once] Cliff made his deal...I said, 'All right, I'll match it,'" Quinn later recalled. "It would have been a PR nightmare for us if Cliff had come back with Makarov and I had come back without Igor." Outmaneuvered by his bargaining partner, Quinn agreed to a matching deal. In time, that agreement would have disastrous consequences.

On July 2, 1989, the Canucks formally signed Larionov. Quinn, meanwhile, was still working on securing Krutov's release. In September Soviet hockey officials—in a tough spot when Krutov refused to play for Tikhonov's national team—essentially offered the Canucks an identical deal to secure Krutov's release. Vancouver accepted, a decision Quinn and the club would come to regret.

The Canucks would field two Soviet players in 1989–90, but the cost of the deals was exorbitant. And even beyond the lucrative transfer payments due to Soviet hockey authorities, the repercussions of the Krutov and Larionov deals would be felt for years to come.

43 Culture Shock: On the NHL Experiences of Krutov and Larionov

From Alexander Mogilny to Sergei Makarov to Igor Larionov, the 1989–90 season was dubbed the Year of the Soviet by TSN's Bob McKenzie. Interest in watching the Russians was sky-high in Vancouver.

The arrival of Larionov and Vladimir Krutov captured the imagination of fans, and the club experienced a significant attendance spike that same year. Enthusiasm reached such a fever pitch that the club had to rework its payment structure for ticket salesmen, lest some of the team's salespeople earn more in commission than Pat Quinn did in salary.

Hyped beyond reason, the impact Larionov and Krutov made on the ice in their initial Canucks campaign was disappointing. Larionov's all-around hockey intelligence shone through at times, but his production was relatively pedestrian until he moved to a line with Trevor Linden and Geoff Courtnall. Krutov, meanwhile, showed up at camp out of shape and was a regular healthy scratch by the 30th game of the season.

Though Larionov and Krutov had been longtime teammates, they grew apart in the course of their first season of North American professional hockey. Larionov was a free spirit, fluent in English, and he acclimated to North American culture with ease. There were still challenges, though. "In Russia, we have small apartment, small car, no food, but we're healthy all the time," Larionov said of his adjustment that first season. "In Canada, we have big house, big car, lots of food, and we're sick all the time."

Food was a mixed blessing for Krutov. A burly, effective bruiser who lacked fitness, he quickly earned the nickname Crouton from Vancouver sportswriters because of his doughy build and soft play.

His teammates had an even crueler moniker for him: Vlad the Inhaler.

Krutov had never experienced freedoms and excesses that were suddenly now available. It also didn't help that his family's immigration status was held up by Soviet bureaucracy, leaving him isolated in a strange land.

Krutov quickly grew fond of hot dogs and Big Gulps. "His bedroom floor was covered with discarded plastic wrappers, pizza boxes, and soft-drink cans," Kerry Banks wrote. "Krutov was so lazy that he used hockey tape to rig a makeshift trip wire to his light switch so that he could simply jerk the tape and turn out the light without rising from his bed."

Managing calorie intake was one thing. Dealing with the concept of earnings and money management was another. During the year, Quinn provided the Krutov family with a checkbook, and when the bank account became overdrawn, they were confused—after all, their book still had checks left!

In Krutov's only season in Vancouver, he managed 11 goals and 34 points in 61 games, but the Canucks had seen enough. They dropped him from the roster and attempted to avoid paying the buyout of his three-year deal. "We wanted Vladimir Krutov to come here and show up in condition…like he committed to in his contract," Quinn said. "That didn't happen.… We believed he was a world-class player who'd come here and play like a world-class player. We gave him every opportunity to do that."

Two years later, a Swedish court responsible for arbitrating the dispute decided in Krutov's favor. The Canucks—who would've owed Krutov and a variety of Soviet hockey interests $1.4 million over the balance of his three-year contract—were forced to pony up $800,000, and were also left on the hook for Krutov's legal fees, which totaled $500,000. The Krutov signing turned out to be a disaster from the standpoint of both hockey and finances.

Larionov's NHL experience was dramatically more successful. Though his best hockey was played in Detroit and he didn't live up to the appreciable hype in his first Canucks season, the Professor grew into his role and eventually found chemistry on a line with Pavel Bure. Larionov later said Bure "brought joy and excitement back to [his] game."

It appeared the Canucks and Larionov had found a solid fit. Those early 1990s Canucks teams were talented but lacked skilled depth at center. Larionov's unique combination of responsible defensive play and sublime passing perfectly complemented players such as Greg Adams, Bure, Linden, and Courtnall. When Larionov's initial three-year contract expired, both sides had interest in an extension.

Once again, the deal that Fletcher negotiated—and Quinn matched—would have disastrous consequences. A clause in the initial deal called for the Russian hockey federation to receive an additional transfer fee—equal to the size of Larionov's next contract—if he signed with Vancouver again.

An independent thinker, Larionov couldn't abide by that on principle. "I don't want to talk about even a small amount of money going to Russia," Larionov said. "They received over a million dollars for three years. Now they want more money. It's unfair. Lots of young people came to the NHL this year to escape from Russia and nobody got any money."

To Larionov, any money the Russian hockey federation received would be akin to a ransom payment. He wasn't wrong. Even when the two sides worked out a buyout of the clause for $150,000, Larionov was obstinate. Unwilling to pay a cent of his earnings to Russian hockey interests, Larionov signed a three-year deal with Swiss league outfit Lugano. This included a NHL out clause, which technically would've allowed Larionov to sign back with Vancouver while avoiding any payments to Russia—but only if he first cleared waivers.

In the fall of 1992, the Canucks opted to leave Larionov unprotected in the waiver draft. The San Jose Sharks selected him in the second round. As such, the Canucks lost one of the most entertaining and unique centermen ever to play the sport over a measly $150,000.

The circumstances of Larionov's departure were so unique and so highly politicized that it seems unfair to blame the Canucks for mismanagement. On the other hand, Quinn's comments suggested the club had no sense the 31-year-old Larionov still had a decade of high-level hockey in him. "We weren't going to bring [Larionov] back, anyway," he said at the time.

It's likely Quinn and the Canucks undervalued what Larionov might contribute going forward. It's also hard to imagine that Larionov's complicated legal situation miffed an organization that overcame greater obstacles in drafting and signing Bure, and in wooing Quinn from L.A. If re-signing Larionov was a priority, surely a club with a rich history of exploiting loopholes could've found another way to do so. In the annals of painful what-ifs, losing Larionov in this manner is rivaled only by the Neely trade.

"I think that was one of the unfortunate blunders," Linden said. "Now, having said that, the situation that Scott [Bowman] created in Detroit, who else was going to do that? They had Fetisov and Konstantinov and Fedorov. Who else could have created that environment? It's easy to say [Quinn] missed, but situations kind of dictate success too."

44 Yes, Joel Otto Kicked It In

Trevor Linden, Kirk McLean, and Bob McCammon's stingy defensive system led the 1988–89 Canucks to the first playoff berth of the Pat Quinn era. Though the team finished underwater by goal differential and only just snuck into the playoffs—the lowest seed in the Smythe Division—the club outshot their opponents by a wide margin and allowed the third-fewest goals in the league.

The Canucks could control games and prevent goals, but generating offense was a slog. But in a seven-game series, a smothering defense and hot goaltending can go a long way. Facing a potent Flames team that controlled a ridiculous 57 percent of shots on goal and finished 43 points ahead of Vancouver in the standings, the Canucks nearly shocked the world.

The series got off to a surprising start when the Canucks contained Calgary's offense and managed to impose a tight-checking flow. The first game went to overtime, and Paul Reinhart—in his first year with Vancouver after nearly a decade with Calgary—managed to beat Mike Vernon with a 15-footer in overtime. "We wanted respect, and this win gives us some additional confidence," Reinhart said at the time.

The additional confidence wouldn't pay off in Games 2 and 3, as the Flames' superior quality shone through. Calgary chased McLean on their way to a 5–2 victory in Game 2 and scored four goals on just 15 shots in a 4–0 victory in Game 3. Calgary's resurgent offense chased McLean from the series, as McCammon opted to start backup Steve Weeks in Games 4 and 5.

In Game 4 Vancouver's super rookie took over. Linden, flashing the "playoff warrior" persona that would characterize his

Canucks tenure, managed a goal and three assists as Vancouver chased Vernon, rebounded from a pair of disheartening losses, and tied the series at two.

"'For me personally, the game was very satisfying," Linden said then. "I feel a lot more confident now about playing with these guys. The pressure's now on them. It's their rink, their fans, their pressure. We just go in to Calgary and see what happens."

In Calgary, the series returned to its predictable equilibrium. The Flames' vaunted offense ran over Vancouver in another 4–0 victory. Once again, McCammon was forced to make a goalie change ahead of Game 6 as the Canucks went back to McLean.

At a sold-out Pacific Coliseum, the Canucks continued to outhustle and outhit the Flames. Having regained his crease, McLean was superb in stopping 29 of 32 shots faced, and Vancouver's anemic offense exploded for four second-period goals to rocket the Canucks to a 6–3 victory. "The series has been a great battle, tougher than anyone expected," McCammon said after the game. That was a dramatic understatement.

The Canucks entered the playoffs with 100-to-1 odds to win the Stanley Cup and were on the verge of beating the best team in the league. One more win, and they'd pull off an upset of historic proportions.

Game 7 was, predictably, a tense and epic affair. The Flames jumped out to an early lead, but the Canucks' power play was firing and continually allowed them to come back. The Flames choked up 1–0, 2–1, and 3–2 leads in regulation. Linden racked up a pair of points, and Doug Lidster's third-period goal forced overtime. Just your typical Canucks-Flames first-round series, really.

Outshot for much of the series, the Canucks peppered Vernon with a flurry of high-quality looks in OT. It was as if the Canucks could smell a historic upset. The Flames, meanwhile, seemed to be wilting in the moment.

As the first overtime period unfolded, the Flames made a ghastly error. An ugly line change resulted in a glorious breakaway chance for Stan Smyl. Charging in all alone off the right wing and with oodles of time and space, Smyl faked a cross-crease deke before pulling the puck back to his forehand and uncorking a wrist shot. Vernon had bit on the deke, but he stayed relatively upright and just managed to snag Smyl's attempt.

Moments later, Vernon robbed Tony Tanti coming in off the right wing. And on a scramble play earlier in the overtime period, the Canucks beat Vernon, but not his post.

As legs turned to Jell-o and the battle of attrition set in, the first overtime period was winding down when Jim Peplinski and Joel Otto skated into the Canucks' end on a two-on-two. There were only about 35 seconds left when Peplinski shot hopefully into the general vicinity of Vancouver's crease. Lidster tied up Otto well, but Peplinski's shot struck the back side of Otto's skate. The puck trickled past McLean for the series-winning goal. The Flames had avoided "a gigantic pratfall" and would go on to win the Stanley Cup.

Canucks fans, players, coaches, and management could only grumble about Otto's questionable positioning in the crease, and how he'd "clearly" meant to kick it in. Today, if you type "Joel Otto" into a Google search bar, "kicked it in" is a popular autofill suggestion. Quinn remembered Otto's goal as the type of bad break that "you never forget and you never forgive."

Linden shared Quinn's thoughts on the manner. "To the last game I played, I'd skate up to [referee] Bill McCreary in warm-ups or at a commercial break and just say, 'Billy, you know that he kicked that in!'" Linden recalled. "It was 20 years later and I was still talking to him about it. I never let him forget it, even if it was mostly for a laugh."

Objectively, it's hard to believe Otto intentionally kicked it in. He was battling for position with Lidster, and Peplinski's shot struck the back side of his skate. Even if the goal was intentional on Otto's part, then it has the virtue of being a remarkable feat (pun intended) of coordination and skill. Whatever the case, the legend of Otto's fat skate is right up there on the list of painful wounds Canucks fans so faithfully nurse.

45 Mike Penny's Fateful Christmas Day Scouting Trip

Taking Pavel Bure in the sixth round of the 1989 NHL Entry Draft is one the biggest steals in Canucks history. And the circumstances surrounding the pick are one of the franchise's greatest mysteries.

That Bure was available late in the draft was due to outdated NHL eligibility rules that governed the selection of 18-year-olds. Players who were 18, like Bure, were generally ineligible after the third round—unless they'd met some very specific games-played benchmarks. Bure had to have played in at least 11 games in 1987–88, which NHL Central Scouting didn't believe occurred. (It officially recognized that he'd played in five games for the Central Army team.)

It wasn't just eligibility concerns, though. Teams could've taken him much earlier and with fewer headaches, but none hazarded an early pick because of widespread skepticism about Bure's ability to get out of his Central Army commitments.

There are competing narratives as to how the Canucks knew Bure was eligible when the rest of the league did not. The most romantic version of the story, though, belongs to Mike Penny.

Penny's hockey operations career in Vancouver spans 20 years. Hired by Jake Milford as an amateur scout, Penny became the Canucks' director of scouting under Pat Quinn, and would later serve as Steve Tambellini's right-hand man during the chaotic season after Quinn's dismissal.

Penny is a gifted storyteller with a keen eye for talent, and it's easy to see how he carved out a 35-year career in the NHL. Today, Penny's still scouting for the Maple Leafs, part of a very select group of scouts who survived Brendan Shanahan's 2015 departmental purge.

In Penny's account, he was on a scouting trip in Finland over the 1987 Christmas holidays when, by pure accident, he came upon a pair of IIHF-sanctioned friendly games that pitted the Russians against the Finns.

"I was in a lower category team's arena, and I was watching some games," Penny recalled. "And Goran Stubb [the NHL's head of European scouting] says to me, 'You know, the Russians are going to play the Finnish national team tomorrow.'

"I said, 'It's Christmas Day,' and he says, 'They're going to play in Vierumaki at the Finnish training center.' So I said, 'How do I get up there?' and Goran Stubb lends me his car. So I drove up."

On Christmas morning as the snow fell, Penny made the two-hour trek north. "The weather was horseshit, like it normally is," he recalled. "It was dark, cold, overcast, a little snowy.

"I get in there, and it's a nice arena once you get in there, but you're driving through the woods thinking, *Where the hell am I going?* So I go to the rink and I get in there and there's nobody in the rink. It's not exactly like the World Juniors these days."

Though tough to find, the training center was a thoroughly modern barn. He was the only NHL scout taking in the games, and Viktor Tikhonov was "pissed off" to see him.

"I thought to myself, *I should get that game sheet*," Penny recalled. "So I went down, and the Finnish guy photocopied it and gave it to me." The next day Penny once again watched a game between the Russians and Finns. And once again, he grabbed a copy of the game sheet.

Years later, Brian Burke would tell the *New York Times* that Vancouver's understanding of Bure's draft eligibility revolved around the fact that Bure "had played 11 games—nine league games and two exhibition games" in 1987–88. That made Bure eligible. If Penny's glorious account is to be believed, only the Canucks knew about those two IIHF-sanctioned games, and they had the game sheets to prove it. A Christmas miracle, if you will.

46 The Controversial Drafting of Bure

On June 17, 1989, the NHL's 21 member clubs assembled at the Met Center in Bloomington, Minnesota, for the draft. Six weeks earlier, Alexander Mogilny had set the hockey world ablaze with his defection, and it had become clear the league was about to take on a more international flavor. In that light, the 1989 draft was unlike any other.

In a bit of symbolism that borders on perfection, several European draftees that year broke down barriers. Sweden's Mats Sundin was selected first overall by Quebec, becoming the first European-trained player to be taken at No. 1. In the third round Detroit selected Nicklas Lidstrom, who would become the first European-born captain to hoist the Stanley Cup.

The Canucks had 11 picks in the draft, and used their first to select Jason Herter, who never carved out a niche for himself at the NHL level. The club picked twice more in the second and fourth rounds, selecting a pair of forgettable prospects—Rob Woodward and Brett Hauer—who combined to play 37 NHL games.

With no fifth-round pick, Vancouver's brain trust—led by Pat Quinn, Mike Penny, and Brian Burke—huddled around the draft table to discuss strategy. By this point, both Burke and Penny had been pushing for the club to draft Pavel Bure since the fourth round. "This guy is the best available by a country mile," Penny said.

Burke and Penny made their case to Quinn. The worst scenario was to take Bure, have it not pan out, and burn a sixth-round pick. Not a huge loss. The potential upside, meanwhile, was certainly worth the risk, and what's more, Penny was convinced Bure was draft eligible. "Jesus Christ, I hope you're right on this one," Quinn told Penny, according to Kerry Banks.

Elsewhere on the draft floor, a variety of other teams—including the Red Wings and the Edmonton Oilers—were similarly engaged in the process of determining whether or not Bure could be taken.

Detroit was ready to make its fifth-round selection when director of player personnel Neil Smith—later the general manager of the New York Rangers—double-checked with NHL vice president Gil Stein. On multiple occasions the league insisted Bure was ineligible. Because of the stern objections of Red Wings European scout Christer Rockstrom, who insisted the league was incorrect, Detroit passed on Bure at No. 95.

Edmonton was also considering Bure in the sixth round. Head scout Barry Fraser was roaming the draft floor, quizzing the league and Goran Stubb on Bure's eligibility. Like most other teams, the Oilers heard the stories and knew how opaque records out of Russia were at the time.

It's unclear if Edmonton would've selected Bure had the Canucks not done so, but it quickly became a moot point. With the 113th overall pick the Canucks selected Bure, who became the most dynamic goal scorer in franchise history and one of the NHL's top 100 players. The pick had barely been announced when the draft floor exploded with recriminations and complaints. "The other teams were tossing expletives at me and everyone else on the Canucks," Burke recalled to Banks.

When order was restored and the draft snaked to its inevitable conclusion, several teams lodged formal complaints about the Bure pick to the NHL head office. League president John Ziegler launched an investigation, and it took a year—and a dramatic 11th-hour reversal—for the league to rule on the matter.

47 We'll Probably Never Know For Sure How the Canucks Proved Bure Was Draft Eligible

As the Soviet Union took its last fitful gasps in the late 1980s, NHL teams wrestled to secure the rights to the best Russian players on the planet. It's one of the most interesting eras in NHL history, characterized by levels of subterfuge and intrigue more appropriate to a John Le Carré novel.

Like the NHL's version of the Wild West, acquiring Soviet players took on a certain lawlessness. Doctors were bribed to render false assessments of players' health. Families were smuggled out of communist countries in the dead of night on Mike Ilitch's private jet. It wasn't unusual to hear a player had simply disappeared from the Russian national team in the middle of an international competition, as Sergei Fedorov did at the 1990 Goodwill Games in Portland.

This sense of cloak-and-dagger permeated Vancouver's effort to prove Bure's eligibility in the face of an official NHL investigation. The entire boondoggle was a product of its time, and as a result, it's extraordinarily difficult to determine how the Canucks proved their selection fell within the rules. Not helping matters? That almost all the principal actors involved seem to have different stories about how it went down.

We've already heard Mike Penny's tale, and it's a great one. There's no doubt Penny's assurances and information were crucial in informing Pat Quinn and the Canucks' decision to draft Bure, though his account has been disputed by former colleagues and other hockey officials.

Mike Murray, for example, an official with the Canadian Amateur Hockey Association at the time, was at the Vierumaki games Penny attended. He has always contended the games Penny saw, and received sheets from, actually occurred in 1988. "Pavel hadn't made the Soviet national junior team [in 1987] and he was just getting ready for the Esso Cup tournament in Quebec," Murray told Kerry Banks.

Murray contended Bure—who would've been 16 at the time—was too young to have played for the national team in 1987. If Murray's timeline is correct and the games Penny witnessed were played on Christmas Day in 1988, then they'd have no bearing on Bure's draft eligibility in 1989.

Burke's version of the story also differs from Penny's, and hinges on the contributions of a paid Russian informant, who Burke referred to in a *New York Times* interview as "our man in Moscow." Burke has never divulged the name of his informant, or the price paid for his information.

Meanwhile the account of Russian journalist Igor Kuperman seems to contradict *both* Burke and Penny and their "two exhibition games and nine league games" theory. Kuperman was brought into this by the Canucks—through Igor Larionov—when the NHL began investigating Bure's draft eligibility.

On Larionov's behalf, Kuperman sifted through relevant files and game sheets. It was a lengthy and difficult process considering the shoddy state of the Russian hockey federation's record keeping. Until he found six additional exhibition games Bure had played in, Kuperman was sure he was on a wild goose chase. "I found six games," Kuperman recalled to Banks. "Not five or seven, but exactly six."

Kuperman and Larionov faxed the relevant information to the Canucks' front office from the Canadian embassy in Moscow. Of course, in Kuperman's account six of Bure's 11 games were exhibition contests, whereas Burke and Penny put the number at two.

Griffiths, the former Canucks chairman, had yet another version of the story. "We did what we could to find the actual game sheets," Griffiths recalled. "I ended up contacting Alan Eagleson, believe it or not, and I said, 'We need to find your contact in Russia that will have access to all the game records to the Red Army team and where they played and when they played.'"

Griffiths couldn't remember the name of Eagleson's contact, though he describes him as "[Eagleson's] Russian counterpart."

Considering the variety of accounts and sparseness of official records, it's probable that we'll never know precisely how the Canucks proved the Bure pick was legitimate. But whatever information Vancouver showed Ziegler, it had the desired effect. Less than a month after announcing the Canucks made an illegal pick and would forfeit their rights to Bure, the league reversed its decision two days before the 1990 draft—which, coincidentally, would be held in Vancouver.

Ziegler's decision was met with a torrent of criticism from other teams. He did what he could to diminish the episode's significance, but two years later, future commissioner Gary Bettman replaced him as NHL president.

Shortly after, Tony Gallagher wrote Ziegler's ruling on Bure played a key role in him losing the confidence of NHL owners. Gallagher's report suggested Ziegler had cut a backroom deal with Quinn, the numbers proving Bure's eligibility never added up and, as quid pro quo for ruling in the Canucks' favor, Quinn agreed to drop a pending Quinngate-related lawsuit against the league. "I don't see John's demise tied to this at all" Griffiths said. "[Ziegler] did the right thing. He said 'Just prove it,' and we did. It was somewhat tense, but we delivered it."

Griffiths has repudiated Gallagher's report in even harsher terms, describing it to Kerry Banks as "an out-and-out lie" in the late 1990s.

For what it's worth, Elite Prospects—an online international hockey database—lists Bure as having appeared in 11 games in 1987–88. The site has Bure appearing in five games with Central Army, which is consistent with official league records, and lists an additional six games Bure played for the Soviet U-18 side.

Do those six games represent Kuperman's findings? We'll probably never know. The only thing we can say with certainty about drafting Bure is it's the biggest draft day steal in franchise history.

48 Quinn Was a Coach First and Foremost

Pat Quinn's tenure as Canucks GM was, in a final assessment, somewhat uneven. His draft record was mixed—the Shawn Antoski and Alek Stojanov selections stand out as particularly egregious—and though his work on the trade market in his first five years in Vancouver was brilliant, the latter stages were marked by a series of iffy win-now deals and misjudged free-agent signings.

Though Quinn's executive work can be second-guessed to some extent, his abilities as a head coach cannot. He was a master motivator and a brilliant tactician, unrivalled in his ability to make mid-series adjustments in the playoffs. You could count on any Quinn-coached team to bring it in a crucial game, and he extended the careers of several less-mobile blueliners with an uncanny ability to pass on the fundamentals of defensive play.

"The thing about Pat is that he loved coaching so much," Trevor Linden explained. "That was his true passion, to be behind the bench—working with the players and in the game. That was his passion and that's why he did it."

Quinn wore many hats in Vancouver—president, general manager, coach—but the position he was best suited for was also the position he loved the most. His heart, his brain and his skill set belonged behind the bench. "If I had to pick a job that was the next-best to playing," Quinn said in 1992, "I think coaching's it. It has the emotional gamut you run through as a player. I love that feeling."

In his first three seasons in Vancouver, Quinn was banned from coaching in the NHL as a result of the fallout from Quinngate. Bob McCammon, Quinn's first coaching hire, was a sturdy tactician and nearly led the Canucks to one of the biggest playoff upsets of all time in 1989. The club regressed the following year, though—Linden didn't improve as hoped, the club's trademark defensive coverage spouted leaks, Igor Larionov and Vladimir Krutov were unable to provide the expected offensive spark, and Kirk McLean struggled—and missed the playoffs. The Canucks were once again limping along under McCammon in 1990–91, when a decision was made. It was time for Quinn to get back behind the bench.

McCammon's last game was supposed to be a home contest against the New York Rangers that preceded a lengthy five-game road trip. The club's success on that trip might determine whether or not the Canucks—carrying a 19–30–4 record at the time—would qualify for the postseason.

The Canucks outplayed the Rangers dramatically in the game, recording 62 shots in 65 minutes of play. And that's when Quinn's loyalty to his longtime coach kicked in and he began to second-guess the decision. "I remember we were going to fire Canucks coach Bob McCammon and we played the Rangers and got [60] shots on net and played great, but we had decided that he'd lost the team," Burke later recalled to Jason Farris. "After the game, Pat said, 'Maybe we give him one more game?' I said, 'Hey, wait a

Pat Quinn acknowledges the crowd after being inducted into the Canucks' Ring of Honor.

second, whoa, whoa. We decided we're firing him. You fire him, or I'll do it.' He said, 'I'll do it.' So he dislikes confrontation with people he likes."

More than four years removed from his expulsion by the league, Quinn was back to doing the job he was best at. But it started under tragic circumstances. Quinn's first game as head coach was set to be played in Los Angeles, the team he'd spurned controversially a few years before. When the Canucks' commercial flight landed at LAX on February 1, 1991, they witnessed a remarkable tragedy. An air traffic controller had made an error that resulted in a Boeing 737–300 and a small commuter plane colliding on the runway.

"The crash happened about 100 yards from the Canucks' plane," wrote Dan Robson in his Quinn biography, "which jolted to an abrupt stop as the pilot hammered on the brakes as the barreling 737 veered in his direction before hitting an airport fire station. The pilot of the Canucks' plane came onto the speaker system and said he was going to get away from the problem, before speeding his plane into nearby grass to distance his passengers from the explosion."

All 12 aboard the small commuter plane, SkyWest Flight 5569, were killed. Meanwhile 23 of the 39 passengers aboard of the 737, USAir Flight 1493, lost their lives, many of them as a result of asphyxiation from the ensuing fire. The Canucks watched helplessly from the window of their plane as the grisly tragedy unfolded. "We might have been the ones," Quinn said. "It makes you think how vulnerable you are when you see those poor people killed like that."

The Canucks' heads and hearts just weren't in the game—a 9–1 drubbing—for completely understandable reasons. That unfortunate start aside, the Canucks were better with Quinn behind the bench. Of that, there was no argument.

"He was a great motivator," Garry Valk told Robson. "His stories were intriguing; they were inspiring. A lot of times, they included past wars or battles. He was a lot like a schoolteacher. Just a really good social studies teacher. You didn't skip his class when the guy was teaching."

Quinn's impact in 1990–91 was limited to begin with. In his first six games, Vancouver lost five times and was widely outshot and outscored. It didn't help matters when Kirk McLean went down with an injury, forcing the Canucks to ride third-string goaltender Bob Mason down the stretch.

In early March 1991, though, Pat the GM did Pat the coach a major solid. In a lopsided deadline deal, Pat Quinn sent Dan Quinn (no relation) and Garth Butcher to the St. Louis Blues for an outrageous bounty of players that included Cliff Ronning, Geoff Courtnall, Sergio Momesso, Robert Dirk, and a draft pick. As you might imagine, adding three top-nine forwards to the roster made a significant impact on the Canucks' ability to drive play.

From then until to the end of the season, the Canucks managed to control better than 54 percent of all shots on goal. If Kirk McLean had been at full health, it's not a stretch to imagine the Canucks could've given the Los Angeles Kings a stern test in the first round of that playoff series. As it was, the Canucks battled to a 2–1 series lead that spring before being soundly beaten in three straight by Gretzky and company.

Despite the loss, the Canucks had their bench boss for the foreseeable future, and the early returns were promising. And the club was about to get a surprise injection of rocket fuel.

49 Clandestine Departures, a Sham Marriage, and a Michigan Arbiter: On Bure's Convoluted Path to the NHL

In the months that passed between the 1989 draft and Pavel Bure's arrival in 1991, the flashy Russian forward built a name for himself on the international stage.

Bure was dominant at the 1989 World Juniors in Anchorage, Alaska. Playing on a line with Alexander Mogilny and Sergei Fedorov, Bure managed 14 points in seven games and was named the tournament's top forward. Bure's game-breaking speed and skill were the talk of the hockey world, and the chatter got louder when Bure starred for the Russian national team at the 1990 and '91 World Championships.

Vancouver wasn't permitted to contact Bure directly after selecting him at the draft but did find a clandestine way to send him some Canucks-branded gear. Still, Bure's sense of the Canucks organization was barely extant.

"The NHL was like the moon to us," Bure's father, Vladimir, recalled to Kerry Banks. "When we heard that Pavel was drafted by Vancouver Canucks, I say, 'Draft? What is draft?'"

Pavel Bure's father—a competitive swimmer who pushed Bure and his brother Valeri hard—tried to keep up with the team's results in the newspaper. He wasn't impressed. "Sometimes I look in the paper and see what happens to the Canucks," Vladimir said. "Lose. Lose. Lose. This is a very bad team."

With Mogilny and Fedorov defecting in 1989 and 1990 respectively, the Central Army saw Bure as the cornerstone of their national program. They attempted to sign him to a three-year extension through the 1994 Olympics, but Bure wouldn't limit his options. In the summer of 1991, Viktor Tikhonov punished Bure by removing him from the national team, which was probably the final straw.

That fall, Bure—without having notified the Canucks of his imminent arrival—showed up at hockey agent Ron Salcer's house in Manhattan Beach, California. Salcer called the Canucks, who were caught entirely off guard. "When Salcer told me that Bure was in L.A., I didn't believe him," Brian Burke told Banks. "I said, 'Bullshit! Put him on the line.' We had no idea he was coming."

Pat Quinn, Burke, and the Canucks weren't just surprised. They were apprehensive about how to proceed. The Vladimir Krutov experience still hung heavy over the franchise. It took more than a week before Burke flew down to meet with the Bure family. Though Burke assured Salcer and Bure that Pavel was a priority for the club, the Canucks didn't inform the league about Bure's whereabouts. NHL president John Ziegler first heard the news from a *Vancouver Sun* reporter.

The relative lack of contact between Bure and the Canucks sowed the seeds for Bure's turbulent tenure in Vancouver. In speaking with the *Sun*, Salcer accused the club of breaking a promise to send Bure equipment, and failing to communicate regularly. "When Brian Burke was down here he told Pavel he was going to make him the top priority and that he was going to send down some equipment. I never heard from him again," Salcer told Tony Gallagher. "He's showing me contempt. I felt I had to speak out. [The Bure family's] spirits are dragging."

Quinn acted quickly to smooth things over, but he also gave a testy quote about the minor kerfuffle to the press. It's fair to describe most of Quinn's public comments about Bure from this time period as notes of caution, with a skeptical tinge.

The process of jumping over legal hurdles extended over the course of a few months. Ziegler said that, in the league's view, Bure was under contract with the Central Army, a view the Canucks shared officially even as Burke was poring over Bure's deal with the Soviet hockey federation and preparing to contest its legality.

To pass the time Bure took to skating with his brother and a 23-year-old woman named Shawn Barfield, who had played goalie for California State, Northridge, and working out. The Bure brothers referred to Barfield as Sean Burke. Bure attended tapings of popular American sitcoms as part of the live studio audience, and posed on the Manhattan Beach pier in roller skates for an iconic hockey card.

As crude deportation insurance, he married a 20-year-old American girl named Jayme Bohn in Las Vegas. They divorced a year later.

Finally the Bures and Salcer—very probably under Burke's advisement—decided to sue the Soviet ice hockey federation. The suit alleged Bure's contract with the Central Army was signed under duress and was thus unenforceable. "He was locked in a room for two and a half hours," Salcer told Iain McIntyre. "They say: 'You sign this. If not, you'll be in Siberia. You have to sign or you'll never see anybody again.'

"He couldn't talk to anyone. He wanted to phone his father, but they wouldn't let him. Pavel held out for two and a half hours."

When the Soviet side answered Bure's complaint, it gave the Canucks some legal standing to force a resolution. It also put the Canucks and the NHL in something of a bind (the league was actually named as the prime defendant in the suit Bure filed).

At issue for the Canucks? If Bure's contract were ruled invalid, it would effectively terminate their exclusive negotiating window with him after 14 days. The Canucks wanted Bure's contract ruled invalid, but if it happened, the prized young winger could become a free agent—free to sign with whichever team he pleased—within two weeks.

For the sake of brevity, we've skirted over Burke's involvement somewhat, but it was central. He'd determined the most favorable jurisdiction for a dispute centered on a contract with a minor was in Michigan, so he flew to Detroit and hired separate representation.

This was a complicated situation, and Burke, to protect the Canucks' interests, was forced to play both sides. He was hoping the club would have an agreement in place with Bure and the deal would be found invalid, of course, but if a contract wasn't agreed to in advance of the hearing—a preliminary hearing gave the Canucks the opportunity to begin negotiating with Salcer—Burke had lawyers at the ready to contest the presiding judge's ruling should it be in Bure's favor.

"[Those days were] probably the most difficult work of my life," Burke recalled to Banks. "I'd begin discussing the case with the two sets of lawyers at 7:00 in the morning and it would continue on until supper time. Then in the evening, I was on the phone with Salcer, negotiating Bure's contract."

The negotiations were tough, and it took until the eve of Bure's arbitration hearing for Burke and Salcer to come to terms—a four-year deal worth a reported $2.7 million. Seven lawyers, three translators, Bure, and a judge ultimately settled the issue during a marathon six-hour arbitration session at the Detroit City-County building on Halloween. The two sides bargained until they were blue in the face but couldn't bridge a $100,000 difference.

A frustrated Bure stood up and, ignoring Burke's advice to "sit down and shut up," volunteered to pay $50,000 out of his own pocket to bridge the gap. Burke later insisted Frank Griffiths ultimately stepped up to cover that $50,000, but it was a committed move from Bure, one that reflected the desperation with which he wanted to test himself in the best hockey league in the world.

It took two months and some unprecedented legal shenanigans, but the Canucks had their man. Burke's work in securing Bure was enormously impressive, particularly considering the complexity of the political and legal issues at stake. The way Bure's tenure in Vancouver played out, however, left some wondering how the club's handling of the young Soviet superstar set the tone.

This period played a big role in shaping the near-persistent acrimony that would characterize Bure's relationship with the Canucks.

50 The Debut

With the hype and fanfare reaching a fever pitch, Pavel Bure arrived in Vancouver on November 1, 1991. He drove up with Brian Burke from Seattle, where Burke had helped him sort through some remaining immigration issues, and arrived in Vancouver in time to watch the St. Louis Blues hand the Vancouver Canucks just their fourth defeat of the season.

Bure hadn't played hockey against high-level players since August and was expected to be a bit rusty. Meanwhile fans and the media were already eager to cast him as a savior, which concerned management.

If fans were in a state of delirium about Bure, Pat Quinn was more circumspect. He'd vowed to be conservative with his team's hottest young commodity and wanted to ease Bure into the lineup. As part of that, Quinn hit the brakes on Bure's debut so that he might practice one more time with his new teammates. Instead of playing his first NHL game against the Edmonton Oilers on November 3, Bure debuted two days later, against the Winnipeg Jets.

"I was in the press box that night," Griffiths recalled of Bure's debut. "I remember watching him step onto the ice for his first shift and I also remember being frustrated because I wanted him to play more, because based on what I'd seen and heard I was convinced he was going to light the world on fire, but Pat was determined to play him in a role and ease him in."

It's remarkable that Bure's debut—which wasn't televised—is such a touchstone for Canucks fans of a certain age. On a typically grim early November evening in Vancouver, 16,000 fans filled the Pacific Coliseum to see a game 100,000 more would later claim to have watched live.

Bure didn't score in his debut, and the Canucks didn't win, but that was beside the point. From the moment he made it onto an NHL sheet, it was clear Bure was a unique player. He was capable of mesmerizing opponents and forcing fans out of their seats every time he touched the puck. "When Pavel came in and you saw him go, you just knew there was something there that was special," Dave Babych later recalled.

Bure possessed an excellent shot, quick hands, toughness, and physical ruthlessness, but those weren't immediately apparent. In that first game, it was all about speed and puck control. The 20-year-old winger got the start alongside Trevor Linden and Greg Adams, but that was just to give fans an opportunity to welcome him to Vancouver in raucous style. He played most of the game with Ryan Walter and Gino Odjick on a depth line, though later in the game, he saw some shifts with Cliff Ronning.

Right from the get-go, Bure's skating velocity permitted him to cut through Winnipeg's defenders like a warm knife through butter. On a second-period rush, he split through Jets defender Fredrik Olausson and partner Shawn Cronin, and after momentarily outskating the puck, he kicked it back to his stick without sacrificing any pace. But Bure couldn't quite pull off the backhand-forehand deke that would later become his signature, and Jets goaltender Rick Tabaracci stoned him.

On another rush Bure took Dean Kennedy out wide. Kennedy had good position on Bure, but the crafty winger made a slick toe-drag move that distracted the veteran defender as Bure gained a step and positioned himself in Kennedy's hip pocket. The Canucks' new prized rookie, whose every touch of the puck was now accompanied by oohs, aahs, and a rising anticipatory cry from the masses, got off a solid snap shot on a partial breakaway. But again Tabaracci turned Bure aside.

Frustrated by the show Bure was putting on, Jets winger Doug Evans mugged him off a neutral zone faceoff. Ultimately Evans got his stick up on the young Canucks winger and appeared to cut his face. Evans was assessed a major penalty and a misconduct.

By the end of his first game, Bure had demonstrated a nose for creating turnovers. While forechecking, he recorded at least four quality scoring chances and he sprung himself for two clean breakaways and another partial one. Regardless of his stat line—which read zero goals and zero points—Bure had thrilled the crowd and demonstrated a level of dynamism that would make him one of the most prolific goal scorers in the history of the sport. "It was very exciting," Bure said through a translator after his debut performance. "I will remember this day all my life. It was beautiful. Beautiful."

Bure's performance in that very first game also earned him a memorable, alliterative nickname. "If Winnipeg are the Jets, then what do you call Pavel Bure?" wrote Iain Macintyre in the lede of his game recap that evening. "How about the Rocket? It fits Bure perfectly. He is the fastest Soviet creation since Sputnik." The Russian Rocket had arrived.

51 Gino! Gino! Gino!

If no former Canuck brings the house down at Rogers Arena quite like Trevor Linden does, Gino Odjick comes close. The Algonquin Assassin was one of the NHL's premier heavyweights during the enforcer-heavy early 1990s. In his first three seasons with the Canucks he fought more than 70 times, but his battle-hardened exterior only served to obscure his sensitivity and kindheartedness. Odjick had a habit of standing up for his teammates on and off the ice, a habit that endeared him to fans.

Standing 6'3" and weighing much more than 200 pounds, Odjick was a physical specimen. An Algonquin, Odjick grew up on the Kitigan Zibi reserve in Quebec. He wasn't very well educated, had grown up without cable television, and found adjusting to big-city life difficult at first.

Odjick—for whom Canucks fans still chant "Gino! Gino! Gino!"—never forgot where he came from. He wore No. 29 in honor of his father, Joe. "When the church sent his father Joe off to residential school," Joe Pelletier wrote, "they took away his name and gave him a number: 29."

During the 1995 off-season, Odjick went on a 500-mile walk through Alberta and British Columbia. It was a "journey of healing" during which Odjick—who by then was speaking publicly and courageously about his struggles with alcoholism—warned aboriginal youth about the dangers of drugs and alcohol.

Over the years, Odjick developed a close personal relationship with Pavel Bure. It was, perhaps, Odjick and Bure's shared status as outsiders that bonded them together so closely. "He came over from Russia, and was a Red Russian, very proud of his heritage, and when he came I knew the feeling he had, " Odjick explained. "We were two people who came from completely different cultures than what we were put into."

Gino wasn't a gifted scorer or skater or puck handler, but his toughness, character, and disposition made him a natural policeman. Though the salary cap and the evolution of the game has recently pushed the one-dimensional enforcer out of the NHL, Odjick's teammates always insisted his presence gave them an added boost of confidence. "Having a guy like Gino around really makes all of us play bigger and tougher," Odjick's diminutive teammate, Cliff Ronning, told the *Vancouver Province*. "We aren't afraid of initiating battles, because we know Gino is with us."

Like most enforcers, Odjick knew what he had to do to stay in the show. And he did it willingly. He had his fans in the organization, Brian Burke and chief scout Ron Delorme foremost among them, and he actually got off to a decent offensive start with IHL Milwaukee in his first professional season. That helped convince Pat Quinn and Bob McCammon that Odjick might be able to

Sour Grapes

When bombastic CBC commentator Don "Grapes" Cherry offered his public reaction to the Bure signing in November 1991, he publicly challenged Odjick to let Bure fight his own battles.

"Think of Odjick—Gino! Gino! Gino! Everybody yells it out there—good Native kid, making $130,000. All right, think about this. Gino—you're watching this, I know you're watching it out there—if a guy is capable of making $700,000, he's capable of taking care of himself. Right, Gino boy?"

It was typical Cherry, and no one was remotely surprised when Bure became a favorite target of Grapes in the coming years. But the basic thrust of Cherry's point, in this case, was remarkably misguided.

Not only did Odjick and Bure become famously close friends and share a Gretzky-Semenko-type bond on the ice, but even if they hadn't developed a special relationship, Cherry's comments suggest a fundamental misunderstanding of the sort of teammate Odjick was.

hold his own at the NHL level. In November 1990, only a few months removed from being a fifth-round pick at the draft, Gino was called up. Though not the most accurate sniper, this was a shot he wouldn't miss.

In Gino's first game, the Canucks were facing the Chicago Blackhawks, a rough-and-tumble outfit at the time. Nine Hawks finished that season with at least 100 penalty minutes, led by a trio of heavyweights in Dave Manson, Stu Grimson, and Mike Peluso.

Odjick knew the stakes. "I was really nervous when I went out on the ice and took warm-up," Odjick recalled to author Justin Beddall. "I was shooting pucks around and I could just tell I had Mike Peluso, Grimson, and [Dave Manson] looking at me thinking, *Who is this kid? Let's fight him tonight and see what he's got.*"

On Odjick's very first shift, he was put to the test. As he skated within spitting distance of the Blackhawks crease, Manson came at the rookie and tested him with a hard crosscheck. Off came the gloves.

The two fought to a draw. Though Odjick had more than held his own, he'd hoped to make a bigger impression in his NHL debut. Later in the game he did just that, lining up Grimson for a big hard hit and then winning a decisive bout against the Grim Reaper—one of the most respected enforcers in the game. "We squared off and got going," Gino recalled. "I hit him with a couple of good punches and kind of buckled him a few times, and as I was walking off the ice, I could hear the 'Gino! Gino!' chant."

In just one game Odjick had fought two of the toughest players in the league and earned himself a signature chant, one Canucks fans would repeat often and joyously for most of the next decade.

As Gino was turning heads in Vancouver as a hard-nosed rookie, the first Gulf War was raging in the Middle East. One night that winter, a fan brought a sign to the game that read: Gino Is Tougher Than Saddam.

As Gino circled the ice during the warm-up skate he spotted the sign. Never one to back down from a challenge, even one with such dire geopolitical consequences, Odjick skated over to McCammon and asked him to point out which player on the other team was Saddam. "I was just coming out of the reserve and we didn't have cable," explained Odjick to Beddall. "I was looking around the ice and saying, 'Where the hell is this Saddam Hussein guy?'"

52 Pavelmania

Long before Pavel Bure cemented himself as one of the league's top goal scorers, he was the object of intense curiosity, scrutiny, and adoration in Vancouver.

The day after his arrival, Bure donned a Canucks sweater and joined his teammates for practice at Britannia Ice Rink. In response, 2,000 fans filled the rink, which wasn't remotely suited to accommodate such numbers. There was an effort to hand out some Bure photographs as souvenirs, but a collective shoving match ensued and nearly turned dangerous.

"Our people were getting mauled," Brian Burke later recalled to Kerry Banks. "We were totally unprepared for it. They mobbed Bure after the practice. We finally had to push him into a car and speed away."

With that, Pavelmania was on. If the level of excitement surrounding Bure's mere arrival in Vancouver seemed over the top, it offered only a perfunctory glimpse of what was to come. "He'd have preferred to have more anonymity," said Griffiths, who remains close with Pavel. "That was hard for him in Vancouver, and I could sympathize with him. He couldn't go anywhere. If he was standing on a street corner, he'd get mobbed. I've seen him run because people have been following him and chasing him down the street for an autograph."

The jubilation surrounding Bure's first few NHL games was evident at the Pacific Coliseum, especially when Bure scored his first career goal against the Los Angeles Kings, beating Kelly Hrudey's backup, Daniel Berthiaume, with a quick backhand deke. The cherub-faced sniper quickly gave his line mates—Gino Odjick and Ryan Walter—a couple wholehearted high fives as the crowd went wild.

Pavel Bure was forced into the spotlight as soon as he first arrived in Vancouver.

Bure's skills and his multiple breakaways per game were enough to win him throngs of adoring fans, but in his first month with the Canucks, he wasn't exactly lighting the league on fire. As November turned to December, Bure had managed only four goals in 11 games—not bad for a 20-year-old but far off the pace of what the future Hall of Famer would manage over the course of his career.

Then things began to change for the better, both on and off the ice. Bure's mother—his father, Vladimir, was already in North America, working for the Canucks—moved to Vancouver in early November, providing a lonesome young man doing his best in a strange land with another friendly face. He enrolled in English classes to try and bridge the gap that existed between him and his teammates.

And in early December Bure was bumped onto a line with Igor Larionov and Greg Adams. Those two were a whole different class of skilled players than Walter and Odjick. The returns of the Adams-Larionov-Bure partnership weren't instantaneous, and Bure continued to produce at a relatively pedestrian rate through December. But once the Professor adjusted, the trio began to make beautiful music.

By mid-January Bure was clicking with Larionov and Adams, and the Canucks were beginning to be taken seriously. With Cliff Ronning and Trevor Linden thriving on the top line and the Bure-Larionov-Adams unit shredding the opposition, Vancouver could score with the best of them, while still playing the solid team defense that was a trademark of the Pat Quinn era.

Bure went on a tear late in the season, scoring 22 goals over the final 22 games. Even a 10-day strike led by Bob Goodenow and the players union couldn't halt the Russian Rocket's progress, as Bure scored in each of his final three games following a 13-day layoff.

The Russian Rocket finished the season tied with Ivan Hlinka for the Canucks rookie scoring record, and was voted the club's most exciting player. He'd also take home the Calder Trophy as the NHL's top rookie.

A general uproar surrounded Bure in the city of Vancouver. He couldn't go out without being mobbed. Teenage girls would shout his name from the street outside his apartment, which forced him to move. He later moved again—to a compound that resembled a military base—after his house was broken into multiple times.

Autograph hounds would hold out Sharpie pens in their pursuit of Bure autographs, which would ruin his best suits—a source of constant consternation for Bure's mother. And after Don Cherry called Bure a "weasel" for slew-footing Keith Tkachuk in the 1992 playoffs, Weasel Power T-shirts sold like hotcakes.

For a young Russian-born forward still learning the language and adjusting to North American hockey culture—Bure's response to Cherry's comments was "What is weasel?"—the attention and adulation must've been overwhelming. Not that it stopped him from scoring against opponents at will.

If Vancouver's hockey fans regarded Linden as one of their own, Bure was almost an alien curiosity. He was a force of nature to be mobbed, and eventually elevated to God-like status. According to Jim Robson, one autograph seeker went so far as to send Linden a piece of fan mail that read, "Dear Trevor: You have always been my favorite Canuck. Can you get me Pavel Bure's autograph?"

53 1991–92: The Canucks' First Winning Season

It took five years, but Pat Quinn had finally delivered the Canucks from the deep thickets of the hockey wilderness. "It was harder than I anticipated," Quinn said to the *Vancouver Sun* in the early 1990s. "I'd always been a person who looked forward to the next day. But when I came in, I saw athletes and an organization that couldn't get its chin off the ground."

By 1991–92, the best moves of the Quinn era had congealed. The blueline was solid and deep and included only one player he'd inherited (Doug Lidster). Kirk McLean turned in his best season, and all Vancouver's top six forwards—Trevor Linden, Igor Larionov, Pavel Bure, Geoff Courtnall, Cliff Ronning, and Greg Adams—scored at least 20 goals and 55 points. Finally, the Canucks were looking down at Edmonton and Calgary from atop the Smythe Division.

In March the Canucks set a franchise record with their 38th win of the season. In April, following a 10-day NHLPA strike, the Canucks won game No. 42—a milestone that passed by without much commentary but which was significant. After 22 seasons, the Canucks had finally managed to win more than half their games in a single campaign.

There is the idea in hockey—possibly an outdated one—that a young team entering its competitive window has to "learn to win." And the way you learn to win is, generally, by losing painfully in the playoffs. It's a notion that undersells and misunderstands the extent to which hockey is a young man's game.

With that in mind, there is a compelling argument to be made that the 1991–92 Canucks were the best team of the Quinn era. It's a notion that's rarely been considered given the following year's team finished with a better regular-season record, and the Quinn era is largely remembered for the 1994 team and its run to the Cup Finals. A variety of facts support the 1991–92 team, though.

Those Canucks controlled nearly 54 percent of shots on goal in all situations, the highest mark of the Quinn era. That shouldn't be a huge surprise, because with Larionov on the roster, the Canucks possessed an unparalleled level of center depth.

Losing Larionov in 1992 was really felt in the defensive end of the rink. His replacement, Petr Nedved, was a scoring ace but never had the same level of hockey IQ as his predecessor. The fact is, the 1991–92 Canucks were consistently able to control the run of play. The 1992–93 Canucks were reliant on Bure's high-flying offensive exploits, which generated against-the-grain offense.

In light of this, the 1992 playoff loss to Edmonton should stand out more dramatically as a blown chance. You don't hear much complaining, or see any hand-wringing, about those Canucks blowing a series against an inferior team, but in looking over the historical record, we suggest that it's one of the biggest missed opportunities in franchise history.

In 1992 Edmonton was a shadow of the glorious Oilers clubs that had dominated the previous decade. Long gone were the likes of Mark Messier, Wayne Gretzky, Paul Coffey, and Jari Kurri. Outshot by a wide margin that season, these Oilers were led by Vincent Damphousse, Kevin Lowe, Craig MacTavish, Joe Murphy, and Scott Mellanby. Esa Tikkanen missed half of the season with injuries. And though the Canucks probably had the superior team from top to bottom in 1992, the Oilers had Bill Ranford.

It all came down, as it so often does, to the first game. The Canucks had home-ice advantage and were known generally to struggle at Northlands Coliseum. At home in Game 1 the Oilers played poorly, by their own admission, but Ranford turned aside 40 of the 43 shots he faced and outplayed McLean in a 4–3

Edmonton victory. In the next game, Vancouver's quality shined through in a decisive 4–0 win.

Though the Canucks rebounded, teams can't afford to blow home-ice advantage in the playoffs, and the Oilers made the Canucks pay with a pair of victories at Northlands. Vancouver managed to force a sixth game, but Ranford again shut the door—making key saves off Courtnall and Ronning in the second period—for a 3–0 shutout that eliminated the Canucks.

Bure took the brunt of the blame for the series loss. The Oilers and Tikkanen, healthy and at his agitating best, had limited the hotshot rookie to just three points in six games. Tikkanen was heralded as Bure kryptonite, but the key to the series was really in goal. Ranford stole Game 1 on the road, and McLean couldn't return the favor at Northlands. That was the biggest difference in the series.

Though overmatched, the Oilers had managed to triumph over the Canucks. Their victory was stunning, but the success was short-lived. In the next round Edmonton was swept by Chicago. The Blackhawks were probably a better team than the Canucks that year, but it's hard to imagine that Vancouver couldn't have given them a run.

Sure, losing in 1992 wasn't a missed opportunity on the scale of blowing a 3–1 series lead to Minnesota in 2003. But it's up there. "I think we were capable of winning, and that's the thing that is most frustrating," Linden said following the Canucks' elimination. "No one was looking to learn anything from this, and basically we were ready to win and thought we were capable."

54 Burke Leaves, McPhee and Nedved Arrive

Pat Quinn's teams were generally well-built but had a fatal flaw: a lack of depth down the middle. This issue was exacerbated by a variety of factors. We'll begin in the summer of 1992, a year of quiet transition for the Canucks franchise. In May, Brian Burke—Quinn's right-hand man—was named the general manager of the Hartford Whalers. It was only a matter of time before Burke, who was in his mid-thirties and was rightly seen as an up-and-coming young hockey manager, got a shot at running his own shop.

"Two years before I got my first GM job, I was asked to interview for the Hartford job and the Ranger job, and Pat refused permission," Burke recalled to Jason Farris. "Pat actually called me into his office when he told the Rangers' president, Jack Diller, 'Go find your own guy and develop him like I did with Brian.' So Pat did not want me to go until I decided to go, and then he couldn't have been more helpful."

When Burke left Vancouver for Hartford, he recommended George McPhee, a hard-nosed forward during his NHL playing days and a recent graduate from Rutgers Law School, to take his place. Burke had described himself as "Pat Quinn's bulldog" during his time with the Canucks, and McPhee brought similar qualities to the role. Quinn required someone to do some of the dirty work so he could appear to be above it all as head coach. Mike Penny was also promoted, and began running the scouting side of hockey operations.

The new-look Canucks front office made several minor trades. The two with the most impact—a deal for Kay Whitmore and another that sent Robert Kron to the Whalers in exchange for defenseman Murray Craven—were with Burke's new club in

Nedved vs. Jagr

The Nedved pick—which happened in front of a partisan crowd at the Pacific Coliseum—has long been a point of contention with Canucks fans. Why? Because three picks later, the Penguins drafted Jaromir Jagr. Though Jagr is one of the greatest players ever, this sort of hand-wringing seems a bit overindulgent in light of two crucial facts.

One, remember that Nedved appeared in 982 NHL games over a lengthy career and managed to produce more than 700 points. Even if his best hockey was played in New York and Pittsburgh rather than in Vancouver, a 700-point NHL career is an indication that a management team selected a very good player who was deserving of his draft slot.

Two, Jagr had informed the Canucks and the other teams drafting ahead of the Penguins that he would only play for Pittsburgh. It took decades for then–Penguins GM Craig Patrick to admit it, but Jagr wanted to join forces with Mario Lemieux. He'd made it abundantly clear to the teams drafting ahead of the Penguins that using a selection on him would be a mistake.

Hartford. For the most part, though, the Canucks were conservative, something that would result in the media branding Quinn as "Stand Pat" Quinn.

The 1992–93 Canucks were an offensive juggernaut. They set a new team record for wins, with 46, and became the first club in franchise history to record 100 points in a season. Led by Pavel Bure, who went off for 60 goals and 110 points, the Canucks appeared to be the best club in franchise history. But there were some emerging structural issues.

The side was more porous defensively than the year prior, and received subaverage goaltending from Kirk McLean, who was outperformed by Whitmore. It probably didn't help matters that Vancouver surrendered nearly 200 additional shots on goal over the course of the season. The special teams also fell off, as their power-play conversion rate and penalty-killing percentage was below league average.

Having a supernova such as Bure helped to patch over some of the club's issues, and the emergence of Petr Nedved as a dynamic offensive producer served to cushion the blow of losing Larionov. It cushioned the blow offensively, anyhow.

Drafted second overall at the 1990 draft, with a pick the Canucks were prepared to use to redraft Bure, Nedved was a willful personality. He defected to Canada as a 17-year-old and demolished WHL competition with the Seattle Thunderbirds. During that time, Nedved's parents were forced by the government to call him and beseech him to return to communist Czechoslovakia.

Nedved had disappointed in his rookie season with the club, but his sophomore campaign was revelatory. While he was still derided for "soft" play, Nedved scored 38 goals and 71 points in his third campaign and did so with only a smattering of power-play time.

55 The Nedved Holdout

Despite a solid junior season, Petr Nedved didn't have a sophisticated feel for the peculiar optics of North American hockey culture and ran afoul of Canucks fans and Vancouver management as a result.

In the 1993 playoffs, Vancouver convincingly bested the Winnipeg Jets before falling to Wayne Gretzky and the Los Angeles Kings in round two. When that series and the best season in team history was over, Nedved asked Gretzky in the handshake line if he might take his stick as a souvenir. While the rest of the team skated off the ice with their heads hanging, Nedved skated off with Gretzky's stick and a conspicuous grin of satisfaction on his face.

Nedved's actions and the skepticism of Canucks management about his ability to play a meaningful role on a winning team, and a relatively inexperienced George McPhee's belligerent negotiating style set the stage for an acrimonious and lengthy divorce from the Czech defector.

The two sides weren't even on the same continent in negotiations. The Canucks tendered Nedved one offer, and when Nedved's representative asked for another, it came in with a salary $50,000 below the first one. It didn't help matters when McPhee sent a letter to Nedved insisting his agent, Tony Kondel, was representing him poorly. In response, Nedved declared in no uncertain terms that he'd never again play for the Canucks. "I don't care if takes one week, one month, or two years, I'm not going to play in Vancouver anymore," Nedved said. "I have a lot of friends on the team and I wish them very well. I have a problem with the management there and a personal problem with Pat Quinn."

The situation festered throughout the season, causing headaches for Canucks management in the press. The Canucks underperformed expectations, which made for a bad look with Igor Larionov thriving in San Jose and Nedved's protracted standoff. It was apparent by mid December that the two-time division winners would not three-peat.

On March 3, 1994, the Canucks hosted the St. Louis Blues and, behind two goals by Pavel Bure, soundly defeated them 4–0. Off the ice Quinn was engaged in trade talks with Hartford GM Paul Holmgren. The Canucks were close to finalizing a deal that would have sent Nedved and defenseman Gerald Diduck to Connecticut in exchange for Michael Nylander, Zarley Zalapski, and James Patrick. But the trade never went through.

On that very day, in secret, the Blues signed Nedved to a lucrative three-year, $4.05 million contract. Quinn and the Canucks were furious. "We have some real questions about what transpired," Quinn said a few weeks later, once the dust had settled. "We want the league to have a look at this. [The process] involves some dirty tricks that were not very savory, and I'm not going to let it go."

Not only had the Blues blown up the Canucks' preferred trade package with Hartford, they'd also signed Nedved to a deal that blew Vancouver's out of the water financially. At that point in the club's history, the Canucks were dealing with perpetual financial headaches. They'd been lowballing Nedved all season, were facing an expensive round of contract negotiations with Bure, and the Blues had just laid bare the club's tightfistedness.

Despite the Blues' agreement with Nedved, this saga was far from over. Because of Nedved's status as a restricted free agent, there was the issue of compensation to work out. The issue was ultimately settled by arbitration on March 14, 1994. At the hearing, the Canucks pushed to secure Brendan Shanahan from St. Louis as compensation for Nedved, but McPhee and Quinn were facing an uphill climb. The Blues pointed to a variety of comments Canucks management had made slamming Nedved's lack of character and skill, including a letter McPhee had written to Nedved's agent.

Ultimately the arbitrator awarded the Canucks a second-round draft pick and physical two-way centerman Craig Janney. Janney, who was in the midst of an 84-point season, refused to report to Vancouver though, causing the situation to drag on for another week. Finally the Canucks agreed to a trade that sent Janney back to St. Louis for Jeff Brown, Nathan LaFayette, and Bret Hedican.

It took three weeks of bad press, arbitration hearings, and acrimonious arguments for the Canucks to resolve the Nedved situation. It was an unfortunate episode for Quinn and Canucks management on a variety of levels—Quinn's annoyance must have quadrupled when Hartford sent Nylander, Zalapski, and Patrick to Vancouver's division rival in Calgary—but the result was a favorable trade that successfully positioned the team well for the playoffs.

"We weren't presented with the best scenario in this situation, but we have acquired a quality defenseman in Brown and up-and-coming young players," Quinn said. "We didn't have Petr and we didn't have Craig, but we do have some players that can come in and help us now."

56 Don't Fit the 1994 Team for Glass Slippers

The popular notion that the 1994 team was a scrappy playoff Cinderella that bested a handful of superior teams on their run to the Cup Finals needs to be reexamined. This was a club with Pavel Bure, a 22-year-old superstar forward at the absolute apex of his powers. Throughout the campaign Bure seemed able to bend both space and time to his will, and there were few, if any, opposing defensemen who could consistently keep up with him.

Trevor Linden, the captain, was 23 and one of the most versatile two-way players in the league. He hit the 30-goal plateau and scored at a point-per-game rate in the playoffs.

Cliff Ronning, Greg Adams, and Geoff Courtnall were dependable, veteran top-six forwards, all of whom could mesh seamlessly with either Linden or Bure. Players such as Sergio Momesso, Tim Hunter, and Gino Odjick were useful role players who brought a physical presence.

Jyrki Lumme and Murray Craven gave the Canucks a pair of 50-point defensemen who could work the power play. Dave Babych, Gerald Diduck, Jiri Slegr, Robert Dirk, and Dana Murzyn provided defensive depth.

In net, Kirk McLean was a reliable starter, and Kay Whitmore proved himself a solid addition. The year prior, Whitmore even outperformed McLean in save percentage. Vancouver rated Whitmore highly enough that they engaged in some roster gymnastics—trading Doug Lidster's signing rights to the New York Rangers for John Vanbiesbrouck—to protect Whitmore during the 1993 expansion draft.

Behind the bench, Pat Quinn had the ingredients of a team capable of winning the Pacific Division (founded when the Smythe Division was renamed in the summer of 1993), and the Canucks started the season as if they'd do precisely that.

To start, the Canucks won eight of their first nine games. A romp to a third consecutive division title seemed to be in the offing. Fate, injuries, and shaky goaltending intervened, however, as the Canucks played sub-.500 hockey the rest of the way. Vancouver still mostly controlled the run of play, but McLean cooled off after a hot start—so much so that by the time the playoffs rolled around, Vancouver fans and media were wondering if Quinn should start Whitmore—and key injuries to Momesso and Adams exposed the club's lack of forward depth. "I remember sitting in the dressing room around Christmas and thinking, *Wow*," Linden said. "Like Greg Adams was out…Petr Nedved was holding out. We had a lot of injuries, and I was thinking, *What happened to our team?*"

Injuries throughout the forward ranks resulted in a mess of call-ups—Mike Peca, for example, made his NHL debut that year—and Odjick, by necessity, spent a large chunk of his season on Bure's wing. The arrangement resulted in a career offensive year for the likeable enforcer, but it was a suboptimal situation for the team.

Quinn, George McPhee, and Mike Penny began to scour the league. The Canucks worked the waiver wire, putting in claims on forward Martin Gelinas, defenseman Kerry Huffman (who went to Ottawa), and defenseman Brian Glynn. Even Jimmy Carson, the once-promising forward who was the centerpiece of the Gretzky-to-L.A. trade, was acquired and given an extended look.

Ultimately it was the resolution of the Nedved situation that gave Vancouver a much-needed boost. Though Quinn would've preferred to add a centerman, Jeff Brown and Bret Hedican gave the blueline a shot in the arm. From the moment the two made their Canucks debut, the team controlled better than 55 percent of all shots on goal in the regular season.

Though Vancouver was the seventh seed in the newly formed Western Conference, by true talent, they were better than their record. In fact, of the opponents Vancouver faced in the 1994 playoffs, only the Rangers controlled a better percentage of shots.

The Canucks were built around young stars and had a deep, mobile defense. Their roster construction was, in fact, quite modern. "Our run to the cup final wasn't a fluke," recalled McPhee. "There were several teams there for several years that could've made a run."

Once McLean got hot—which happened midway through Vancouver's epic first-round series against Calgary—the Canucks were nearly unstoppable. And it had nothing to do with pumpkin carriages or glass slippers.

57 The Adjustment

Know this: any time Vancouver and Calgary meet in the opening playoff round, there will be fireworks. By virtue of their seventh-place finish, the Canucks were set to lock horns against the Flames in 1994. It was billed as yet another referendum on Pavel Bure's ability to produce in the postseason, and a rematch of the storied 1989 series.

The Flames were favored once again, but this time the talent level between the two teams was a push. Vancouver underperformed in the regular season for a variety of reasons but was better than their record indicated. What's more, moves made on the waiver wire and at the deadline were really starting to pay off.

In the series opener, the Canucks showed they shouldn't be counted out. Kirk McLean was great, stopping 31 shots, and the Canucks demolished the Flames 5–0 behind power-play goals from Cliff Ronning and Jeff Brown.

It was a different story in Game 2, as Calgary had its revenge. Behind a dominant Al MacInnis effort—the hard-shooting defender recorded five points and seven shots on goal—the Flames jumped the Canucks with four first-period markers. Vancouver rallied but couldn't get the score within two, as the Flames won a violent, penalty-filled affair.

As the series shifted to the West Coast, the Flames' strategy of shadowing Pavel Bure with Mike Sullivan—who'd later go on to coach in Vancouver—and Zarley Zalapski continued to frustrate. Game 3 was a tight-checking affair, with the Flames opening the scoring midway through the third period, building on their lead late, and winning yet again.

With their backs against the wall, the Canucks came out and dominated Game 4. Bure managed a whopping seven shots on net and the Canucks managed 44 as a team but could only beat Mike Vernon twice—and Bure was once again held off the score sheet. The Flames won 3–2 and dug their boots into Vancouver's neck.

Down 3–1 in the series, the Canucks were in trouble. Desperate for an answer, Pat Quinn made a crucial adjustment ahead of Game 5. The top end of the Flames' roster was wreaking havoc on the Canucks, and Theo Fleury and Gary Roberts appeared particularly unstoppable. So Quinn decided to shift Trevor Linden into the middle of his forward group, pairing him with Greg Adams and Bure on a new-look first line. "Pat was a tactical magician," Linden said. "At the time we were searching for answers; it was a huge part of [our turnaround]."

Quinn's adjustment paid immediate dividends when Bure scored his first goal of the series, beating Vernon with a lovely one-timer assisted by both Adams and Linden less than five minutes in. Just more than 60 seconds later, German Titov answered on a three-on-one to tie the game, which remained deadlocked into the overtime period.

Though the Canucks controlled the fifth game decisively, the Flames had their chances, and McLean bailed out the Canucks with key stops on Roberts and Robert Reichel.

Nearly eight minutes into overtime, Courtnall took advantage of an iffy Flames line change and streaked down the left wing. The skilled left winger, who always seemed to save his best games for the postseason, uncorked a wicked slap shot that whizzed past Vernon. Game over. Canucks win. The tide was turning, and Quinn knew it.

"Pat and I were having dinner after the game, and he just turned to me and said very quietly, 'They won't beat us now,'" George McPhee said. "Pat just seemed to know that the Geoff Courtnall overtime goal was going to be the turning point for us, and it was. After that game, and for the rest of the playoffs, we played terrific hockey."

In the confines of the raucous Saddledome, the Canucks had earned the right to play another game. And as the series shifted to another do-or-die game, this time at the Pacific Coliseum, the Canucks were poised to play like a team of destiny.

Vancouver jumped all over the Flames early in the first period of Game 6, dominating the first 20 minutes and testing Vernon with a flurry of scoring chances. Only a Gerald Diduck drive managed to find the back of the net, though. With time expiring in the frame, the Flames managed to draw even, as Roberts scored with just tenths of a second remaining.

The Flames ambushed the Canucks early in the second period, building on the momentum of the Roberts goal. Vancouver took the lead against the grain, though, when some nifty forechecking by Nathan LaFayette pushed the puck to Courtnall just below the Flames' goal line. Courtnall made a perfect pass to find Jose Charbonneau drifting through the slot, and Charbonneau—the roller hockey legend who later plied his trade for the Vancouver Voodoo—converted as Vancouver took a 2–1 lead.

Writhing with tension and excitement, the fans who filled the Pacific Coliseum waited to exhale as the Flames stomped the Canucks in the final 20 minutes. Wes Walz deflected a Zalapski point shot past McLean to tie the game early in the period, and the Flames only poured it on from there. Under siege in a period in which the Canucks were outshot 10–2, McLean held the fort and preserved the tie through regulation.

The Canucks' season was hanging by a thread, but the Flames remained the better team early in overtime. Theo Fleury and Robert Reichel tested McLean with 10-bell scoring chances, only to be robbed by the Canucks goalie.

Once again, an iffy line change did in the Flames. With just fewer than five minutes to play in the first overtime period, the Flames were assessed a bench minor penalty for too many men on the ice. Calgary head coach Dave King was running a system in the series whereby his left wing would change and Sullivan—tasked with shadowing Bure—would jump onto the ice whenever Bure did. Though Sullivan held Bure off the score sheet early in the series, one is left to wonder whether King's clever scheme was somewhat *too* clever. This crucial bench minor was Calgary's third infraction for too many men on the ice in the series.

"We were starting to get to them a little bit because they were really trying to match against Pavel, myself, and Greg Adams," Linden recalled a decade later. "We were getting to them and confusing them with our line changes."

On the ensuing power play Bure was controlling the puck near the half wall when he turned away from a Flames penalty killer and skated to the left point. While Jyrki Lumme raised his stick to call for the one-timer, Bure unleashed a wrist shot through a crowd.

The puck hit a body and fell right at Linden's feet. Linden found it a split second quicker than any Flames defender, hacked at the puck to get it in front of him, and sent a soft backhand along the ice at Vernon. The sprawling Flames netminder stopped Linden's first attempt, but the captain kept crashing the crease and got off a second backhand shot, willing it past Vernon to force Game 7. The stage was set.

58 April 26, 1994

With the benefit of hindsight, big events can feel inevitable. That's true in hockey and in life. To even force a seventh game of the 1994 Western Conference Quarterfinals, the Vancouver Canucks required consecutive overtime goals. Down by a goal on the road late in Game 7, a breakdown by the Calgary Flames defense permitted Greg Adams to waltz into the slot untouched for a crucial game-tying goal. In overtime, Kirk McLean robbed Gary Roberts on a partial break and bent the forces of geometry to his will to stone Robert Reichel on the save.

Then Bure, quiet all series, etched a beautiful goal onto the face of hockey history when he took a perfect hook pass from Jeff Brown and beat Mike Vernon on a breakaway chance with his signature backhand-forehand deke.

Bure's goal was the culmination of an extended series of unlikely events, but for the Canucks players and coaches who lived it, something about that moment felt predestined. "Even when we were down, I felt something was going to happen," Canucks assistant coach Ron Smith told Kerry Banks. "It's almost metaphysical, something cosmic."

It's remarkable how many members of the 1994 Canucks—players, executives, coaches, and owners—share a similar story about the Flames series. Kirk McLean later remarked he felt the Canucks were getting under the Flames' skin as Game 7 went along, a sign things were moving in Vancouver's favor. Quinn had quietly, calmly called the series over a beer with his assistant general manager, George McPhee, following Geoff Courtnall's overtime winner in Game 5.

Of course Vancouver's Game 7 victory over the Flames wasn't preordained or written in the stars. It was the confluence of some fantastic puck luck and a series of excellent performances. It easily could've gone the other way.

The Flames, in fact, were the better team for most of the contest. Vancouver had the first prime scoring chance of the contest when Linden fooled a Flames forechecker with a neutral-zone deke and found Bure streaking down the right wing. Bure tried his signature move, the one that would end the series a few hours later, but lost control of the puck. Instead it was Calgary who opened the scoring when Theo Fleury beat McLean.

Vancouver answered on the power play with a stunning bit of puck movement that began with a Linden drop pass in the neutral zone to a streaking Geoff Courtnall. Courtnall carried the puck into the offensive zone and wound up for a slap shot but was hooked by Fleury and fell to the ice. Courtnall got off a quick pass that Linden overskated, but the pass was hard enough that it found open space on the right wall and Bure picked it up. Bure put a high-risk deke on a Flames penalty killer while pushed up against his own blueline and made a tricky pass to Jyrki Lumme on the other side of the ice, which Jeff Brown left cleverly. Lumme sent a shot on net that ricocheted off Vernon onto Bure's stick at the side of the net and into the Flames' goal for the game-tying marker.

The Canucks added to their lead a little more than two minutes later when Courtnall was first to a Murray Craven rebound and sent a quick snap shot past Vernon. As the buzzer fell on the first period, the Canucks led the Flames 2–1 with 40 minutes left to play.

Calgary outshot Vancouver 16–8 in the first 20 minutes of Game 7 and duplicated their margin in the second. Under almost constant siege, McLean turned away quality Fleury drives and five-alarm Gary Roberts chances in droves. Calgary tied up the game midway through the second, though when a Kelly Kisio pass attempt deflected off Ron Stern and past McLean; 64 seconds later, Fleury gave Calgary the lead when he brought the Saddledome crowd to its feet with a 15-foot blast that McLean barely had time to react to.

As the contest morphed into a nervy affair, the Flames had opportunities to ice the Canucks. Robert Reichel missed wide on a gimme setup by Fleury, and Wes Walz nearly converted on a two-on-one, but his shot hit the iron. As the game clock wound down in the third period, the Canucks needed a goal to force a third consecutive overtime.

With three minutes left in the game, Jyrki Lumme skated behind the Flames' net and initiated the cycle while protecting the puck from Zarley Zalapski. Bure flew by, and Lumme dumped the puck off to his forward, who promptly carried the puck to the point. Reading off his preternaturally skilled teammate, Lumme wisely cut to the slot, forcing Zalapski to follow him.

The tricky little switch Bure and Lumme pulled off caused the Flames defenders to confuse their assignments. Zalapski followed Lumme and ended up on his off side, and his defense partner, James Patrick, was too slow to pick up Greg Adams along the half wall. When Adams received the pass from Bure, there wasn't a Flames defender within two strides of him.

Adams struggled with injuries and production throughout the 1993–94 regular season, but he was an enormously skilled forward and relished attacking the crease with the puck. In this moment, Adams didn't hesitate. He just attacked the Flames defense and carried the puck straight to the net.

As Adams moved across the crease, he deked to his backhand to avoid a Vernon poke check and shot a low backhander that trickled past Calgary's netminder. A deflated Saddledome crowd yawned.

"People talk about Pavel's overtime goal, so it gets lost," Linden recalled of Adams' game-tying marker, "but Greg tied that game up with three minutes to play in Game 7. We're down 3–2 and it's over if he doesn't score there. It was a massive, massive goal."

The series was getting the overtime period it deserved.

59 Overtime: "The Save" and the Hook Pass

Late into the night on April 26, 1994, the Canucks and Flames traded chances with their season on the line. Kirk McLean stoned a hard Al MacInnis drive from the point and made an excellent save off a Robert Reichel wraparound attempt in the first overtime period, after Reichel spun off Trevor Linden. Mike Vernon, meanwhile, turned aside a deft Gerald Diduck tip and made consecutive saves off Geoff Courtnall and Murray Craven, the latter chance springing a three-on-one the other way when Dana Murzyn pinched and got caught.

Theo Fleury was skating down the right wing with Gary Roberts trailing and Robert Reichel charging hard down the left wing. Only Jyrki Lumme was back for the Canucks as Geoff Courtnall scrambled helplessly to get back into the play. Lumme kept his eyes on Fleury the entire way, getting low to the ice and never retreating below the hash marks. Fleury, one of the best puck handlers of his generation, passed into the circle, and the three-on-one flattened out. McLean retreated from a three-quarters depth posture.

Fleury never seemed to seriously consider shooting the puck, and at the last moment sent a pitch-perfect saucer pass over Lumme's stick and found Reichel open on the left wing. Reichel directed a shot low and toward the bottom of the net near the left post as McLean desperately lunged in a two-pad stack across his crease.

The red light went on. Half the Saddledome crowd erupted in celebration. The other half had witnessed the Save. "They turned the red light on, but that wasn't a goal," Jim Robson exclaimed on the CBC broadcast. "That was a spectacular save by Kirk McLean!"

"I kind of read it at the right time and came across with the puck and was able to get my toe on it," McLean recalled to Canucks TV a decade later. "If you really look at it, what works out great for me is the fact that my pad was meeting the shot right on—[Reichel] didn't have a lot of time to get it up or put it back far side.... There was some good timing there."

McLean's save was heralded immediately as an absurd piece of clutch larceny by the Vancouver netminder. "You watch hockey for the next 100 years and you'll never see a better save," exclaimed Don Cherry.

"Every time I see that save on video, I go: 'Oh my God, I can't believe Kirk got it,'" Courtnall told the *Vancouver Sun* 20 years later.

As if buoyed by McLean's gallantry, the Canucks pressed. Sergio Momesso beat Vernon with a quick snap shot off an offensive zone draw but hit iron. Martin Gelinas handcuffed the Flames netminder with a hard slap shot from the left point, but Vernon managed to hang on. McLean meanwhile had one last big stop to make. He somehow stoned German Titov from point-blank range with his pad, then stopped a second wraparound attempt. Game 7 would require double overtime.

Two minutes into the second overtime period, Trevor Linden dumped the puck in for Greg Adams to go chase, but the Canucks winger was tripped up by a Flames defenseman, and the puck rimmed around the Flames net where Vernon played the puck to Flames winger Paul Kruse. Linden was bearing down on Kruse, who took the puck on his forehand with his back facing up ice. His only play was to dump the puck out of Calgary's zone.

Unable to get off on a change, the Flames were scrambling. Recovering the puck in the neutral zone between the benches, Dave Babych made a heads-up play with a D-to-D pass on his backhand to Jeff Brown. It was a pass designed to keep the pressure on, a sequence Pat Quinn had drilled his team on throughout the series.

Brown took his time. He looked up ice and calmly controlled the puck. Then he fired a strike of a hook pass, catching Bure just inside at the Flames blueline behind Zalapski and James Patrick. Mike Sullivan, Bure's shadow throughout the series, never had the opportunity to get off Calgary's bench.

Bure received Brown's pass and with two lightning-quick strides pulled away from Zalapski as the Flames defender (who was so nearly Bure's teammate six weeks earlier) did everything he could to get a stick on Bure and slow him down. When the Russian Rocket went supersonic, there was no catching him. Trying in vain to hook one of the fastest skaters in the history of the sport, Zalapski's final attempt to lay his stick on Bure whiffed so completely that he knocked himself off balance.

Bearing down on Vernon, Bure pulled off his trademark backhand-forehand deke at full pace. Vernon bit to his left then sprawled to his right, flailing to get his paddle down and stop Bure's shot. Vancouver's superstar winger was just too fast, his hands too sure. As the puck trickled over the goal line for the game winner, Zalapski barreled into Vernon, knocking the net off its moorings. The Flames were defeated. Vancouver's run to the Stanley Cup Finals was on.

60 Liftoff

The Vancouver Canucks' thrilling comeback over the Calgary Flames in the first round electrified the city of Vancouver ahead of the club's second-round series against the Dallas Stars. The Stars were coached by legendary defensive ace Bob Gainey, which perhaps explains why they were widely seen as an imposing defensive club, even though they'd permitted an above-average number of shots and goals against throughout the 1993–94 season. Fresh off a first-round series sweep of the St. Louis Blues, the Stars held home-ice advantage in a second-round series that followed a 2–3–2 home-and-away format.

If the Stars—by virtue of their superior regular-season record and their convincing victory over the Blues in the first round—were seen as favorites going into the series, that was probably an error on the part of handicappers and hockey pundits. Dallas had some big-name players, Mike Modano foremost among them, but they didn't employ mobile defenders of the caliber of Al MacInnis or Zarley Zalapski. Though Derian Hatcher was widely seen as the gold standard of NHL shutdown-type defensemen at the time, Dallas' blue-line group was long on size and short on skating ability, which made them a poor matchup for Bure and the Canucks.

The first game in Dallas was a rousing affair. Vancouver jumped out to an early lead behind goals by Murray Craven and Geoff Courtnall and built a commanding 4–1 advantage by midway through the second period. The Stars battled back, though, capitalizing on the man advantage with Tim Hunter in the box and getting two goals from Mike McPhee.

As the game settled into a more traditional, tight-checking playoff affair, the Stars held a narrow edge in play but were unable to beat Kirk McLean. With five minutes to play in the third period, Martin Gelinas beat Darcy Wakaluk with a quick shot off an offensive zone draw that dribbled by the Stars netminder. Trevor Linden added an empty netter and the Canucks had a 6–4 victory and the series lead.

Bure scored a goal in the first game, waltzing into the slot and freezing multiple Stars defenders and Wakaluk with a flurry of shot fakes before blasting the puck home, but he was only just beginning to assert himself in the series. From Game 2 through to the handshake line, the Stars series morphed into the Bure Show.

Cliff Ronning opened the scoring in the first period of Game 2, but it was Bure who padded Vancouver's lead, finding a loose puck in the slot and rifling it past Andy Moog. Bure's celebration was significant, partly because of some memorable dramatics earlier in the frame.

In the first period the Stars were clearly following a game plan of challenging Bure physically. Craig Ludwig landed a big hit on Bure, which could have been called boarding or crosschecking, that went unpenalized. Just as Bure was getting to his feet, Stars right wing Shane Churla came in from Bure's blind side and drove the Russian winger to the boards with his shoulder.

Obviously Bure took note of Churla's number. On a sequence later in the frame, Churla challenged Dave Babych along the wall while forechecking and poked the puck past the Canucks defender. Churla had barely touched the puck and was moving to get himself into formation to defend the Canucks breakout when Bure came flying in from center ice and delivered a brutal leaping elbow that knocked Churla out cold.

"It was an awful hit," recalled Linden.

"Nowadays, Pavel would get life for that," Dave Babych joked to Elliott Pap of the *Vancouver Sun* 20 years later.

Though Babych was kidding about Bure's life sentence, there's probably some grim truth to his assessment. Nearly five seconds elapsed between when Churla last touched the puck and when Bure blinded him. Bure led with his elbow and left his feet for a retributive and predatory hit. The elbow literally ticks every single box on the Department of Player Safety checklist. "I had no choice," Bure said. "They [were] trying to kill me. I'm lucky I didn't get hurt."

In actual fact, Bure was lucky he didn't get suspended. For a play so dirty it has almost no contemporary analog, Bure was fined only $500 by NHL vice president Brian Burke—two years removed from working with the Canucks—and that was the extent of it.

Bure's elbow served to obscure, to some extent, his magnetic performance in the contest. With time ticking off the clock in the second frame, Bure took a lead pass from Craven and sped off. Hatcher was the last man back for the Stars, but he appeared to be skating in quicksand next to Bure. By the time Bure crossed the Dallas blueline, Hatcher was choking on the fumes from Bure's tailpipe.

With Hatcher cleanly beaten, Bure skated right across the Stars' net, pulling Moog into no-man's-land before calmly depositing a shot up and over the flailing Stars netminder. The goal gave the Canucks a commanding 3–0 lead, and Vancouver went on to win Game 2 by that precise margin.

Linden came to refer to Game 2 of the Stars series as the best game Bure ever played. "He had the puck the whole game," Linden recalled. "He was just a man amongst boys. You couldn't get it from him, and that's when he was unstoppable."

As the series shifted to Vancouver, the Stars battled back. Dallas overcame an early 2–0 deficit in Game 3 by scoring four consecutive goals. The Stars' defense held the fort in the third period, as the Canucks mustered just two total shots on goal in the third frame in an anemic comeback attempt.

In Game 4 the Stars had every opportunity to change the arithmetic of the series. They imposed their preferred, plodding pace on the game, limiting Bure to just a couple breakaway attempts, and the game was tied 1–1 at the end of regulation. It was a typical overtime winner, a garbage goal whacked in by Sergio Momesso, that allowed the Canucks to put the Stars in a vise grip with a 3–1 series lead.

In the decisive fifth game at the Pacific Coliseum, Bure once again led the way. Nathan LaFayette opened the scoring in the first period and Bure converted a perfect Linden feed from the corner to give Vancouver a 2–0 lead and some breathing room. Modano cut into the lead late in the first frame, but Craven restored the two-goal cushion in a second period that the Canucks dominated.

As the clock wound down in the third period, Canucks fans reached back 12 years and began serenading the Stars with the "Na Na Hey Hey Kiss Him Goodbye" chant. Modano, desperate to make something happen, cut into the Canucks end and unleashed a shot that McLean easily kicked aside. The puck rimmed around the boards to Greg Adams, who found Bure in space.

Bure skated in on Moog, with only a back-checking Modano in pursuit. Like Zalapski before him, Modano tried to hook Bure, but the effort felled him. The American-born superstar watched from a prone position as Bure went to his backhand and beat Modano cleanly. It was an appropriate final nail in Dallas' coffin, an exclamation point on the most dominant individual performance in a single series in Canucks franchise history.

61 Greg Adams! Greg Adams! Greg Adams!

Between the second round and the Western Conference Finals, the Vancouver Canucks had an opportunity to lick their wounds and rest while the San Jose Sharks and the Toronto Maple Leafs duked it out. When the Maple Leafs prevailed, it set the stage for the first and only playoff series between the Maple Leafs and the Canucks in the history of the respective franchises.

Once again the Western Conference Finals (absurdly named, because they featured a team that played home games in Southern Ontario) followed a 2–3–2 home-road format, and once again the Canucks opened on the road, in Maple Leaf Gardens, one of hockey's most hallowed grounds.

Western alienation, as a sociocultural subcurrent, thoroughly permeated the series. It was aided by some members of the Toronto press corps, such as *Toronto Star* columnist Rosie DiManno, who described Vancouver as a "blond bimbo" of a town. The usual conspiracy theories ran wild—every missed call was evidence of a sinister plot against Vancouver's Stanley Cup hopes—and there was little sense of objectivity on either side. Tom Larscheid even described an iffy call as "bullshit" on live radio during the series.

The Maple Leafs took the first contest by the skin of their teeth. Nursing a late third-period lead, Maple Leafs forward Mike Gartner was penalized for holding with 102 seconds remaining in regulation. Vancouver's power play went to work, and Linden managed to tie it up with just 30 seconds remaining. The Canucks' furious comeback fell short in overtime, when Peter Zezel beat Kirk McLean on one of the very few soft goals McLean allowed throughout that fateful postseason.

In Game 2 the Canucks battled back, led by Bure, who was on an unholy tear. With points in nine consecutive games, Bure's confidence was running high. At one point early in the contest Bure attempted to flip the puck to himself from behind the net. The "fancy" self-pass worked, in that Bure managed to test Felix Potvin with a quality look, but it didn't result in a goal. Bure opened the scoring late in the frame, undressing several Maple Leafs defenders and beating Potvin to extend his playoff point streak.

The Maple Leafs battled back in the second period, briefly taking the lead behind a pair of Dmitri Mironov power-play markers. Several minutes later the Canucks got two quick goals from Jeff Brown and Murray Craven and took a 3–2 lead into the visitors' dressing room during the second intermission.

In the midst of a hard-fought playoff game, a special teams contest had broken out. Toronto tied the game in the third period when defenseman Dave Ellett scored for his third power-play point of the evening, but a late Jyrki Lumme power-play goal stood up as the winner. The Canucks were headed back to Vancouver having earned a split at Maple Leaf Gardens.

In the 1994 Stanley Cup playoffs, Kirk McLean put together one of most spectacular playoff runs in the history of goaltending. The Canucks starter stopped pucks at an average rate throughout the 1993–94 regular season, but he was nigh unbeatable once the playoffs started. And his best run of form in those playoffs—even more impressive than his ridiculous performance in Game 1 at Madison Square Garden, and more spectacular than the Save—came against the Maple Leafs in the Western Conference Finals.

Having allowed a third-period power-play goal in Game 2, McLean wouldn't fish another puck out of the Canucks net until the first period of Game 5. Bure tortured the Maple Leafs for two goals in Game 3, and the Canucks were outplayed soundly in Game 4 before Cliff Ronning took advantage of Toronto's one mistake in the game's 58th minute, but the goal scorers barely matter: McLean had simply closed the door on Toronto's Stanley Cup hopes.

If the Canucks hoped to avoid a return trip to Maple Leaf Gardens with a Game 5 victory, the Maple Leafs weren't going to make it easy on them. Vancouver had two glorious early chances, but Brian Glynn put a backhand wide and Greg Adams couldn't convert a gimme chance on a two-on-one with Trevor Linden.

Then the Maple Leafs took over. Toronto's goal-scoring drought had extended past the 140-minute mark when center Mike Eastwood took advantage of a failed Canucks clearing attempt and finally solved McLean on the short side to give the Maple Leafs an early lead. Before the period was over, Doug Gilmour and Wendel Clark added two more goals—scored within 45 seconds of each other—to give Toronto a commanding 3–0 lead after 20 minutes.

The 1994 Canucks, as they so often did that spring, found a way to battle back. Murray Craven jumped all over a Geoff Courtnall rebound less than 100 seconds into the second frame to get the offensive onslaught started. Midway through the period, after McLean had made a very fortunate sprawling save off Rob Pearson, Nathan LaFayette walked past the Leafs defense and beat Potvin with a gorgeous move to make it a one-goal hockey game. Then Adams got into it on the power play, picking up the loose change after Potvin couldn't control a Bure blast, to level the score 3–3.

On the brink of a Stanley Cup Finals berth, the Canucks pressed in the third period and overtime but couldn't solve Potvin. Meanwhile McLean was counted upon to make a series of crucial stops, his best off a sneaky Dave Andreychuk wrist shot in overtime. Twenty minutes of overtime slipped by without a game winner. Double overtime would be needed. "It was the start of the second overtime, and I was tired," Adams recalled in 2014. "I remember thinking, *God, I hope somebody scores early.* It felt like the game was going to go on all night."

As fans made their way back to their seats following the fourth intermission—the city of Vancouver was peppered for days afterward with stories of missing the game winner while waiting in line for the bathroom—the puck was dropped and the Maple Leafs promptly turned it over in the neutral zone. Linden played the puck back to Babych, who uncorked a shot Potvin couldn't handle. The puck bounced tantalizingly in front of the Maple Leafs goaltender, and a charging Adams got to it first. Adams slipped a soft backhand under an exhausted Potvin as the Pacific Coliseum erupted and radio broadcaster Jim Robson, in an iconic moment, yelled, "Greg Adams! Greg Adams! Greg Adams!" repeatedly into the microphone.

"The rest of the call—'The Vancouver Canucks are going to the Stanley Cup Final!'—was clear," Robson later recalled, "but just saying 'Greg Adams' over and over again wasn't too imaginative, I guess."

Imaginative or not, it captured the spirit of the moment. As spontaneous celebrations engulfed Renfrew and Robson Streets, Linden lifted—and broke—the Clarence Campbell trophy. Perhaps it was a bad omen, but it didn't matter in the moment. Toronto was vanquished. For just the second time in franchise history, the Canucks were going to play for hockey's ultimate prize.

62 The Best Game in Franchise History

The 1994 Stanley Cup Finals are regarded as one of the finest in league history. There was major star power. The series went the full seven. And while the Canucks may not have registered on the national radar, their opponent certainly did. The New York Rangers entered the series with tons of hoopla. They'd been the class of the NHL, racking up 52 wins on the strength of a bunch of personalities fit for Broadway. There was "Iron" Mike Keenan, the club's notorious hardass coach. There was captain Mark Messier, a four-time Cup winner in Edmonton. Sergei Zubov and Brian Leetch were two of the best offensive defensemen in hockey. All told, the playoff roster had three future Hall of Famers.

The Rangers were also tasked with winning Lord Stanley's Mug for the first time since 1940. For an Original Six team in a massive media market, it was a huge storyline.

Then there was Vancouver. Though the Canucks had impressed in their run through the Western Conference, early previews suggested they would largely be a footnote as New York snapped its Cup drought. Many made note of the fact that New York finished the season with 112 points to Vancouver's 85—a 27-point differential. And many of those same folks also noted it was the largest differential between Stanley Cup finalists since 1982 when—oh, yeah!—the Canucks were swept by the Islanders.

It's almost unfair to gloss over the first five games of the series, but it's requisite to get to the heart of this chapter. If there was an overriding theme from those five games, it was that Vancouver was more than equipped to battle the Rangers tooth and nail. New York's long-awaited coronation wasn't going to be easy.

Greg Adams, at this point a folk legend in Vancouver, scored the OT winner in Game 1 as the Canucks stunned the Rangers at MSG. From there, the Blueshirts asserted their dominance, rattling off three straight wins while outscoring the Canucks 12–4 in aggregate. That set the stage for a potential series clincher in Game 5 at MSG, and the city prepped for celebration.

The Rangers were feeling it. Perhaps too much. The Canucks jumped out to a 3–0 lead in Game 5, squandered it, then rebounded and went on to a 6–3 victory. It was a stunner. "All my family, my parents, sister were coming to the game, so my focus was not on the game," New York forward Stephane Matteau recalled to the *Hockey*

News. "I was worrying about them driving from Noranda, Quebec, to New York. But when we got to the game, I had no legs. I think a lot of players felt that way and we lost."

New York's loss was Vancouver's gain for Game 6, in that the city was treated to the best game in franchise history. Facing elimination in a second straight contest, the Canucks put forth an unforgettable effort in front of a frenzied Pacific Coliseum crowd. The energy was palpable to start as Vancouver fired everything it could at Rangers goalie Mike Richter. Jeff Brown opened the scoring, then added his second in what was one of the finest games of his career. Not to be outdone, Geoff Courtnall added a pair of his own, including the infamous second tally.

With just less than two minutes remaining and Vancouver clinging to a 3–1 lead, Nathan LaFayette's diving swipe pass on a choppy two-on-one found Courtnall, who deked backhand and flipped the insurance marker past a sprawling Richter. But there was just one problem. The puck hit the back bar and quickly bounced out. Officials, unclear if the puck had crossed the goal line, allowed play to continue, and seconds later, Messier scored to cut the lead to one.

Hold on a sec, though. The goal judge threw the red light on for Courtnall's shot. That warranted a review. While the referees went to the penalty box to contact the NHL head office—arguably the most important phone call ever made from Vancouver—the CBC broadcast showed multiple replays confirming that, yes, Courtnall's goal was a good one.

"The score is 4–1, Mr. Keenan," said Neale, the former Canucks coach and GM who had since transferred to the TV side of things.

"Vancouver is gonna win this hockey game!" cried play-by-play man Bob Cole, Neale's partner in the booth.

Messier may have been denied his goal, but he wasn't finished making his mark, parton the horrible pun. As time ticked down on the clock, Adam Graves ran into Trevor Linden at the Vancouver blueline, sending the Canucks captain to the ice. While he was there, Messier delivered a second hit, enraging the Canucks while forcing Linden to crawl back to the bench in obvious pain.

To call the atmosphere charged would be a massive understatement. The audience was going wild at the prospect of a Game 7… and going crazy because Messier had just nailed Linden.

If there was anyone fit to capture the moment, it was longtime Canucks play-by-play man Jim Robson. And capture it he did. "I didn't see who hit him the first time, but Messier hit him when he was down the second time. Sergio Momesso is really upset at the Vancouver bench," Robson said. "But there is going to be that seventh game! We'll hope they can patch Linden up and get him in that one."

Then Robson seemed to realize what he might have just inferred. Like there was any chance of Linden not playing. Like he was going to miss this. "He will play!" Robson bellowed. "You know he'll play! He'll play on crutches! He will play, and he will play on Madison Square Garden on Tuesday night! The game is over!"

At that point in the broadcast, Robson fell silent and let the deafening roars of the Coliseum take over. In the upper corner of the camera, a frenzied fan—who had somehow gotten onto the playing surface—dropped to his knees and slid across the ice, pumping both fists skyward in a moment of unhinged celebration.

That wasn't the only indelible image from Game 6. Linden, bleeding from the mouth and literally looking dead on his feet, skated out onto the ice and threw his right arm around an equally exhausted Kirk McLean. One keen-eyed photographer snapped a shot, and with it captured one of the most unforgettable moments in franchise history. "It was just one of those exhausted, relief feelings," Linden recalled to the *Vancouver Sun*. "The photo really captured that moment. Like they say, one picture is worth a thousand words."

"Trevor and I didn't really say anything after the game," said McLean. "Obviously he has the blood dripping off his chin and on his shirt, and his arm is up around my head pushing my mask halfway across my face. We were both mentally spent at the moment.

"The photo has taken on a life of its own. People love that photo, and it really does show a lot of what we went through—and what Trevor went through as far as taking a beating and continuing."

63 LaFayette and the Final Gasp

"You don't know this, but Trevor Linden had cracked ribs and torn rib cartilage for the last four games of the 1994 Stanley Cup Final. You can't imagine what it's like to hear your captain, in a room down the hall, screaming at the top of his lungs as they injected the needle into his rib cage. Knowing him, he probably thought we couldn't hear. He would then walk into our dressing room like nothing had happened. That was inspirational."

—Cliff Ronning, to NHL.com in 2008

Given Cliff Ronning's admission, Game 7 was quite literally Vancouver's final gasp. Yet coming off the greatest contest in franchise history, the Canucks had time to catch their breath. Game 6 was played on June 11, but because the series had to shift back to New York, Game 7 wasn't scheduled until June 14.

That gave both teams extra time off between contests. One would think Vancouver would have relished the rest, given Trevor Linden had been beaten to a pulp and Kirk McLean was on the brink of exhaustion. Not the case, however. "We always believed that if it weren't for having two days off between Games 6 and 7 that we would've won it," George McPhee said. "We had so much momentum at that point."

The extra day off only added to the nervous energy in New York, which at that point could have lit up Times Square. The Rangers had a 3–1 series lead, and were on the verge of snapping their 54-year Stanley Cup drought. Now they were one loss away from blowing the whole thing.

Needless to say, the city was watching. "I remember going to the rink," Dave Babych said, per CBC. "They had barricades all over the place and the police were corralling people. We needed a police escort to get to the rink. Once you got in the rink and the dressing room, a little more calmness set in."

Nerves were palpable for both sides, but it was New York that channeled them into an early positive. The Rangers jumped out to an early 2–0 lead, only to see Linden cut that in half with a shorthanded marker in the second period. Answering the Canucks captain tit for tat, Messier scored early in the third to make it 3–1, and then—as if to answer Mark Messier—Linden scored again to make it 3–2.

Then Nathan LaFayette became a household name in Vancouver. A 21-year-old rookie who wasn't even in the lineup at the start of the playoffs, LaFayette found himself in the biggest moment of his career. He took Courtnall's centering pass with 70 seconds left and one-timed the puck past Richter…and, *ping!*, hit the goal post.

It was, without a doubt, Vancouver's last quality chance to tie the game. A few half-opportunities presented themselves in the

A dejected Kirk McLean hangs his head after Game 7 of the 1994 Stanley Cup Finals.

dying moments, but for most Canucks fans, Game 7 ended when LaFayette hit the post.

For LaFayette, it was an ignominious way to be cemented in history. He's not to Vancouver what Bill Buckner is to Boston—not by a long shot—but years later he admitted the stigma never went away. He told the *Globe and Mail* he still gets a lot of attention when he returns to Vancouver and that, when in New York, even the occasional Rangers fan will come up to thank him.

When asked if the Canucks one day winning a Cup would act as a reprieve, LaFayette didn't shy away. "I'd love to see the Canucks win, because I think there's no better hockey town," he told the *Globe and Mail.* "But no question, [it] would also help me to kind of move on, to get rid of that collar. Absolutely."

The 1994 loss, when the Canucks gasped for that last breath but failed to find it, has stuck with a number of players. Years later, Babych said it still made him feel bad. "Guys were torn apart," he said. "You don't know what it's like to win, and that's probably the part that hurts the most."

64 The Riot

In the aftermath of Game 7, Vancouver and New York had very different reactions. New York waited three days to demonstrate its feelings, and did so with a memorable ticker-tape parade down the so-called Canyon of Heroes, in front of an estimated crowd of 1.5 million. Adam Graves said it was one of his favorite memories as a Ranger.

Vancouver, meanwhile, wasted little time with its response—immediately embarking on the city's first riot in more than 20 years. Bruce Arthur later recalled in the *National Post* at the time: "Vancouver hadn't seen a proper riot since a Rolling Stones concert in 1972 devolved into a melee that saw 200 concertgoers firebomb a police car and put 13 officers in the hospital with rocks as big as footballs. There had been a few others, including one that saw more than 300 people get arrested for hurling beer bottles at police on the eve of the 1966 Grey Cup game between the Saskatchewan Roughriders and the Ottawa Rough Riders at Empire Stadium;

171 were arrested in riots after the BC Lions lost the 1963 Grey Cup to Hamilton, too."

Though there was that history, Vancouver didn't exactly have a reputation as an overly riotous city. That all changed rather quickly. Reports estimated between 50,000 and 70,000 people converged downtown, causing an approximate $1.1 million in damages. The epicenter was at the intersection of Robson and Thurlow Streets, with a number of Robson's retail outlets receiving the majority of the abuse. Eaton's, once one of Canada's largest department stores, reported 80 windows broken.

Around 10:00 PM the riot reached a "flash point," as later described by the British Columbia Police Commission report. One man, who'd scaled the guide lines that supported trolley wires, fell sharply to the ground and required medical attention. Paramedics arrived, and while they attended to the injured individual, members of the crowd began climbing on the bumpers of one of the ambulances.

Shortly thereafter, the police's crowd-control unit made its move. The members donned their tear gas masks and began dropping smoke grenades, but the effort failed to achieve the desired result of taming the crowd. In fact, as the BCPC report later stated, the situation was deteriorating.

Then came the tear gas. And with it more chaos. The crowd was young, and they were energized and invigorated by participating in something they hadn't experienced before. Alcohol, unsurprisingly, was pegged as a major riot fuel.

In the end, more than 500 police officers were involved in the incident. St. Paul hospital treated approximately 90 people for injury, and an additional 100 suffering the effects of tear gas or pepper spray. CBC reported that 150 arrests were made.

But those were the numbers. They didn't do much other than illustrate the scope of civic unrest, and certainly didn't tell the whole story. What everybody wanted to know was, how did this happen? And why?

Vancouver, it turns out, was short on answers. Some pointed to the year prior, when Montreal experienced a significant and similar riot following the Cup Finals—though not *that* similar, because the Habs were the victorious side. But still, maybe there was a copycat trend at play. Philip Owen, then Vancouver's mayor, said the riot was indicative of "deep social problems across the country."

Light was cast on the media for potentially inciting the public. In a piece titled "Inciting a Riot, Hypocritically" the *Times-Colonist* claimed local media outlets "whipped the community into a frenzy" over the Cup Finals, adding the coverage appealed "to the lowest common denominator in their readers, viewers, and listeners."

No single theory seemed to adequately explain what happened, which is fair. Incidents of this nature are complex and multifaceted, and sometimes it's tough to rationalize irrational behavior.

The hope was that Vancouver would learn from the riot and that the public shame and humiliation would prevent it from ever happening again. That hope was not to be realized.

65 Bure Didn't Threaten to Hold Out in the 1994 Playoffs

Pavel Bure is at the center of some of the most riveting and unsolvable mysteries in franchise history. From the murky circumstances surrounding his draft eligibility to the way his mammoth five-year extension with the club came to be to his precise reasons for holding out in 1998–99, there was an almost constant level of noise, controversy, and speculation during the Bure era.

Of all the crazy stories that stuck to Bure during his dynamic, memorable Canucks career, though, the playoff blackmail story is perhaps the toughest to understand. Everyone involved, including Bure; George McPhee; Pat Quinn; Bure's agent, Ron Salcer; and Arthur Griffiths, insists the story isn't true, but it was reported by three different reporters—Damien Cox, Al Strachan, and Tony Gallagher—in late May and early June 1994.

Let's go through what we know, and then we can get theoretical about precisely how Bure's contract negotiations became so public and so messy.

It's well accepted at this point that Bure's relationship with Canucks management started fraying almost immediately upon joining the club. After Bure's ridiculous success in his rookie season, he and the Canucks acknowledged his contract required renegotiation, but nothing came of it. "In my first year [the Canucks] admitted my first contract was not enough," Bure told Strachan and Gallagher during a 1999 sit-down. "But when we went to talk about it, they said, 'Hold on, you have to play a bit more; you have to prove it to us.'"

Finally in 1993 the two sides agreed in principle to a five-year deal worth just less than $15 million, an identical contract to what Bure's former Central Army linemates Alexander Mogilny and Sergei Fedorov had signed in Buffalo and Detroit, respectively. When Bure went to sign the contract, though, the amounts were listed in Canadian dollars rather than in greenbacks. This 1993 kerfuffle resulted in Bure's first trade request.

"We should've done it a little bit earlier, probably could've done a better deal if we'd done it earlier," McPhee said later. "But that's business. Sometimes you wait and it works out; sometimes you wait and it costs you more money. When you're paying one guy so much money, there isn't a lot to go around. It turned out to be hard on the team."

Now let's fast-forward to the spring of 1994. Canucks management was reluctant to offer Bure a lucrative extension, and Bure had no desire to commit long-term to the Canucks; in fact, he'd already requested a trade. Despite this asymmetry, business realities intervened to make a lucrative contract extension all but inevitable.

In an effort to build a downtown arena, Griffiths had overextended his family's empire and put the Canucks in a perilous financial situation. The cost of the land for the barn that would eventually be named GM Place was exorbitant, and the construction of the arena ran overbudget (a situation that was exacerbated by a variety of strikes at the city docks).

Griffiths' construction of a privately financed downtown arena was a boon to the public—particularly when viewed against the trend for professional sports leagues and clubs to raid and extort city coffers to build multimillion-dollar rinks—but it precipitated the sale of the team to John McCaw and Orca Bay in the mid-1990s.

The costly construction of GM Place is crucial context. Bure was the club's biggest draw, and as Griffiths' empire required additional financing, locking in the club's biggest star became imperative. Despite management's skepticism, the Canucks would make Bure an offer too lucrative and favorable for him to refuse. "It had to be done; he was the star player," McPhee recalled. "It helped get the new building built."

Bure has often insisted the contract was agreed upon prior to the 1994 playoffs, but the deal—a five-year contract that paid Bure at least $6 million per season and guaranteed he was paid as much as the third-highest-paid player in the league—wasn't signed until before Game 3 of the 1994 Stanley Cup Finals. And even then, Bure insisted Quinn—who was at best lukewarm on making such a major commitment to one player—be present in the room when the deal was signed.

Why a contract that was apparently agreed to in mid-April would go unsigned until mid-June is hard to fathom. Over the intervening eight weeks, though, a variety of rumors and reports surfaced that accused Bure of effectively blackmailing the Canucks organization.

Damien Cox of the *Toronto Star* dropped the first such report on May 31, 1994—immediately preceding the opening of the 1994 Stanley Cup Finals. "News that the 23-year-old Bure has apparently signed a monstrous contract rumored to be worth US $30 million over five years retroactive to this season, stunned the hockey world on the eve of the Stanley Cup Final," Cox wrote. "Now there is rampant speculation that Bure's California-based agent, Ron Salcer, threatened to have Bure sit out playoff games, including last week's Game 5 against the Leafs, if the contract wasn't finalized."

It's interesting to note Cox was pretty close on the actual value of Bure's contract (though the deal was only partially retroactive) but didn't quite have the timing of the signing down.

The very next day, *Toronto Sun* columnist Al Strachan picked up the baton and ran with it. In comparison with Cox, Strachan had the timing of the signing right but didn't quite have the terms or the dollar value. In Strachan's version, Bure threatened to withhold his services ahead of either Game 6 or Game 7 of the club's first-round playoff series against the Calgary Flames. "Salcer presented Canucks coach and GM Pat Quinn with a demand," Strachan wrote. "Either Quinn would sign Bure's new contract, or else the Russian Rocket would not be playing that night. Quinn went wild, as might be expected, and said that he would not give in to extortion. He told assistant GM George McPhee to call team owner Arthur Griffiths and explain why Bure would not be in the lineup that night. McPhee returned with a message from Griffiths. 'Sign it.'"

Salcer, Griffiths, and McPhee have consistently disputed this version of events and continue to do so to this day. "I don't think there's any truth to it," McPhee said. "I don't think there was any truth to the whole thing."

"There is absolutely no way that that story is true," Griffiths added. "I don't understand sometimes why stories sometimes get written and repeated."

There are a variety of theories as to the source of the leak, but all the principals agree that the meat of the story is false. Bure never threatened to withhold his services during the 1994 Stanley Cup playoffs.

The fallout from these reports and Pat Quinn's failure to repudiate them with sufficient force at the time may have led directly to Bure's holdout half a decade later.

66 The Canucks Could've—and Should've—Signed Wayne Gretzky

In the summer of 1996 the Vancouver Canucks set their sights on the biggest-name unrestricted free agent in hockey history: Wayne Gretzky. In mid-July the two sides—owner John McCaw, GM Pat Quinn, assistant general manager and lead negotiator George McPhee, and Orca Bay deputy chairman Stan McCammon on the Canucks side and Gretzky, lawyer Ron Fujikawa, and player agent Mike Barnett on the other—met in Seattle for a marathon bargaining session.

Gretzky had every intention of doing a deal if the money was right, even bringing a suit for a potential press conference. At the 11th hour, it appeared the two sides were close and the framework of a potential deal was set. And then it all fell apart at about 1:30 AM, as a result of a misguided phone call.

In the annals of painful what-ifs in Vancouver Canucks history, the misguided middle-of-the-night ultimatum to Gretzky stands alongside "What if the Canucks had won the 1970 draft lottery?" "What if Nathan LaFayette had put that shot an inch to the left?" and "What if Alain Vigneault had pulled Roberto Luongo after the second period in Game 3?" as an absolute all-timer. It was just one phone call, but it completely altered the trajectory of the franchise.

The doomed meetings in Seattle have been spun far and wide in the two decades since, and a peculiar mythology has attached itself to the series of meetings in mid-July and the fateful phone call in particular. To get a better sense of the competing narratives involved, it's best to simply lay them out side-by-side.

In Dan Robson's Pat Quinn biography, *Quinn: The Life of a Hockey Legend*, the story goes that Quinn made contact with Barnett about Gretzky and the conversations proceeded fruitfully. With the deal moving along, Quinn offered to cancel a planned trip to Singapore to get the deal done but was told that wouldn't be necessary.

While on vacation, Quinn received constant requests for updates from McCammon, demanding to know how negotiations were proceeding. Eventually Quinn cut his trip short, partly on advice from Arthur Griffiths, who warned his hockey czar that the Orca Bay crowd was beginning to whisper that Quinn wasn't serious about getting a deal done.

Tony Gallagher's reporting differs from Robson's account in a few subtle but significant ways. On July 15, 1996, Gallagher reported that Gretzky had met with "McCaw and other high-level officials from Orca Bay within the last four days." Gallagher suggested that if the deal fell apart, it would be "because of an emerging gap between the ownership and the hockey department," and even went so far as to pass along a note that McPhee and

Quinn "expected to be able to talk ownership out of the notion [of pursuing Gretzky]."

It's certainly known that McCaw met with Gretzky without Quinn at his retreat in Sun Valley, Idaho, that summer. By the time Quinn rushed back to Seattle, it's unclear that he was leading the negotiations. "We were there; it was mostly [Mike Barnett] talking to [John McCaw]," McPhee recalled. "It got past a certain level."

It's at this point that the accounts really begin to differ. Robson's account features Gretzky and McCaw going for a late dinner, comfortable with the notion that a deal was essentially in place. But as the other parties to the negotiations broke to have their dinner, Robson suggests McCammon told Quinn he was worried about Gretzky's camp using their offer as leverage to squeeze the New York Rangers into offering more.

Around midnight, the two sides parted ways, confident a deal was close for something in the neighborhood of $5 million per season over three years. In Robson's account, however, McCammon and Barnett remained behind to discuss bonuses and marketing details. At about 1:30 AM, Barnett said he thought they'd worked it all out and that Gretzky would agree to the deal in the morning. It was at this point that McCammon insisted on waking Gretzky and getting the deal signed immediately. When Gretzky refused to do the deal on the spot, the Canucks pulled their offer. Three days later, Gretzky signed a two-year, $10 million deal with the New York Rangers.

According to Gallagher, on the other hand, substantive negotiations took place past midnight, at which point the Canucks significantly raised their offer from $4 million per year to $5 million per year, which really brought the two sides close to an agreement. Barnett and Fujikawa woke Gretzky and apprised him of the new developments. After huddling briefly, the Gretzky group

What could have been. The Greatest scores his NHL-record-setting 803rd goal against the Canucks in 1994.

broke up, believing a deal was close and that it would be resolved in the morning.

At 1:30 AM, however, Barnett received a phone call from Canucks management informing him the offer was of the "take it or leave it" variety. Barnett woke Gretzky, who wasn't prepared to do the deal that night, and in the morning it was off the table.

McCammon certainly doesn't recall any one-on-one meeting with Barnett and remembers the ultimatum being delivered over the telephone, after the Canucks' side huddled together as a group. "I don't remember any one-on-one discussions with anybody," McCammon said. "I was there to essentially say, 'Does this fit within whatever plan we'd outlined?' The discussions were largely led by George and Pat, and largely by George because that's sort of the role he played at the time."

George McPhee remembers the crucial moment somewhat differently. "They sat down in another room and the owner decided to pull the plug at a certain point, and we didn't have much say in the matter," McPhee said. "It wasn't Pat or I [who woke up Gretzky], it was [Stan McCammon]."

That it was McCammon who made the fateful phone call is beyond dispute. The question, really, is whether McCammon and McCaw acted without taking advisement from their representatives from the hockey operations department, or if McCammon bit the bullet and made the phone call based on a more collective decision. "I have a lot of respect for George and Pat as hockey people, but I think in this instance they felt strongly that there was risk to a deal getting done if it didn't get done and signed that night," McCammon said. "So it was left to me to make the phone call."

It's hard to imagine why negotiations would have persisted into the wee hours were there not substantive issues—terms and salary in particular—being haggled over. On that front, Gallagher's reporting seems more persuasive. As for whether Gretzky and Barnett were making a leverage play, an insecure notion crucial in preventing an agreement, was driven by McCaw and McCammon or by Quinn and McPhee, it's impossible to know for sure.

That Quinn and McCaw's Orca Bay proxies weren't on the same page in the latter stages of Quinn's Canucks tenure is well documented. In fact, Quinn later publicly disavowed moves like the Alexander Mogilny trade and Mark Messier signing as moves that the "suits" pushed for. That gap between ownership and hockey operations is crucial context in picking through the wreckage of what exactly occurred in the early-morning hours on July 19, 1996.

We'll probably never know the full story of how exactly things fell apart on the Canucks side of the equation. What we can say with confidence is failing to land Gretzky compounded the loss of Cliff Ronning, weakening the Canucks down the middle and firmly closing the competitive window on the Pavel Bure–Trevor Linden core.

67 Grand Larceny: How the Canucks Landed Markus Naslund

The core of the fondly remembered early 1990s Vancouver Canucks teams was constructed by Pat Quinn, largely through excellent work on the trade market. Some of Quinn's trades were for pure prospects, guys such as Kirk McLean, but more often, Quinn rolled the dice on skill players who needed a new opportunity and a change of scenery: players such as Cliff Ronning, Greg Adams, Jyrki Lumme, and Geoff Courtnall.

By the late 1990s the Quinn era was winding down in Vancouver. The general manager, who had enjoyed an enormously friendly working relationship with the Griffiths family, began to clash with new owner John McCaw's proxies with increasing frequency. He had one last trick up his sleeve, though: a trade in a similar mold of some of the best deals he made early in the decade. Though Quinn wasn't running the Canucks by the time the move paid serious dividends, it might have been his finest deal as Vancouver's general manager.

The story of the most lopsided deal in Canucks history begins, as many Canucks stories do, with a Mike Penny scouting trip. During a game in Pittsburgh, Penny noticed a young Penguins winger named Markus Naslund was being bumped further down the lineup as the game went on. "I happened to be passing through Pittsburgh the week before [the trade]," Penny recalled. "And I thought of Naslund, *Eddie [Johnston] doesn't like this guy.*' You could just see it."

Naslund was 22 years old and in his third professional season. He'd scored 19 goals for Pittsburgh, getting a look on a line with Mario Lemieux and Tomas Sandstrom. On a Penguins team loaded with future Hall of Fame talent, though, Naslund's offensive prowess was occasionally seen as redundant, and the skilled Swedish winger struggled to earn the trust of his head coach. "I felt that I had a decent first half of the season and obviously it helps playing with great players like Mario and Tomas," Naslund recalled, "but then things were starting again to get back to me getting less and less ice time."

Eager to prove himself at the NHL level and stuck behind oodles of talent on a team with five 70-point forwards, Naslund needed a new opportunity and actively sought it out. "I didn't feel like I was one of Eddie Johnston's favorites, and he had lots of forwards to choose from," Naslund says. "At that point I did feel like I had to ask for a move to have a chance to make it in the NHL."

That Naslund requested a trade out of Pittsburgh is a too-often-ignored aspect of the lopsided deal that ultimately brought a future captain to Vancouver. It's crucial context that helps to explain why Penguins general manager Craig Patrick prematurely parted ways with the talented young forward.

There was a good deal of familiarity between the Canucks and Naslund when the Swedish forward went on the block ahead of the 1996 NHL trade deadline. Not only had Penny watched Naslund play a week prior, but Thomas Gradin was familiar with Naslund from his Ornskoldsvik connection, and Gradin's mother even occasionally babysat Markus for Naslund's parents in his youth.

Still, Quinn wasn't completely sold. "Pittsburgh saw a potential [Cam] Neely in big Alek [Stojanov], and they were willing to give up this skill guy," Quinn recalled to Iain MacIntyre some 15 years later. "You're always concerned about doing another Neely deal and giving away a guy too soon, especially some of these big kids."

Alek Stojanov was the seventh overall pick at the 1991 NHL Entry Draft. Where Quinn excelled at taking a chance on overlooked skill players on the trade market, his habit of drafting one-dimensional physical forwards too early on draft day (Stojanov, Shawn Antoski) was arguably the Achilles' heel of his managerial tenure with the Canucks. In this case, at least, he cashed in his chips at the exact right moment.

"Pat called me up and says, 'What do you think of Markus Naslund?' and I said, 'He's a pretty good player,'" Penny recalled. "Pat says, 'He isn't scoring much for a goal scorer,' and I said, 'I don't care,' and Pat said, 'We can get him for Alek Stojanov.' I was shocked. I said, 'I'll pick him up from the airport.'"

On deadline day in 1996, the Canucks completed the fateful swap of a pair of 1991 first-round picks. Stojanov went to Pittsburgh in exchange for Naslund, and the rest is history. Stojanov got injured in a serious automobile accident the following season, effectively ending his NHL career. He went on to score just two goals for the Penguins. Naslund, meanwhile, became the face of the Canucks franchise during the West Coast Express era, and his No. 19 hangs from the rafters at Rogers Arena. It was

Quinn's last bit of trade market larceny in Vancouver, capping off an impressive run.

68 Wooing Mark Messier

It seems unfair when you consider the big picture of Vancouver Canucks history, but John McCaw and his Orca Bay sports ownership group aren't too fondly regarded in Canucks lore. McCaw's ownership tenure is often unfairly remembered for the negatives, for the fact that his proxies "pushed out" Pat Quinn and Brian Burke. For whatever reason, the Orca Bay years tend to be associated with Mark Messier and Mike Keenan and the Todd Bertuzzi punch, rather than with the dawn of the West Coast Express or for the financial heft and stability McCaw and his partners brought to the franchise. It should be harder to ignore the fact that McCaw sold a better-positioned club to the Aquilini family than the one he acquired piecemeal from the Griffiths family, but for whatever reason, that tends to go unmentioned.

During the 1980s, the Canucks had a nauseating habit of finishing second in the running for free agents. They just couldn't keep up with the haves of the league and made a point of subtly publicizing it.

Whatever you think of McCaw's stewardship of the franchise, during the Orca Bay years, the Canucks were real players. This was a team that suddenly carried a well-above-average payroll every year (despite losing money, especially in those early seasons). They could afford to land the big-name coach or the top free agent. The Canucks found themselves regularly bidding against the New York Rangers for top talent.

On the heels of the Wayne Gretzky debacle and following the departure of perpetually underrated pivot Cliff Ronning, the Canucks' overall weakness down the middle of their forward group was exposed during the 1996–97 season. Though the club was relatively loaded on the wings with Alex Mogilny, Marty Gelinas, Trevor Linden, Pavel Bure, Markus Naslund, and Geoff Courtnall, and scored goals at an above-average clip, the Canucks struggled to control play and finished four points out of a playoff spot. It didn't help matters that their goaltending tandem of Kirk McLean and Corey Hirsch combined to post a well-below-average .892 save percentage.

So Canucks management and ownership went searching for a top centerman. The Canucks were connected to former Canuck Igor Larionov, an unrestricted free agent, that summer before he signed an extension in Detroit. And the club ultimately put on a full-court press in an effort to woo Mark Messier to western Canada.

It's believed that Quinn was skeptical about the notion of pursuing Messier, but he agreed to accompany John Chapple to the Messier compound in Hilton Head, South Carolina, to meet with Mark and his agent (and brother) Doug Messier. On July 21, 1997, the Messiers met with Quinn and Chapple at a local pub and discussed leisure sports and hockey and spoke philosophically. At a subsequent meeting, the two sides broached the topic of compensation. By the second meeting, "Already, in my view, we had crossed the threshold that this clearly made sense for Vancouver," John Chapple later told the *New York Times*.

Following the second meeting between Messier, Chapple, and Quinn, Quinn returned to Vancouver, but Chapple stayed on and convinced Messier's camp to join John McCaw and Vancouver's management and ownership groups on McCaw's sailboat in San Francisco. According to Dan Robson, Quinn was livid.

Quinn called McCaw, according to Robson, and asked, "Who's doing this deal? I want to know who's doing this contract!"

"That's what I want to know," McCaw apparently replied. "Who's doing this contract?"

"It better be me," Quinn is said to have responded.

It can be a bit tough to separate fact from myth in the latter stages of Quinn's Canucks tenure. Though Quinn went on to express skepticism about the Messier signing, he was absolutely involved in the negotiations in both Hilton Head and San Francisco, and seemed to take credit for the genesis of the pursuit at Messier's introductory press conference. "I phoned John [McCaw] and explained to him what I wanted to do in going after Messier, why I thought it was a good idea and how much it was likely to cost," Quinn said the day after Messier signed. "He listened and said, 'Let's try for it.'"

Quinn also was actively counseling the Canucks' moneymen on their chances at a favorable outcome. When Messier made stops to meet with the Detroit Red Wings and the Washington Capitals prior to heading west to San Francisco, Quinn suggested he still liked Vancouver's odds, according to Chapple. "Pat said Mark wouldn't get on a plane unless [he was] giving this real serious consideration," Chapple recalled.

Ultimately Messier's camp—including his father, brothers, and an accountant—joined McCaw, Chapple, and Stan McCammon on McCaw's sailboat in San Francisco. Later that afternoon, after a sail around the San Francisco harbor in which it was observed that a container ship named *Vancouver* was providentially moored nearby, the two sides came to an understanding. Messier would give the Rangers one more chance to come close to matching Vancouver's deal but resolved to leave Manhattan for Canada's west coast if New York's final offer came in low (which it did, at a relatively paltry one year at $4.6 million).

The deal with Vancouver, once agreed to, called for Messier to earn an NHL-record $20 million over the span of a three-year pact that included two team option years that could have pushed the deal's value into the $30 million range and a variety of bonuses, both performance-based and tied to a potential sale of the team, the latter of which Messier would contest in court (and ultimately win) nearly 15 years later.

Messier's agreement with Vancouver sent shock waves of excitement through the market and across the industry. In Canadian media circles the deal was hailed as a sign that smaller-market teams based in Canada might survive and even remain relevant, despite the recent relocation of the Quebec Nordiques and Winnipeg Jets.

The rest of the hockey world, meanwhile, recoiled in sticker shock. Ken Holland suggested "Vancouver blew everyone else out of the water" in the Messier negotiations, and then–Rangers general manager Neil Smith described the contract as "mind-boggling." In fact, the Capitals are believed to have offered slightly more than Vancouver, but Messier didn't have much interest in playing in the same division as the New York Rangers.

Even Quinn seemed to hedge when asked if Messier was going to be overpaid in Vancouver. "That's a difficult question to answer," Quinn answered. "But we believe he's the player we needed."

"I think everybody thought it was a boatload of money," McCammon recalled of the sticker shock factor, "but if Pat didn't want to sign it, it wouldn't have gotten done."

With Messier in the fold, expectations for the Canucks were sky-high. Burke joked to Quinn that the Vancouver media were already planning the parade route. In the lead-up to the 1997–98 season, Messier essentially became his own cottage industry. Messier was 36 years old and was expected to single-handedly lead an undermanned Canucks team to glory. The Canucks may have landed their $20 million man, and the Moose may have cashed in, but both parties had also set themselves up to fail.

69 Know Why Messier Is So Widely Detested by Canucks Fans

Mark Messier is revered throughout the hockey world for his two-way prowess, his overall public amiability, his unmatched leadership skills, and his legacy as a winner and a champion. He's the third-highest-scoring player in NHL history and one of the most recognizable faces in the sport.

Talk to a hardcore Vancouver Canucks fan, though, and they'll discuss Messier's tenure in Vancouver in the sort of dark, hushed tones you'd expect a citizen of the wizarding world to employ when discussing Lord Voldemort.

The widespread dislike of Messier in the Vancouver market has proven durable. Two decades later, Messier still ranks alongside Brad Marchand, Mike Keenan, and Duncan Keith on the Mount Rushmore of all-time Canucks villains.

When Messier became a pitchman for Rogers GameCentre LIVE at the start of the 2014 season, for example, commercials depicted the all-time great walking through the homes of hockey fans as they engaged in a wholesome manner with NHL content on a variety of platforms—smartphones, televisions, laptops, and tablets—with their families. In response to one image of Messier walking through the living room of an affluent-seeming Canucks jersey–clad nuclear family, @CanucksArmy tweeted, "'Because they're Canucks fans, I'm not actually welcome in their home!'—a more realistic Mark Messier Game Center Live commercial." The joke was retweeted or favorited more than 150 times.

Messier's detested status in Vancouver is a fact the rest of the hockey world—who can never seem to quite wrap their fingers around the many peculiarities of the Vancouver market—seems to find enormously confusing. In fact, it's not all that surprising, even if Messier's Vancouver legacy is often regarded unfairly.

In hockey there are few problems winning can't cure, and at the end of the day, that's the most fundamental reason for the dislike Canucks fans have for Messier. His tenure is associated with the low point of the franchise's contemporary history, his three seasons in Vancouver representing the black hole that existed between the Quinn era and the West Coast Express era.

Vancouver failed to make the postseason in all three of Messier's Canucks seasons, and the club began to improve almost immediately upon his return to New York. That legacy of losing isn't entirely Messier's fault—by 1997 the club was far past its "best before" date and in desperate need of a rebuild—but it's at the rudiment of the municipal dislike for Messier in Vancouver.

It should also be noted that the city was perhaps predisposed to disliking Messier. He is, after all, the man who captained the Rangers to a victory over the Canucks in the 1994 Stanley Cup Finals and played a major role in toying with overmatched Canucks teams throughout the 1980s during his time with the buzz saw Edmonton Oilers. Perhaps winning could have cured that, but there should be no doubt that a preexisting basis for enmity was exposed when Messier's Canucks teams proved to be feckless.

For a variety of reasons—some fair, some unfair—the extent of the animosity Vancouver harbors toward Messier goes well beyond wins and losses, though. Vancouver is a different sort of hockey market, with its own subtleties, and Messier proved to be tone-deaf in his handling of public perception. A variety of early decisions Messier and the club made served to inflame the skepticism of Canucks fans.

On the day Messier was introduced as a Canuck, for example, he was introduced to the public wearing the No. 11 he'd worn throughout his storied NHL career. To an outsider, that was of little significance. Of course Messier would wear No. 11, right?

To hardcore Canucks fans, however, it was a sign that Messier saw himself as being above the team and the team's history, a subtle indication he was an outsider. At the time of Messier's introduction, no Canucks player had worn No. 11 in 23 years, since original Canucks forward Wayne Maki died in May 1974. Chris Oddleifson wore No. 11 for 21 games in the 1973–74 season, but after Maki passed away, he wore No. 14 for the rest of his Canucks career.

No. 11 doesn't hang from the rafters, but in practice the number was retired. That the Maki family—who would later refer derisively to Messier in the press as Mr. Wonderful—was never contacted about Messier's use of the number beforehand, and was treated rather brusquely by Pat Quinn when the club finally got around to making the telephone call, only compounded the insult.

Messier ran afoul of the sensibilities of Vancouver hockey fans again immediately prior to his Canucks debut in Japan in the fall of 1997. Before that game, Trevor Linden decided in a tearful address to his teammates to hand over the captain *C* to Messier. The decision to make Messier captain was ultimately Linden's, and if there was any internal pressure on him, it was self-generated. "I could read the tea leaves," Linden recalled of wrestling with the idea of giving up his captaincy. "I could play this out a little bit, and quite honestly I could see that it was a reality: something was going to have to [give]. I talked to Pat about it, and the reality was that there was a sense that Mark did feel like for him to come in and do what he wanted to do, that he needed to be captain. I downplayed it at the time and probably still would downplay it."

Still, Messier should never have accepted the *C* from the most popular Canucks skater in the franchise's history. It's a fact he's

Messier's eye-popping deal was the biggest headline he grabbed during his time in Vancouver.

come to admit openly. "If I changed one thing," Messier told a Reddit poster during an Ask Me Anything session in 2014, "I would not have accepted the captaincy from Trevor."

"I thought it was interesting," Linden said of reading that quote nearly two decades on. "We all do things that we look back and say, 'I probably would've done something different.' We've all been there. There's a healthy respect between Mark and I today. He came here and had an expectation to fill and felt a certain way about how he needed to do that."

The Canucks struggled enormously in Messier's first season in Vancouver, and massive changes shook the franchise. Quinn and Tom Renney were both fired in the fall of 1997. Steve Tambellini and Mike Penny replaced Quinn as GM on an interim basis, while Mike Keenan replaced Renney.

The vacuum created by Quinn's dismissal and the club's decision to hire Keenan, Messier's former coach, created a common perception that Messier was more than just a "player" but had in fact become part of management. It was a perception many of Messier's veteran Canucks teammates shared. "It was a common theme from the guys," Linden recalled, that "Mark was part of management, not just a player."

Penny, who spent much of the 1997–98 season as a co–interim general manager, similarly felt Messier held a good deal of sway with ownership. "I knew we were in trouble the day Messier was in the offensive zone taking a faceoff and Renney sends Mike Sillinger out to take the draw and Messier wouldn't come off the ice, so Sillinger comes back to the bench," Penny recalls. "And I thought, *Tom, you're done. This ain't going to work.* Not long after that Messier, of course, is on the phone to McCaw and out the door goes Tom Renney and in comes Keenan."

And of course Quinn didn't mince words. "Messier was consulted by ownership on personnel decisions," he told the *Globe and Mail* in 1998. "When that happens, it's deadly."

The idea of Messier as a sort of player–general manager exploded into a high-profile tit for tat between Messier and some of his ex-teammates as the season went along. "He didn't break a sweat for the first 10 games and just waited for Tom Renney and Pat Quinn to be fired," Gino Odjick told Tony Gallagher after he was traded to the New York Islanders. "They signed him to help us, but all he wanted was most of us out of there so he could bring in his own people. He talk[ed] to ownership all the time, and he [was] responsible for Keenan being [t]here, and he [was] part of most of the trades. Messier just want[ed] to destroy everything so he [got] the power. Everyone [was] brought in to play for Mark."

When Messier fired back at Odjick, he did so by taking an implied swipe at Linden, who had similarly been dealt to the Islanders in a separate deal. "I think this is a lot more than Gino Odjick coming forward," Messier said. "I think there's a lot of people who don't have the courage or guts to say it to my face, and they used Gino as a vehicle to do it. It shows you the kind of people who were here and why we needed changes."

Implying Odjick—an enormously popular Canuck, a free-thinker, and his own man—was being used as a pawn didn't go over well with Canucks fans. Nor did Messier's implication that Linden lacked "courage" and "guts."

By the time the Canucks hired Brian Burke as general manager in 1998, the savvy executive—a public relations heavyweight if ever there was one—clearly knew he had to push back on the idea that Messier was calling the shots. He publicly suggested Messier should "just play" and focus on his on-ice performance.

Meanwhile rumors surfaced in the summer of 1998 that Messier regretted his decision to sign in Vancouver. Messier went to great lengths to deny that was the case but was left carrying the fallout with Odjick and Linden well into the off-season. "Looking back at Gino's remarks, I'm not really upset," Messier told Elliott Pap in the summer of 1998. "It was a tough year for a lot of people.

There were a lot of players who were in Vancouver for a long time and had great careers here and then things changed.... Change isn't easy, but it's inevitable. It had to be done here in Vancouver."

Rumors of Messier's unhappiness persisted throughout his three seasons in Vancouver, and surfaced again in a most public fashion when it was widely reported at the 2000 NHL All-Star Game that Messier was openly talking to fellow players about being dealt to a contender at the deadline (an episode similar to Ryan Kesler's situation at the 2014 Winter Olympic Games in Sochi). Burke and Messier met to clear the air, with Burke declaring thereafter that he'd never ask Mark if he'd accept a trade, because he earned his no-trade protection.

Messier wasn't traded that season, though the Canucks mercifully declined to pick up the option on the fourth year of his contract. In fairness to Messier, he probably played his best hockey in the closing months of the 1999–2000 season as Vancouver made an exciting push to the postseason that fell just short.

The myriad PR blunders stand out in the minds of Canucks fans and have eclipsed the extent to which Messier was still a pretty useful piece. He logged major minutes and didn't play nearly as badly as many remember.

Yes, Messier's two-way assertiveness and goal-scoring abilities were in decline, but he remained a sturdy defensive player, an ace faceoff man, and an excellent playmaker. And though Messier alienated the Quinn-era core that was in place when he first joined the team, there seems to be a bit of a generational split between the likes of Linden and Odjick and the younger players whom we associate with the West Coast Express era. Most of those players will tell you Messier's leadership was genuinely helpful as they learned the ropes at the NHL level. "I know he wasn't loved there," said ex-Canucks defenseman Jason Strudwick, "but he had a big impact on [Markus] Naslund, [Todd] Bertuzzi, myself, [Ed] Jovanovski."

Naslund, who really established himself as an NHL star while playing on Messier's wing during the season Bure held out, echoed Strudwick's assessment. "Messier took a hit for everything that went wrong during his time in Vancouver," Naslund said. "It was a transition period and there were a lot of other factors, but Mark was really well-liked by my generation of players and the guys that ended up being the core of the next five or ten years. He showed us a lot that was valuable. And looking back at his age when I got there, he played at a high level, and really showed a lot of professionalism during his time in Vancouver."

In the final analysis, Messier came to a franchise that needed to rebuild and was anointed the savior. It was an impossible situation that was exacerbated when Messier picked fights with beloved franchise icons and fumbled the public perception game on a variety of fronts.

That Messier came to be personally associated with some of the painful decisions and the losing that characterized his three years in Vancouver is probably unfair to some extent. Unfair or not, though, that Canucks fans consider him an archvillain in franchise history really shouldn't be so surprising to the rest of the hockey world.

70 Why 1997–98 Was Linden's Toughest Season

Usually cast as the golden boy throughout his Canucks tenure, Trevor Linden filled the role of Job during the 1997–98 season. Beset by myriad injuries, belittled in public and private by his new head coach, and traded to Long Island, it was the season from hell for one of the classiest players in Vancouver Canucks history.

The story of the most challenging year of Linden's professional career likely began on the day Mark Messier signed with the Canucks. Driving back from Whistler with his wife, Christina, Linden heard the news on the radio. Like most Canucks faithful, his initial reaction was excitement. "I was pumped," Linden recalled. "I though, *That's great. This is the guy we need. We have Pavel, we have Alex, we're bringing in a leadership structure. It's great.* Pumped. Immediately it pops into my mind, *Okay, now what?* Because I'm the captain, so what does this mean? That's the second thing I thought."

Linden spoke to Quinn and wrestled with the notion of whether or not to give up the captain *C* for the rest of the summer. He wasn't necessarily pressured to give it up by anyone within the organization, but he ultimately figured that if he decided to hold on to the *C*, the issue might linger.

"I knew that if this was a situation that would continue to bubble, and if there was any part of Mark that felt he should be the captain, then let's deal with it now, or else it was going to continue to be an issue," Linden recalled. "And I didn't want that going into the season. I didn't want that for the guys, the team, or myself."

The longtime Canucks captain informed his teammates of the decision in a speech prior to the team's season-opening game in Japan. It was a tearful speech, and Linden—a poised and polished speaker—didn't get through it. "I wanted to downplay it, but I think…no, I remember…being pretty emotional with that whole situation," Linden said.

The Canucks' top-heavy roster got off to a woeful start to the season, winning just three of their first 15 games. It was at this point in the season that Pat Quinn, a father figure to Linden, was relieved of his duties as general manager. "When Pat got let go in Washington, that was a dark day," Linden recalled. "Pat was a big figure in my life." It was still November, but Linden had already lost his mentor and friend, and his captaincy, and the darkest days were still ahead.

When Vancouver hired Mike Keenan, most expected the Russian-born superstars—Alexander Mogilny and Pavel Bure—to be the focus of his ire. Instead Keenan, a man Brett Hull once described as "the sort of guy who will stab you in the back right to your face," focused his abuse on Martin Gelinas and Linden. "If everything pointed left, he would point right," Linden said of Keenan. "And this was a common theme for me and him. Because I was well-liked, he was going to flip things on [their] ear. I was an easy target."

Less than a week into Keenan's tenure, Linden pulled his groin during a particularly tough practice. Keenan reacted by suggesting to the media that the former Canucks captain—a legendary fitness nut—wasn't in game shape. "The two things [my fitness level and the groin pull] had nothing to do with each other," Linden said later. "[My] VO_2 max, which was important to him and to hockey, was in the top 2 or 3 percent in the league!"

The groin injury cost Linden eight games before he made a fateful return on December 8 in a game against Keenan's former club, the St. Louis Blues. Linden wasn't right yet and struggled in the first 40 minutes, as Keenan shuffled his lines. "I come back from this groin tear, which was significant, I come back early to play," Linden recalled of the game that evening. "And there were things at play there—St. Louis, his former team—and we were down three and I was just back for my first game, trying to get my legs under me. And he attacked me."

Gary Mason, writing at the time for the *Vancouver Sun*, got the full story of what went down during the second intermission. Linden was congratulating Vancouver's makeshift fourth line (which included defenseman Steve Staios playing out of position), when Keenan snapped. "Sit down, you fucking idiot!" Keenan yelled. "Shut the fuck up! Just shut the fuck up! Who are you, anyway? What have you ever done?"

Going from Quinn's good graces to Keenan's house of horrors gave Linden a serious sense of whiplash. If he didn't already suspect it, this incident convinced him it wasn't going to work out with him and Keenan, and his agent began to get involved. "It was the most chaotic…when I think back to it, it was just the most crazy, chaotic time," Linden recalled. "We had no system, no plan, no plan to get the puck. It was just work hard, work out intensely…. We were a disaster. It was chaos in the room. There was no stability whatsoever. It was crazy."

An untenable situation continued on fitfully for a couple months, with Linden being benched regularly and Keenan continuing to call his effort into question. It got to the point where some of Linden's teammates began to defend their former captain in the press, including Gino Odjick and Jyrki Lumme.

Meanwhile the Canucks continued to lose games, and the behind-the-scenes discord escalated further. Mason wrote of an incident in-game when Donald Brashear challenged Keenan to a fight on the bench, and Odjick and Keenan had a tense exchange after Odjick was described by the head coach as "one of Pat Quinn's boys" (a compliment in any other era of Canucks history).

A steady stream of leaks describing emotional behind-the-scenes incidents between veteran players and the coach served to undermine the struggling club further. Core players—and Linden loyalists—such as Gelinas and Kirk McLean were shipped out in trades. Mark Messier did his best, using bland hockey-style quotes Tony Gallagher came to term *captainspeak* in an intentional allusion to George Orwell, to defend Keenan in the media. "Unless we're willing to change the behavior that's been here a long time, things aren't going to change in the standings," Messier said.

In reference to Keenan's tirade at Linden in St. Louis, Messier again had the head coach's back, saying, "Sure, it's tough, but you have to be able to accept criticism and accept the truth."

There's a pretty distinct line between criticism and cruelty, and in the case of Keenan's treatment of Linden, it's pretty clear the coach crossed it repeatedly. Linden was named to the 1998 Olympic team in December, but his participation was in doubt when he sustained a knee injury in Phoenix in late January. "I was just devastated in Phoenix. I'd hurt my knee again, I thought I was going to miss the Olympics," Linden recalled. "And [Grant Ledyard], who was a whipping boy as well…came in to talk to me, as guys often do when their teammate is injured."

With the playoffs firmly out of reach, Keenan—who by now, most agree, was in control of player personnel decisions—began to dismantle the team in earnest. With a flurry of moves in early February, Keenan shipped out Mike Sillinger, Geoff Sanderson, and some mid-round draft picks in exchange for Brad May, Peter Zezel, and some mid-round picks. Those moves didn't really move the needle, but the Linden trade—a ballsy move, and one of the best trades in franchise history—returned Todd Bertuzzi, Bryan McCabe, and a third-round pick.

"It was terrible," Linden recalled later. "I remember being traded and how empty that felt. I knew it had to happen, but I was devastated." He continued, "It was weird because I got traded and I was going to the Olympics, so I needed to skate, but I had no team. I remember Darren Granger and Patty O'Neal being so good to me and really supporting me, giving me a 'Skate here; we'll take care of you' kind of thing. I went to the Olympics, which was strange. And then walking in after the flight to New York and walking into the Long Island Marriott for the first time and thinking, *Wow, this is real.*"

Linden's storied Canucks tenure, which started out with so much hope and burned so brightly for a time, came to an end in the most painful and acrimonious manner imaginable.

"What happened there that year hurt," Linden said. And then it was over, or at least for a while.

71 Trading Blows: How Gino Odjick Got to Know Jason Strudwick

Trevor Linden had about a month to get acclimated to his new surroundings in Long Island before he was scheduled to return to Vancouver for a game between the New York Islanders and the Vancouver Canucks, in late March 1998. "I remember having a conversation with Trevor before we got to Vancouver," recalled Linden's then–Islanders teammate Jason Strudwick. "As the days counted down before that return to Vancouver, I don't want to say it rattled him, but I don't think he was comfortable; he'd played there for so long and got traded away. You could tell it was working up. I felt for him. I thought Trevor handled that day really well, but as a guy on the inside, I could tell that it was getting to him."

Strudwick grew up admiring Linden's tenacious game and was 23 years old at the time. A rookie defenseman, he'd only appeared in 18 NHL games in his career. He seemed an unlikely suspect to upstage Linden in the beloved Canucks forward's return to Vancouver, but life and hockey have a funny way of upending expectations.

The 1998 NHL trade deadline was set for March 25, and the Islanders arrived in Vancouver just two days before. There was a multitude of rumors surrounding both teams, as neither was playoff bound. On the morning of March 23, as Strudwick was sitting with his roommate, Claude Lapointe, in his hotel room, he received an ominous telephone call.

"I jumped up as the young guy and answered. 'It's Mike Milbury. Jason, thanks for everything; we've traded you to Vancouver.' And that was it. *Boom*," Strudwick recalled. "Claude look[ed] at me and [said], 'What happened?' and I [said], 'I think I just got traded.' Five minutes later Mike Keenan calls, and they get me to a press conference at GM Place, tell me to get downstairs in five minutes."

Strudwick strolled into the bowels of Rogers Arena just as an emotional Gino Odjick was finishing his outgoing availability with Vancouver media. Upset, angry, and fed up with his own club's management, Odjick didn't pull any punches during his conversation with the press. He explicitly said he was angry about the trade and didn't take it as a compliment that he was dealt for Strudwick, or as Gino called him, "someone I'd never heard of."

"I get to the scrum," Strudwick recalled, "and one of the first questions someone asks is, 'Jason, do you know Gino said he didn't mind getting traded, but he didn't want to get traded for a nobody?' Obviously on the inside I felt a lot differently than what I said, which was just the basic: 'Whatever, these things happen; I'm sorry he feels that way.' So I went home to my new hotel, and I'll be honest, it really bothered me. To be a hockey player, you have to a certain amount of arrogance and confidence, and I was fired up."

Strudwick laughed, "The problem was it was Gino Odjick. I wish it had a been a 5'10" guy, 160 pounds. Not a 6'4" monster and a guy who fought and played like an animal for years in the NHL. So the next morning I go into practice, and Mike Keenan says, 'You're playing,' and I made up my mind right then and there: 'I'm going to fight Gino.'"

"Some people [think Odjick is] not a great hockey player, but he's one of the toughest guys in the NHL, and he got 15 goals when he played with me," said Pavel Bure of the decision to trade his best friend and roommate. "He's part of Canucks history."

Though Trevor Linden's return was still big news, Odjick was a similarly beloved Canucks icon. His off-the-cuff comments about Strudwick, and Bure's emotional reaction to the deal, came to dominate the pregame attention.

As the game approached, Strudwick knew he had to make an impression. He'd just been acquired at the price of one of the most popular Canucks of all time, and that same Canucks legend had publicly insulted him. The stakes were high.

"I challenged him right away, but he wanted to play and didn't want to go," Strudwick recalled. "I understand now, being an older guy, that he was going through a lot of emotion, and fighting some 23-year-old wasn't high on his priority list. Anyway, we got caught up on my first shift and I gave him a couple of whacks, and gave him a tap. He knew. We know the tap. If you've ever been in a hockey fight before, you know. Nothing needs to be said. It's a look and the body language. He wasn't scared, that's for sure, but he had other things going on. Part of me was happy about that, honestly, but part of me wanted to go."

Midway through the period, Strudwick had another opportunity. He took it, and this time Odjick indulged him. Gino was one of the most accomplished fighters in the game, and to begin the fight he hugged Strudwick close and kept his right arm locked in a vise grip between his left arm and his body. Strudwick struggled to escape so that he could throw a punch, but Gino was too strong. "I was thinking, *God, why is this guy holding my hand? Why isn't he throwing punches?* So I'm trying to get my hand free, and just before I realize it, he releases my hand and just starts teeing off on me," Strudwick said. "I'm like, *Oh, that's why. He was letting me get tired so he could beat me up.*"

Odjick got in three good punches to the side of Strudwick's head, and the rookie defenseman fell as the linesmen intervened. But Strudwick gamely stood right back up and the two continued to throw punches with on-ice officials in the middle. "He didn't really thrash me, but he definitely got the decision," Strudwick recalled. "And…after, we both kind of go to the penalty box and just played our games the rest of the way. A few months later we met up, and he said, 'I want to apologize for what I said,' and I said, 'No problem, Gino.' So it was nothing malicious."

The footage reveals nothing extra was said in the penalty box. The Canucks faithful at GM Place treated Gino, their old favorite, to an appropriately rousing good-bye, but the rookie defenseman, the guy nobody had heard of, succeeded in making the impression he was looking for.

"I do remember after I came back from the penalty box, Mike Keenan came down and tapped me on the shoulder," Strudwick recalled. "Then Brad May comes down and says, 'I didn't know you could fight that well! Good to have you on the team!'"

The Canucks managed a rare win over the Islanders, clad in their unsightly fish-sticks sweater, that night. Asked about the fight afterward, Strudwick continued to introduce himself to Vancouver's hockey-watching public with a quality one-liner. "He didn't know who I was," Strudwick told the Vancouver press corps, "so I thought I would introduce myself."

72 Eat Like John Garrett (If You Dare!)

Since the 2008–09 season, John Garrett and John Shorthouse have served as the voices of Vancouver Canucks regional broadcasts on Sportsnet Pacific. Affectionately known as "the Johns" among Canucks fans, Shorthouse and Garrett have a particular type of odd-couple chemistry and lean on a variety of regular bits during the broadcast.

Perhaps their most famous bit comes attached to a variety of promotional spots for the Safeway grocery chain. Safeway sponsors a variety of giveaways, and certain products are specifically name-checked by the Johns during local broadcasts.

"The local broadcasts have all those Safeway promos or food promos or pizza promos, and when I was doing both—the national broadcast and the local stuff—you would look forward to the national games because you'd have 10 more replays per game, instead of the local promos," Garrett explained.

Rather than allowing the regional broadcast to get bogged down by product placement, the Johns have turned it into a regular highlight. The bit is simple. Shorthouse plays the straight man, while Garrett goes off on a salivating Scooby Doo routine discussing his love of ketchup on macaroni and cheese ("Even without ketchup, it's good stuff," he adds), his Omar Little–esque obsession with Honey Nut Cheerios, the quasi-religious virtues of Cheez Whiz, or the joy he gets when eating a cheeseburger that's topped just right.

"I like Shreddies," Garrett will announce in uncommonly pedestrian fashion, following a Safeway promotional spot announcing a sale on the popular cereal. "You can add sugar."

For a time, Shorthouse's bio on Sportsnet's website even listed "introducing John Garrett to Five Guys Burger and Fries" among his career highlights, which is a bit rich. Yes, occasionally the bit verges into self-parody. It's mostly charming, though.

What's perhaps most remarkable about Shorthouse and Garrett's routine is that it's completely genuine. Garrett's love for fast food runs deep, as a glance at Sportsnet Pacific's host Dan Murphy's Twitter feed will reveal in convincing fashion.

"I grew up in a family with seven other kids," Garrett explained. "Ketchup wasn't a condiment; it was part of the main diet. Our diet wasn't great to start with as kids, and it just continued on."

Garrett continued, "I remember when I first started playing. We got six dollars for food, and we'd go to the Woolworth's lunch counter and get the daily special. It was heavy stuff, but it was delicious, and then we'd save the rest of our per-diem money so we could have beer after the game."

So how does such a dedicated lover of corn syrup and butter-fried anything stay relatively svelte? "I don't eat a whole lot on the road," Garrett explained, "which is why I'm not 300 pounds."

It's true that the life of the traveling hockey journalist or broadcaster lends itself well to soft bodies and clogged arteries. There's a lot of travel and a lot of late nights. There are a lot of sources to cultivate, with alcohol and red meat as lubricants.

Even among battle-hardened hockey pundits, however, Garrett's love of fast food is legendary. There's a particular tale in media circles about how Garrett covered an entire playoff run without ever eating a meal that required him to touch a utensil. We always believed that tale to be urban legend, but when we asked Garrett about it point blank, he didn't hesitate to confirm it.

"Chris Cuthbert, myself, and Scott Russell got going in the playoffs, and my diet isn't great anyway, but we ended up on a 42-day playoff run," Garrett recalled. "There were all these seven-game series, and I never got a chance to get home. And I told them, as a lark—because they'd order me salads and stuff, and I'd never eaten a salad—and so I told them I would order food where I never would touch utensils the entire playoff run. Sure enough, I did it," Garrett recalled with pride. "And it just kept on going. Day after day: pizza and hamburgers and junk food for 42 days."

73 On Burke's Return, and the Start of a Rebuild

The 1997–98 season was an unmitigated disaster for the Vancouver Canucks franchise. Repeated off-ice turmoil had seriously damaged the credibility of the organization, and the club struggled enormously. Despite signing the biggest-name free agent on the market the previous summer, Vancouver finished with the fourth-worst record in the league.

In June 1998 the organization made a key decision that would begin to restore sanity, hope, and profitability. The decision was made to hire former Pat Quinn lieutenant and NHL chief disciplinarian Brian Burke as general manager and president.

Burke broke into hockey management with the Canucks in the late 1980s, but had mostly worked for the league since. He dubbed Vancouver's hockey operations "the asylum" and began to work toward restoring the club's reputation in the market and around the hockey world. "I hope my first impact is to stop the waves this organization has been through, battered by storm after storm," Burke said in his introductory press conference. Burke had no way of knowing that some of the biggest storms, in fact, lay ahead.

The task Burke faced was gargantuan. He inherited a coach, Mike Keenan, who was already loathed in the market and strongly believed that he should have input into player personnel decisions. Burke said the right things in public, but it's now widely believed that Orca Bay insisted on retaining Keenan. "I'm thrilled of have Mike Keenan as my coach," Burke said tactfully. "It's not something that I am saddled with. It's something I have been blessed with."

No one was really convinced. The *Vancouver Sun*, citing unidentified sources, later reported that in Burke's initial meeting with Keenan, Keenan defiantly asked the incoming general manager, "Have you seen my contract? It says I get to approve all trades."

"Yes, I have, Mike," Burke is reported to have responded in classic fashion. "Have you seen mine? It says I get to hire and fire the coach."

Keenan had already begun the work of scorching the earth and rebuilding the club, jettisoning veteran players such as Martin Gelinas, Kirk McLean, Trevor Linden, Gino Odjick, Mike Sillinger, Grant Ledyard, and Dave Babych. The fact of the matter is that with the exception of the Linden deal, those deals returned very little of relevant value.

The Gelinas-McLean deal with Carolina was particularly disastrous. Though Keenan fared well in the initial deal, which netted Vancouver Sean Burke and Geoff Sanderson, two players who would continue to be productive for the next five to six seasons, he'd subsequently trade both players for lesser pieces such as Garth Snow and Brad May.

Brian Burke had a decent foundation to work with, particularly along the blueline, where 21-year-old Mattias Ohlund was coming off a solid rookie campaign, 22-year-old Bryan McCabe had proven himself a player with star potential, and 24-year-old Adrian Aucoin had acquitted himself well over the latter half of a losing season. Despite some signs of life from a 24-year-old Markus Naslund and a 22-year-old Todd Bertuzzi, though, Vancouver's forwards were aging rapidly, and Vancouver's goaltending situation was tumultuous as the club used five different goaltenders during the 1997–98 campaign.

There was a lot of work to do, which was made even more difficult by Pavel Bure's decision that he would never suit up for the Canucks organization again. When Burke accepted the job, he made no secret of his desire to keep Bure—coming off another 50-goal season—in the fold. "Our reluctance to trade this player should be obvious to everybody," Burke told the press. "We go to sleep at night dreaming of getting players like Pavel Bure."

Burke's effort was frustrated by Bure's staunch refusal to report to the Canucks next season, which he communicated to Vancouver's incoming general manager early in July 1998.

Reeling, Burke asked for more time, but Bure was done playing ball. He'd been requesting trades out of Vancouver on an almost annual basis for nearly five years, but the club always dragged its feet. (The club nearly dealt him to the Islanders at the 1998 trade deadline but couldn't work out the details.) There would be no more patience from Bure's camp.

In August Bure made his trade request a matter of public record. If Burke was hoping to steer the Canucks to calmer waters, he'd have to weather a few additional storms yet.

74 Accept That We'll Never Know Exactly Why Bure Held Out

Pavel Bure's face was splashed across the front pages of newspapers across British Columbia in August 1998. The greatest, most entertaining player in franchise history wanted out. "I'm not going to play for the Canucks for personal reasons," Bure said vaguely. "The reasons are my own, and I don't really want to discuss them. I love the fans here, and I love the city. I want to thank them for the seven years they supported me, but I really feel it's time to move."

Bure's public trade request and his refusal to report to the team put new Canucks GM Brian Burke in the mother of all binds. As newspapers on the East Coast insisted the Maple Leafs would be able to pry Bure out of Vancouver in exchange for the bargain price of similarly disgruntled goaltender Felix Potvin, Burke was left with few options aside from public declarations of obstinance. "I'm not operating with any artificial timetable, and I'm not making any promises," Burke said defiantly. "If a trade is not made, he'd better have a good TV set."

During the 1997–98 season, Bure had hit a variety of key performance-based benchmarks that triggered a clause in his deal stipulating he had to be paid as well as the fifth-highest-paid player in the sport. Player salaries had inflated appreciably in the years since Bure first signed that contract during the 1994 Stanley Cup playoffs, and the Russian Rocket was now due more than $8 million for the 1998–99 campaign. For personal reasons he wasn't eager to discuss, however, Bure wanted out badly enough that he was willing to leave $8 million on the table.

Considering the salary level involved, Bure's decision to hold out during the summer of 1998 was and remains entirely without precedent. In recent years we've seen players such as Kyle Turris refuse to come to terms on a second contract as a restricted free agent, and we've seen players such as Alexander Radulov head to the Kontinental Hockey League rather than fulfill their entry-level deal. In neither case was a player walking away from a top-five NHL salary.

In theorizing why exactly Bure wanted to hold out, many have pointed to the usual things. It's said Bure didn't like playing in a fishbowl market such as Vancouver, that he wanted more privacy, and that he detested the travel burden associated with playing on Canada's west coast. Arthur Griffiths, who is still close with Bure, suggested a big part of it was Bure felt an urgency to win and didn't see the Canucks as having the requisite pieces to contend in a credible way.

Griffiths said, "Ultimately he was just done, I think, with feeling like there were no extra pieces for the team to go forward. In a way, I'm sure that was part of it, but I think there was the other part, which was his privacy. When you're expected to do certain things on the ice and then more things off the ice. So there was no rest, no downtime."

It's difficult to imagine walking away from $8 million over privacy issues, travel complaints, and skepticism about the quality of the team. Just considering the $8 million in foregone salary, those theories really don't strike one as credible. It seems likely, rather, that the root of Bure's discontent was something more personal, even something ancient, which is what Bure seemed to allude to in an interview that his agent, Mike Gillis, arranged with writers Al Strachan and Tony Gallagher following his trade to the Florida Panthers.

"I was down there for two weeks before anyone showed up," Bure recounted of how he felt the Canucks had been indifferent to him upon his arrival in North America in 1991. "It was really hard. I thought they'd be waiting for me when I got there, but there was nobody."

Bure waxed on apoplectically about how the team never believed he was more than a flash in the pan, always suggesting in contract negotiations that he'd been lucky to put up the gaudy goal-scoring totals he managed early on in his career. He was also still sore about the leaked story regarding his supposed threat to hold out during the 1994 playoffs. "Somebody from management planted that story," Bure insisted to Gallagher and Strachan. "But the story was out all over, and by the time it was denied by [Pat] Quinn and everybody else, it was too late. It looked like a cover-up."

The "by the time" element of Bure's quote is perhaps what's most interesting. Though Quinn eventually went to the mattresses for Bure on live television on precisely this subject, Quinn's initial round of denials were relatively tepid.

Bure also said he felt like Quinn didn't want to give him the contract back in 1994, which we now know with some confidence is in fact true. That deal was very probably at the behest of ownership, a transaction driven as much by a need to secure financing on the construction of GM Place as it was by any on-ice rationale.

We'll probably never know exactly why Bure ultimately held out. The notion that it must have been something sudden or dramatic or secret is appealing, just based on how dramatic it is to willingly walk away from $8 million in salary.

A dramatic reason isn't always required, though. Sometimes a relationship—even a personal services relationship such as that between a professional sports team and a professional athlete—can be frayed for much simpler reasons. If it was instead a collection of incidents in which the proud, talented Bure detected a trend of disrespect from his employer, surely that is sufficiently compelling.

75 Why the Bure Deal Wasn't as Bad as It Looked

In the summer of 2016, Brian Burke recorded a video tribute that was played at a gala in honor of longtime Ottawa Senators general manager and former Florida Panthers executive Bryan Murray. "We made the trade for Pavel Bure," Burke told Murray. "You kind of fucked me on that one."

Always a colorful quote, Burke was being generous to his longtime rival executive. The Panthers got the best player in the Bure deal—of that there can be no doubt—but considering the circumstances, Burke made out as well as could be expected.

The Bure saga unfolded in slow motion, against the backdrop of one of the most depressing losing seasons in Canucks history. With Bure out of the lineup and the team struggling, there was enormous pressure on Burke to pull the trigger quickly and end the lengthy stalemate. That pressure came from without and from within, as Mike Keenan lobbed the occasional bomb at his general manager, publicly bemoaning his club's lack of offensive push and pointedly noting the Canucks "franchise [couldn't] afford to miss the playoffs for a third straight year."

"We have nothing beyond the first line until we make a Pavel Bure move," Mike Keenan said after a late October loss in Nashville. "We have no depth."

Burke held firm, though, mostly refusing to comment publicly. "It's not like I'm going to stand by and watch Rome burn," said Burke, a noted history buff, invoking Nero. "But it's not a time for anyone to panic. Panic should not be in the lexicon of the general manager."

As Bure, who was suspended without pay after leaving training camp in September, trained with the Central Army team and newspaper columnists lobbed bombs at Burke for badly botching the situation, the first-year Canucks general manager gamely refused to accept one of the anvils being offered.

The rumor mill churned into hyperdrive, and Bure was linked to the New York Rangers, the New York Islanders, the Florida Panthers, and the Washington Capitals. It was said that Burke wanted a young goaltender, a centerman, and above all else an offensive defenseman, and it was reported that he was particularly interested in Washington's Sergei Gonchar.

As the months dragged on, however, key pieces the Canucks had been linked to were shopped elsewhere. Now general manager in Washington, George McPhee denied his interest. The Canucks, who reportedly offered the Rangers Bure in exchange for goaltender Dan Cloutier, Alexei Kovalev, and Adam Graves—rumors Burke denied, suggesting he'd much prefer forward prospect Manny Malhotra—saw the Rangers ship Kovalev to the Pittsburgh Penguins in exchange for former Canucks holdout Petr Nedved.

Meanwhile, the losses continued to pile up and the pressure continued to build. "I'm not making a crappy deal because Mogilny got hurt," Burke told the press after the club's best winger sustained a significant injury. "I don't care if five more guys get hurt, and I don't care if we lose five games in a row." Those comments were seized upon by frequent Burke nemesis Al Strachan, who criticized Burke's flippancy at length in the *Toronto Sun*. "Burke...delivered a slap in the face to every one of his players on Monday when he said 'I don't care if we love five games in a row,'" wrote Strachan, who quoted an unnamed player in the piece who was critical of Burke's approach.

"To [the players], a flippant statement of that nature is a betrayal," Strachan continued later in the piece. "[It's a] statement that in order to prove a point, Burke will let the team lose."

Finally, after much bluster on both sides, a deal began to take shape. At the World Junior Championship tournament in Winnipeg that year, just as Burke was watching a pair of Swedish brothers underwhelm against Canada and the United States, Murray and Burke began to discuss the possibility of a Bure deal.

News of the Panthers' interest first broke in Toronto newspapers in early January, but Murray denied them. Informed by a local beat reporter that the Rangers and the Panthers were said to be front-runners in the Bure trade sweepstakes, Murray protested too much, answering, "Well, then I guess the Rangers will get him."

By mid January, however, reports began to surface in local Florida papers that indicated in a well-informed manner the sort of pieces that were being discussed. "[Pieces under consideration] would probably be a No. 2 center, which means Rob Niedermayer, a British Columbia native, or rookie Oleg Kvasha, who has more raw talent," David J. Neal wrote in the *Miami Herald* on January 14, 1999. "The Canucks also want a young defenseman, which would indicate Ed Jovanovski or Rhett Warrener. Also thrown into the deal could be center Dave Gagner."

Three days later, after trying once more to broker a more favorable deal with the Rangers, Burke and Murray agreed to the deal that would send the Russian Rocket to south Florida. The final deal sent Bure, defenseman Bret Hedican, junior defenseman Brad Ference, and a third-round pick to the Panthers in exchange for Ed Jovanovski, Dave Gagner, Kevin Weekes, Mike Brown, and a first-round draft pick.

Even before Burke could finish his memorable assessment of Gagner as "not just a throw-in," initial reviews excoriated the Vancouver general manager. "On paper it looks like Murray committed highway robbery," opined Michael Russo of the *Sun-Sentinel.*

"I didn't come here anticipating they'd plan a parade route for me," Burke told reporters during a press conference that, according to Kerry Banks, "had the smell of surrender."

"We're ecstatic," Burke continued. "We believe this is the best deal for our team for both right now and for the future."

Having lost out on Bure, Rangers general manager Neil Smith grumbled publicly about Burke not giving him a chance to match Murray's final offer. The Rangers' best offer included 24-year-old winger Niklas Sundstrom, a first-round pick, and Dan Cloutier, but Burke always preferred to get a defenseman in the deal, and at least wanted hotshot prospect and future Canuck Manny Malhotra in addition to those other three assets. If Smith had been willing to throw Malhotra into the deal earlier, Bure might have been a Ranger. Once Jovanovski was on the table, though, it's very likely Burke would have preferred Florida's package no matter what.

On paper it was a losing deal for Burke, but over the medium term, the trade paid significant dividends for the Canucks. Bure continued to dominate in Florida after the trade, but the Panthers never really contended during his time there. Within a couple years the Canucks were the better team.

Though Weekes, Brown, and Gagner were never significant contributors, and Vancouver used the first-round pick to select Nathan Smith—more famous for his streaking antics than his on-ice play—Jovanovski was a big part of Vancouver's success over the next decade. The puck-moving defenseman had a stellar Canucks tenure, jump-starting the up-tempo West Coast Express era teams from the back end and playing a physical, if occasionally marauding, style of defense. Perhaps the biggest short-term impact the acquisition of Jovanovski had, however, was in further bolstering Vancouver's blueline depth.

By adding Jovanovski, Burke had successfully created a genuine abundance of quality young defensemen. Burke inherited Mattias Ohlund, Adrian Aucoin, and Bryan McCabe—all under the age of 25—and then used the fourth overall pick at the 1998 NHL Entry Draft to select Bryan Allen. Once Jovanovski was thrown into the mix, Burke had a level of surplus, particularly on the left side of his defense corps, that provided him with a valuable trade chip to play. At the 1999 NHL Entry Draft, Burke cashed in that chip to franchise-altering effect.

76 Välkommen Till Laget

Pavel Bure may have shone brighter, Roberto Luongo may have dominated more headlines, Todd Bertuzzi may have more thoroughly tapped into the zeitgeist of the city, and Trevor Linden may have been more universally beloved, but there is no doubt that Henrik and Daniel Sedin are the greatest Vancouver Canucks of all time.

The twin brothers hail from Ornskoldsvik, a tiny town in northern Sweden. Don't let the size fool you, though. When it comes to churning out NHL talent, Ornskoldsvik—home of Victor Hedman, Markus Naslund, and Peter Forsberg—punches well above its weight. It's the Swedish equivalent of London, Ontario, or Magnitogorsk, Russia—an elite hockey player assembly line masquerading as a midsize community.

When he returned to Vancouver as the Canucks general manager, Brian Burke inherited a team in disarray. The club was losing money, a situation exacerbated by the weak Canadian dollar. The head coach he inherited was widely loathed in his marketplace and believed he should have a big say in player personnel decisions. Meanwhile, Vancouver's most recognizable face, Pavel Bure, was dominating headlines by foregoing $8 million in salary, holding out, and publicly demanding a trade.

As Burke rode out myriad controversies, the Canucks were on their way to a bottom-of-the-table finish. The club would have a top pick, and Vancouver's scouts were hard at work, seeking to unearth the sort of star player who might play a crucial role in reversing the franchise's flagging fortunes.

The industry as a whole considered the top end of the 1999 NHL draft class to be below average, and Burke shared that opinion. Taking in the U20 World Junior Championship that year in Winnipeg, Burke didn't like what he saw from any of the top prospects. He left the tournament resolved to trade the third overall pick.

He'd been particularly unimpressed with the performance of a pair of Swedish brothers, identical twins named Henrik and Daniel Sedin. "They had had a poor World Juniors that year in Winnipeg," Burke recalled to *Global News* in June 2016. "I think they finished second and third in scoring in the tournament, but they scored a lot of points against, you know, Bulgaria and Panama and some of the other teams. Against Canada and the US, they had a real hard time."

Burke is famous for his decisiveness. He's claimed at length that he decided to use a first-round pick on Ryan Kesler after watching just one shift the two-way centerman played at Ohio State. In another well-publicized incident, Burke signed Kevin Bieksa to a professional contract because of a favorable outcome in a bar fight.

In this case, thankfully, Burke changed his opinion. He was convinced to take another look at the twins by Thomas Gradin, Vancouver's longtime ace Swedish birddog. "I saw them a few times," Gradin told *Global News*, "and the only two players that had the puck the whole game was them."

Though there were question marks about their skating ability and their size—concerns that Burke shared—even then the Sedin twins had this subtle ability to control the run of play. It's an uncanny ability Henrik and Daniel honed over decades of playing together, working the puck along the wall and moving the puck into the middle of the ice with unpredictable rapidity to find soft spots in their opponents' defensive zone coverage. This unique skill set became less subtle as Daniel and Henrik's powers increased over the course of their NHL careers.

"You could see that crazy thing they do for the first time, and I came back from Norway and said, 'I've got to get them,'" Burke said of watching the twins play at the 1999 World Hockey Championship. "There was no question about it."

Now that Burke knew he wanted the twins, he had a problem. He had only one top-five pick, and what had impressed him about the twins was the way they played with one another—their sonar-like ability to find each other all over the ice and convert the cycle into high-danger scoring chances. It wasn't enough to get Henrik *or* Daniel; he needed to get them both. "One twin standing alone had very little value," Burke said after the 1999 NHL Entry Draft. "There was a chemistry they have. The sum of the two was greater than the individual parts broken down."

Arriving at the 1999 NHL Entry Draft in his hometown of Boston, Burke knew he had to pull off a coup. If he could do it, it could define his career and the future of the Canucks franchise. If he failed, he'd have some more awkward explaining to do.

Twin brothers Daniel (left) and Henrik Sedin are the best Canucks of all time.

Having stared down Mike Gillis, Pavel Bure, Mike Keenan, and a smattering of local media in his first full year as Canucks general manager, Burke now had to cut a multitude of deals with a variety of similarly struggling teams. According to his own account, Burke arrived in Boston and immediately declared to his fellow general managers, "No one is walking out of here with the twins but us." Fortunately for Burke, there was a widespread sense of skepticism regarding the value of the top picks at the 1999 draft. Opportunity was knocking.

To get the ball rolling, Burke agreed to send Bryan McCabe and his first overall pick in 2000 to the Chicago Blackhawks for the fourth overall pick at the 1999 NHL Entry Draft. It was a steep price to pay and a big brass-balls gamble.

The twins endured enormous scrutiny and criticism in their first few seasons in Vancouver, but imagine how much worse it could've been—shades of Phil Kessel for Tyler Seguin, really—had the 1999–2000 Canucks sputtered and part of the acquisition cost to bring the twins to Vancouver had included the pick that brought Dany Heatley or Marian Gaborik to Chicago, rather than Pavel Vorobiev. It's unimaginable, really.

"Bob Murray is a tough man," Burke told *Global News* of the current Anaheim Ducks general manager and then–Blackhawks executive. "Even though we overpaid, that took a lot of time. It started probably three weeks before. At first, he was like, 'No, we'll wait and see what happens.'… Then it was me trying get him off Bryan McCabe, who I loved as a player, and [Murray] wouldn't move. So finally we made a decision."

Acquiring the Chicago pick gave the Canucks a fighting chance, but there was still work to be done. Burke and then–Tampa Bay Lightning general manager Jay Feaster talked about the first overall draft selection into the wee hours the night before the draft, but they couldn't work it out.

"We talked till late in the night and hung up on each other, cursing and swearing," Burke told *Global News* in 2016. "I went to bed and I didn't have this deal. And I'm thinking if I gave up Bryan McCabe and a first, and I've got to take one of these other players at four, I just made a horrible mistake."

Negotiations—which Burke later recalled were "like a chess match"—continued on the draft floor the next morning. Microphones captured the culmination of Burke's negotiations with Feaster, when he summarized the gentleman's agreement he'd come to with Atlanta Thrashers general manager Don Waddell, and how that would affect Tampa if they agreed to move down three draft slots. "So you get [the fourth overall pick] and two third[-round picks] in return for the first pick overall, OK?" Burke told Feaster. "You've got my word, so Jay's heard it, we're not taking anyone but the twins, and [Don's] promised me he's not taking anyone but [Patrik Stefan]."

The deal with the Thrashers was indeed a pure gentleman's agreement, designed with Burkean theatrics in mind. In return for agreeing not to take either Sedin twin with the first overall pick, Burke would allow Atlanta to announce their pick first, which would permit Vancouver to select the Sedin twins at the same time as consecutive picks. The real loser in this deal was Stefan, who is now included on every list of "bust first-overall picks" alongside Alexandre Daigle, even though he was drafted first overall on paper only and not in spirit.

With the Atlanta deal consummated, the Canucks had their twins. It went down to the wire, though; the deal with Tampa Bay that set it all up was only finalized minutes before the start of the NHL draft. "Five minutes before it started, Thomas [Gradin] walked up to us," Henrik Sedin recalled to *Global News*. "He was yelling from the floor, telling us that it was going to happen."

Gradin, the scout who always believed in the greatest players in Vancouver Canucks history, was yelling at the twins in Swedish.

"*Välkommen till laget,*" he said, which translates precisely to: "Welcome to the team."

The impressiveness of Burke's series of deals on the draft floor shouldn't be understated. Burke rolled the dice in a big way by trading his 2000 first-round pick and a very promising defenseman who would go on to play 12 more seasons, recording more than 40 points five times, for the fourth overall pick in a draft class widely believed to be weak (a perception that turned out to be true, aside from Henrik and Daniel Sedin). If the 1999–2000 Canucks hadn't improved to the extent that they did, or if Burke hadn't successfully twisted Feaster's arm on the draft floor, Burke's wheeling and dealing would be remembered very differently.

As it turned out, Burke's calculated risk paid off. He brought the greatest players in Canucks history to Vancouver. The magnitude of Burke's accomplishment isn't lost on him. In the foreword to Jason Farris' book *Behind the Moves*, Burke isolated the series of Sedin trades on the draft floor as the best of his career. "My own best move, I think, in terms of setting up the team and changing its fortunes," Burke wrote, "was trading for and drafting the Sedins for Vancouver in 1999."

That Burke singled out his draft floor moves in 1999 rather than anything that had to do with assembling the 2008 Stanley Cup champion Anaheim Ducks is enormously telling. The complexity, the pure brashness, and the outcome of the series of draft floor moves that brought the Sedin twins to Vancouver are, in retrospect, almost as unique and unbelievable as Henrik and Daniel themselves.

77 The Dawn of the West Coast Express

Opened in 1995, the West Coast Express is an interregional commuter railway linking downtown Vancouver with some of the Fraser Valley's largest cities. It's one of the busiest public transit services in British Columbia. But ask Canucks fans about the West Coast Express, and their answer doesn't involve trains.

For them, the West Coast Express is Markus Naslund, Brendan Morrison, and Todd Bertuzzi, a high-flying offensive trio that took Vancouver by storm in the early 2000s, emerging as one of the NHL's best and most exciting lines.

Much like the aforementioned railway, the Canucks' West Coast Express took time to build, and the process wasn't easy. Construction began in March 1996, when Quinn sent one of his former first-round picks—Alek Stojanov, taken seventh overall in 1991—to Pittsburgh in exchange for Naslund, a talented but underachieving Swedish winger.

It wasn't exactly roses to start in Vancouver. In fact, Naslund almost never made it to play alongside Bertuzzi and Morrison. Not long into his tenure as a Canuck, he clashed with then–head coach Mike Keenan and, as was often the case in Keenan-related clashes, the player quickly checked into the coach's doghouse. Keenan dropped Naslund from the lineup on several occasions, prompting the 25-year-old to request a trade out of Vancouver. "It was nothing personal," Naslund said later, to ESPN. "I just thought I could do more if I was given the opportunity."

Fortunately for Naslund—and the Canucks—circumstances intervened. A slate of injuries allowed him to move up the lineup, play more minutes, and shoulder more offensive responsibilities. And then Big Bert arrived.

In one of the most profoundly altering moves in club history, Trevor Linden—the captain and face of the franchise—was flipped to the Islanders at the 1998 trade deadline for a package of players that included Bertuzzi, a hulking, enigmatic talent labeled by the *New York Times* as "an underachiever."

Bertuzzi stood 6'3" and weighed 230 pounds, and had all the markings of a prototypical power forward. He was a huge net-front presence, blessed with quick feet, great hands, and a mean streak. Yet nothing ever seemed to click on Long Island. He played to middling reviews and was ultimately classified as a guy with maximum potential who yielded minimal results.

Bertuzzi knew he needed a change. "Things weren't working out here," he told the *New York Times* upon being dealt. "I'm a little rattled, but looking forward to the new start, nothing but good things." If only he knew then how prescient that was.

Bertuzzi and Naslund clicked almost immediately in Vancouver. In 1998–99, the two skated on a line with Alexander Mogilny, and while Bertuzzi missed time to injury, signs suggested the Canucks had found something special. Naslund—buoyed by the firing of Keenan, who was turfed in late January—finished the year with a career-high 36 goals, emerging as one of the club's leaders, while Bertuzzi had nearly as many goals in 32 games (eight) as he did in his last full year with the Isles (10, in 64 contests).

At this stage, it's fair to assume Morrison was targeted as the final piece of the puzzle. But in a familiar refrain with the West Coast Express, it didn't exactly start that way.

At the 2000 deadline, Burke—having taken over from Quinn two years earlier—flipped Mogilny to the Cup-contending New Jersey Devils. The Devils, in turn, were willing to part with Morrison, a decorated NCAA talent out of the University of Michigan who captured the Hobey Baker Award in 1997.

A local kid, Morrison grew up in Pitt Meadows—one of the cities on the actual West Coast Express!—and played junior for

BCHL Penticton before starring with the Wolverines. All of it made for a nice narrative, but nobody was sure what the Canucks were actually getting. Morrison wasn't big, and had a modest body of work in New Jersey, but was praised for his heady play, quickness, and hockey IQ.

Morrison's first full season with the Canucks came in 2000–01. At the time, minutes at center were hard to come by, with future Hall of Famer Mark Messier and trusty veteran Andrew Cassels in the mix. For more than a year Morrison bounced around the lineup, seemingly without a set role…until January 9, 2002.

That night, head coach Marc Crawford put Morrison at center between his two top scorers, and the train left the station, so to speak. The trio scored a pair of first-period goals in an eventual loss to the powerhouse Red Wings, but the result was almost secondary. The chemistry on the new-look top line was immediately evident, and only seemed to get stronger in the following weeks. Everybody realized something special was happening. Not long after, the West Coast Express moniker was attached.

In that first season together, the WCE had a coming-out party. Naslund, Morrison, and Bertuzzi combined for 99 goals and 242 points and threw a scare into the eventual Cup champion Red Wings in the opening playoff round, jumping out to a 2–0 series lead before eventually falling in six games.

The second year of the West Coast Express? Naslund, Bertuzzi, and Morrison rewrote the franchise record books, and provided the kind of highlight-reel hockey Vancouver hadn't seen since the peak Bure years. They accounted for a staggering 45 percent of the team's goal production—and that was on a very good Canucks team that racked up 45 wins, finished with 101 points, and won its first playoff round in eight years.

All three established career highs in scoring (Morrison with 71 points, Bertuzzi with 91, and Naslund with 104), and both Naslund and Bertuzzi were named to the NHL's First All-Star team. Naslund also won the Lester B. Pearson Award, given to the league's best player as voted by the NHLPA.

It was fitting that Naslund took the biggest haul. He was the first West Coast Express member to arrive in Vancouver and, fittingly, inherited the captaincy from Messier in 2000, wearing the *C* during some of the most prolific moments in Canucks history. He also embodied the *theme* of the West Coast Express. Naslund, along with Bertuzzi and Morrison, never forgot the teams that drafted them ultimately discarded them. In an interview with *Sports Illustrated*, Morrison noted, "All three of us are castoffs." That feeling of failure in their first stops fueled them to succeed in their second.

Bertuzzi agreed, citing Naslund as the figurehead. "He's been the best player in the league the past couple of years—by far," Bertuzzi told *Sports Illustrated* in 2003. "We've had to work from the bottom up. His accomplishment is bringing this team to where it is now."

In the early 2000s the Canucks were one of the best teams in the NHL, and the West Coast Express was a big reason why. But it wouldn't be that way for long.

78 Dan Cloutier, the Flub, and the Importance of Playoff Success

Goaltending has been a relative strength of the Vancouver Canucks now for about a decade, but when Brian Burke famously dubbed Vancouver "a goalie graveyard" in the early 2000s, most Canucks fans grimly nodded in agreement.

Kirk McLean and Richard Brodeur remain well regarded in Canucks lore, and earned their status as "the exceptions to the rule" in the pre–Roberto Luongo era with stellar playoff runs in 1982 and 1994, respectively. Both netminders were likable and memorable, but their popularity was a double-edged sword for the team. Both goaltenders also turned in a number of subaverage seasons in the latter stages of their Canucks tenure as the team held on to them well past their primes.

As any Canucks fan older than 25 can tell you, goaltending was a massive issue for the team throughout the mid-1990s. Though most will trace those struggles as spanning from the McLean trade right through to the lopsided Luongo trade, it's actually a bit more complicated than that.

McLean's epic, historic run through the 1994 Stanley Cup playoffs obscures the fact that, really, his last full season as an average starter by save percentage was the 1992–93 season (it should be noted that McLean posted an above-average save percentage during the lockout-shortened 1994–95 season as well). As save percentages rose with the more widespread adoption of the butterfly technique throughout the mid-1990s, McLean's more traditional stand-up style became outdated. By the mid-1990s he was an .890 goaltender in a .905 league.

Poring over McLean's performance relative to the league average is worthwhile because it reveals a startling fact: Vancouver's issues in net predated the McLean trade by about five seasons. The Canucks, in fact, went a remarkable 11 full years between seasons in which their goaltenders combined to post a save percentage above the league average, stretching from 1992–93 through to 2003–04. If you want to understand the genesis of the "goalie graveyard," that's it right there.

Some of the club's struggles to find saves were issues of the team's own creation—the club jettisoned Arturs Irbe and Sean Burke in the late 1990s, for example, and the goaltenders went on to post a number of excellent seasons for the Carolina Hurricanes and the Phoenix Coyotes, respectively. But there's no denying that a variety of other goaltenders—Felix Potvin, Garth Snow, Peter

Skudra, Fredrik Norrena, Corey Schwab, Bob Essensa, and Kevin Weekes—just weren't up to the task in Vancouver.

It's also worth considering that Vancouver's save percentage finally stabilized well before the Luongo trade. The goaltender who really ended Vancouver's lengthy subaverage save percentage drought is a player who probably deserves wholesale reexamination, because it's ironically his name that's most associated with memories of the Canucks' puck-stopping ineptitude, not to mention uncharitable beach ball memes. We're talking, of course, about Dan Cloutier.

Cloutier was long said to be the apple of Burke's eye, and as a member of the New York Rangers, he was a key part of trade packages that Rangers general manager Neil Smith and Burke discussed in a potential Bure trade.

Raw and athletic, Cloutier was a highly touted young goaltender, and he performed well in a limited run with the Rangers from 1997 to 1999 before being dealt to the Tampa Bay Lightning when the Rangers shipped essentially the same package they'd been offering Burke for Bure (Niklas Sundstrom, Cloutier, and a first-round pick) to Tampa Bay in exchange for Pavel Brendl, the fourth overall pick at the 1999 NHL Entry Draft.

As a starter in Tampa Bay, Cloutier handled a bigger workload, and over a larger sample size (and with opposing clubs prescouting his game more rigorously), the young netminder began to be exposed by NHL-level shooters. Relying on instinct and his natural athleticism, Cloutier's technique and positioning lagged well behind his natural gifts. Over nearly 80 appearances with the Lightning, Cloutier managed an .887 save percentage in an era when the league average save percentage was 15 points higher.

Finally in February 2001, Burke evidently got frustrated watching his struggling tandem of Bob Essensa and Felix Potvin cost his club games. By the 2000–01 season, with Marc Crawford firmly in place and the West Coast Express era clubs beginning to solidify, the Canucks ably controlled play and inched toward the top 10 in NHL scoring. Goaltending remained the club's Achilles' heel, though, so Burke made a deal with the Lightning, sending Adrian Aucoin and a second-round draft pick to western Florida in exchange for Cloutier. Even without using the benefit of hindsight, it was a bad bet on Burke's part.

By the time Cloutier arrived in Vancouver, he'd appeared in more than 100 NHL games and was carrying a career save percentage of .881. He didn't appear to be a strong candidate to morph into a league-average starting goaltender. Aucoin, meanwhile, was 27 years old, a sturdy defensive piece, and had a big right-handed blast that was a genuine weapon on the power play.

Yes, goaltending was an urgent issue for the Canucks, and the emergence of Brent Sopel provided Vancouver with a reason to consider Aucoin expendable, but it's hard to endorse any move that results in a club giving up a quality blueliner for a goaltender with a subaverage track record. Aucoin went on to play top-four minutes for another 11 seasons, scoring more than 10 goals on four occasions and successfully driving play from the back end until his retirement.

Though Burke made a questionable bet on Cloutier, it should be noted that it actually kind of worked out. After all, Burke wasn't betting against Aucoin so much as he was betting on Cloutier, and Cloutier genuinely improved in Vancouver. The newly anointed Canucks starter struggled over the balance of the 2000–01 campaign, but thereafter he put in the work and improved his technique, and one can reasonably argue that he morphed into a low-end but bona fide NHL workhorse starter.

"When I came in [to the NHL], I was more of a battler, a gamer; I just went in there and competed," Cloutier recalled of his formative NHL years. "I just tried to stop pucks, I didn't really have a plan. If I had to dive, I just dove.

"When I came to Vancouver I worked with Andy Moog and Ian Clarke and refined my game technically, and all of a sudden I became more consistent. I had something to fall back on. I had a plan," Cloutier continued. "It allowed me to play more games, and I became a more legitimate starter."

In Cloutier's first full Canucks season, he managed to stop more than 90 percent of the shots he faced, though he was outperformed by his backup, Peter Skudra, that year. And of course the whole season is remembered for just one moment: when a bouncing shot from center ice by Nicklas Lidstrom got by him late in the second period of Game 3 against the Detroit Red Wings.

It was an iconic flub, and the Canucks, who were up 2–0 in the playoff series at that point, went on to lose four consecutive games to the eventual Stanley Cup champions. For fans and media it was seen as the turning point in the series. The sequence took on a life of its own and is memorialized to this day online with the famous beach ball GIF.

To a man, the players on that team, head coach Marc Crawford, and Burke refused to blame Cloutier. It was a bad bounce at a big moment, but those sorts of bounces happen. "It was one of those bounces that you rarely see," Markus Naslund recalled. "Obviously it ended up being a bit of a letdown, but we still had plenty of opportunities to win that series even after that goal. I know Dan took a lot of heat for that particular goal, and the media made it out to be the turning point, but there were other factors as well—we couldn't score on the power play and [Dominik] Hasek played some unreal hockey."

In evaluating goaltending legacies, though, playoff performance is weighted heavily by fans. In some ways, Cloutier's Canucks legacy never recovered from the impression left by that one fateful play during the 2002 Stanley Cup playoffs. "People like to talk about that goal, but you know, I'm a goalie, and every goalie understands that you let in those bad goals and you forget about it right after," Cloutier told the Canucks website in 2010. "It's just hard to make other people forget about it."

It didn't matter that the Red Wings were the superior club or that Cloutier continued to improve subsequently, morphing into an average starting goaltender. And it doesn't matter to most fans that just as Cloutier had figured out the technical side, he was betrayed by a series of hip injuries that plagued him for the next five years and ultimately forced him into a premature retirement.

Cloutier wasn't a star-level netminder, and goaltending was a big reason the West Coast Express era Canucks never went on a deep playoff run. Cloutier followed up the Red Wings series with another shaky playoff performance in 2003, as the Minnesota Wild overcame a 3–1 series deficit to defeat the Canucks. By then, most Canucks fans had determined Cloutier didn't have "the stuff" to win in the playoffs, and when an injury in the third game of the club's first-round series against the Flames in 2004 ended Cloutier's season, Cloutier never got another chance to prove them wrong.

It's a fine line that separates success and failure in hockey, though. Cloutier wasn't a great goaltender by any means—he wasn't even an above-average starter—but it's only a couple bad bounces that result in him being remembered by Canucks fans as totally hapless, which in fact he wasn't.

The truth is that during his Vancouver tenure—and before hip injuries permanently derailed his career—Cloutier improved his technique and developed into a roughly average starting goaltender, the sort of netminder capable of sustaining a decent save percentage and outperforming his backups in heavy usage over multiple seasons. There's a lot of value in that sort of player.

Obviously Cloutier's regular-season reliability and his technical improvement won't make anyone forget how he flubbed that Lidstrom shot or came undone against the Wild in 2003. That's life for a professional hockey goaltender. Cloutier isn't even the most egregious example of how a small sample of playoff performances can skew the way Vancouver's hockey-watching public evaluates and remembers a goaltender.

Even so, it's reasonable to suggest Cloutier is a goaltender who performed better in a Canucks jersey than anyone could've reasonably expected when he was acquired, despite a series of memorably iffy playoff performances.

79 End of the Line: Steve Moore and Derailing the WCE

Most dynasties don't end with a single moment. They're often whittled away by time, age, or a confluence of circumstances. That could be said of the West Coast Express, but no singular moment defined the end of the era more than what transpired on March 8, 2004.

That night's game, between Vancouver and Colorado, was a rematch of a few weeks prior, when Avalanche forward Steve Moore hit Markus Naslund in the head, knocking him out with a concussion. Moore went unpenalized, and the Canucks were enraged. Veteran tough guy Brad May put a bounty on Moore, while Todd Bertuzzi—Naslund's linemate, and close friend—called Moore "a piece of shit." That set the stage for one of the ugliest moments in Vancouver's history. Not Vancouver *sports* history, but Vancouver's history.

The rematch was a blowout, with Colorado leading 8–2 midway through the third period. Moore, who'd already been challenged to (and accepted) a fight—scrapping with Matt Cooke in one of four tilts in the opening frame—was in the midst of a shift, and being constantly harangued by Bertuzzi, who was seemingly determined to administer additional frontier justice. Then it happened.

Bertuzzi grabbed Moore from behind and punched him in the head, then fell on top of the Avalanche forward as he hit the ice. The impact of the blow and fall was cataclysmic—Moore lay prone on the ice for 10 minutes while paramedics moved him onto a stretcher and rushed him to local hospital.

There, Moore was treated for injuries normally reserved for multi-vehicle accidents: three fractured vertebrae in his neck, a concussion, ligament damage, and facial lacerations. He would never play another game in the NHL.

For Bertuzzi and the Canucks, the fallout was immense. Two days after the attack, Bertuzzi openly wept at a press conference, apologizing to Moore and everyone who witnessed the attack. "For the kids that watch this game, I'm truly sorry," Bertuzzi said. "I don't play the game that way. And I'm not a mean-spirited person."

Bertuzzi's apology did little to calm the firestorm. The incident—a premeditated one—made headlines and led TV broadcasts throughout North America, embodying all that was wrong with hockey's inherent violence. To give an idea of how frenzied the media blitz was, *The Oprah Winfrey Show* covered Bertuzzi-Moore. Yeah, Oprah.

With his league in the most unfavorable of spotlights, NHL commissioner Gary Bettman had no choice but to come down hard on Bertuzzi—and he did, suspending him for the remainder of the regular season and playoffs, while fining the Canucks $250,000.

Vancouver's season was, unsurprisingly, thrown into disarray. The top team in the Northwest Division and a legit Cup contender, the Canucks won just seven more games down the stretch and were upset in the opening playoff round, losing to the sixth-seeded Calgary Flames.

The season was over. But Bertuzzi's suspension—and the Moore incident—would linger for much, much longer. The 2004–05 NHL campaign was lost to labor strife, and Bertuzzi was unable to play anywhere in the interim as the International Ice Hockey Federation banned him from all international competition. All told, his suspension from professional hockey lasted 17 months and accounted for more than $500,000 in lost salary.

And when Bertuzzi came back, things weren't even close to being the same. He, Naslund, and Morrison tried to rejoin forces for the 2005–06 campaign, yet it was clear the stain of the Moore incident had marred him and the entire franchise. Bertuzzi had to face reporters' questions about the attack wherever he went, and

Bertuzzi's mugging of Steve Moore changed the course of Canucks hockey forever.

both he and the team were met with jeers in nearly every visiting arena. What's more, the lengthy layoff took its toll, as West Coast Express was no longer a formidable offensive force (all three failed to crack the 80-point plateau in 2004–05, and Vancouver missed the playoffs for the first time in five years).

That off-season, the Canucks knew things had to change. It began with the firing of Marc Crawford, who had constructed the West Coast Express. (Years later, Crawford acknowledged the West Coast Express had been surpassed that year by Daniel and Henrik Sedin as the club's "top guys.")

Then GM Dave Nonis made the move everybody knew had to happen—Bertuzzi was traded. The blockbuster deal saw him flipped to Florida in exchange for prized goalie Roberto Luongo.

All told, it was an ignominious end to the West Coast Express, and fans were left with the lingering question of what could have been. Between injuries, suspension, and the lockout, the trio only had three full seasons together and—fairly or not—will be remembered for its failures in the postseason as much as it's regular-season success. To wit, the WCE never advanced past the second round of the playoffs.

As for the Bertuzzi-Moore incident itself? It dragged on for 10 years, going through a litany of legal motions before an out-of-court settlement was reached between the two parties in 2014.

For Naslund, the guy Bertuzzi was trying to defend, the sting of the incident may never go away. "It still bothers me what Todd has had to go through over this, and the way it's dragged on over the years," Naslund told the *Province*. "There's no question he was standing up for me and for his teammates when it happened. It all went too far."

80 The Return of Linden, Vancouver's Prodigal Son

The Vancouver Canucks made a quick turnaround from a cellar-dwelling, dysfunction-ridden club in 1998 and 1999 to a young, up-tempo, fun-to-watch team in 2000 and 2001. It all happened quickly enough to give Vancouver's hockey fans whiplash.

With Marc Crawford behind the bench and Brian Burke as GM, Vancouver identified a new core, integrated the Sedin twins, and quickly became an offensive force. Those early versions of the West Coast Express era Canucks possessed team speed throughout the lineup and a tough-to-contain cycle game that left opponents spinning. Even before any expectations attached themselves to those clubs, the Canucks were resonant again in the Vancouver market.

In the fall of 2001, however, only a year removed from a brief playoff berth the previous spring, the Canucks stumbled out of the gate. The Sedin twins didn't appear to be taking the big step forward that was expected of them as sophomores, Andrew Cassels got hurt, and Todd Bertuzzi took a 10-game suspension for leaving the bench to fight in a game, perhaps prophetically, against the Colorado Avalanche. A team that was expected to make noise didn't look ready for prime time.

Publicly, Burke expressed confidence, even signing Crawford to a contract extension at a time when his club was reeling. Still the club's early-season issues were seen as a major step back. In a market where an effervescent love of Canucks hockey was on the verge of a renaissance, there was a significant sense of "here we go again."

Whether Burke felt the team needed more maturity or a figure who could help take some of the media glare off his still-young core group, or perhaps just a veteran checking center to supplement the more skilled profile of his other centermen, Brendan Morrison and Cassels, the Canucks general manager pulled the trigger on a trade to bring Trevor Linden back to Vancouver.

"Players like Trevor Linden were more than a hockey player or an asset to me," Burke told Jason Farris 10 years later. "All of these young people are. You don't easily suggest that teams and people don't mean something big to you. That's where your hope for success lies—that people do well."

The cost was relatively high, a first-round draft pick in 2002 and a second-round draft pick in 2003, in exchange for Linden, a conditional second-round pick and an agreement that the Capitals would pick up some of the $8.5 million Linden had remaining on a contract that ran through the 2002–03 campaign.

"I went out for a game in Washington on Saturday night, came out for warm-ups, and Ron Wilson said I wasn't playing," Linden recalled of hearing the news. "I said, 'What are you talking about?' So I went into the room, sat in the room by myself, and thought, *So...I've just been traded.* I watched the game the night before, the Canucks were in Chicago, and they talked about their lack of penalty killing and how they didn't do well on faceoffs. George McPhee comes in and says, 'You've been traded to Vancouver.' So I got on the phone with Burkie."

For Linden, who still made his summer home in Vancouver, it was indeed like coming home. On the other hand, this wasn't just some player returning to Vancouver. As the meaning of it all sunk in, so did the pressure. "I was scared shitless, oh my God," Linden said. "I remember thinking, *I can't go back there.* I had 10 great years there. I didn't sleep that night. I was scared to death thinking that [I was] just going to screw this up."

He continued, "I came back like a kid going to kindergarten. I remember being back here thinking I wasn't comfortable here at all: the players were new, the coach was new. I wanted it to work.

It wasn't like I was slapping backs and laughing, I was focused. It was not a comfortable spot to come back to, but it became one of the most rewarding years I've ever had. It was so much fun."

It was probably fun because the Canucks—6–11–1 at the time of the trade—promptly found their rhythm. The club went on a three-game winning streak immediately following the Linden acquisition and lost just 19 combined games the rest of the way. By season's end the Canucks led the league in goal scoring and roared into an extremely difficult postseason matchup with the Detroit Red Wings, surprising everybody by taking a 2–0 series lead. Even the early season Cassels injury, seen as a body blow at the time, became a positive development when Morrison found chemistry on one of the most beloved forward lines in team history with Todd Bertuzzi and Markus Naslund.

From a contemporary vantage point, we're left to wonder how much the experience Linden went through upon his Vancouver return—and the instantaneous impact he seemed to have on a still-green group of core players—informed his later approach as Vancouver's president of hockey operations.

As an executive, Linden's Canucks have gone to great lengths to bolster the club in the short term, steadfastly refusing to tank and placing a major premium on veteran leadership. Is it possible that this approach has its genesis in the remarkable turnaround the 2001–02 club made after adding Linden to the roster? "I did see that I was definitely an important piece to that," Linden said when asked this very question. "We had such a young group...that I think I was an important piece. And it was the perfect fit for me. The importance of having guys that are leaders and mentors and professionals...I mean, it's massive. I see the change in our guys just from having that, and it's important. It's culture."

81 Make the Provies

At the height of the Mike Gillis era, when the Vancouver Canucks were regularly storming their way through the Northwest Division and were a common pick to win the Stanley Cup, the sheer volume of quality content on offer—from traditional and nontraditional sources alike—was staggering.

The two local newspapers still employed multiple beat writers in those days, and with the advent of social media, any Canucks fan could start a blog, and most seemed to. After any given Canucks game, fans could read the standard journalistic game reports from the *Vancouver Province*, the *Vancouver Sun*, the *Globe and Mail*, and the assorted wire services. Canucks fans could also go online and read *Pass It to Bulis*' incomparably funny "I Watched This Game" postgame piece, or check in on what the fancy stats said and what the scoring chance differentials were over at CanucksArmy.com.

Starting in about 2012, though, the Death Star of unique Canucks-focused postgame content emerged. Known to die-hard Canucks fans as "the Provies" this must-read postgamer is written by Jason Botchford, with Wyatt "the Stanchion" Arndt pitching in about a dozen times per season. Designed as an informal post-game awards show—each Provies segment is technically an award given out for Best Sound Bite or Best Sequence—the Provies were originally included in the print edition of the *Vancouver Province* starting in 2007. In the early years, though, Botchford's missives were truncated so as to fit in the paper.

In 2012 the Provies became untethered from print and evolved into something entirely different. Existing in a digital-only format, Botchford's Provies expanded into snarky freeform dispatches. Eventually the staple postgamer evolved into a must-read broadsheet, incorporating rumor, fan tweets, original reporting, player quotes, in-depth coverage of in-game happenings, and in jokes. Lots and lots of in jokes.

"In 2012 [my editors] came to me and said, 'We don't have any space for [the Provies] in the paper anymore. Why don't you just take it online?'" Botchford recalled. "That was when I was able to start flexing and expanding, and that's when I got to thinking, *What do I want this to be?*

"There were three things that I grew up reading or listening to: I listened to Howard Stern, I listened to Jim Rome, and I listened to the band Phish. All of them had this payoff if you were a long-term fan, like a secret language that only you could understand. If you ever flip on Stern or Rome, there's a bunch of stuff that doesn't make any sense to a neophyte or a newbie."

The sprawling focus of the Provies allows Botchford to go in-depth on relatively minor occurrences, such as a Murphy bed management during the Gillis era had installed so John Tortorella (the "commuter coach" in Provies parlance) could take midday naps, what fans are discussing online, or whether or not Derek Dorsett is a fan favorite.

"There are moments, like Provies moments," Botchford said of how he decides what to include. "One of them was when Cody Hodgson scored a couple of goals, and when the media [was] let into the dressing room, Roberto Luongo [was] chanting, 'More ice time! More ice time! More ice time!' That chant [was] hilarious and kind of thread[ed] into this whole Cody Hodgson saga with a three-word chant. I immediately [thought], *That's a moment that's great for the Provies*, and honestly, that's something fun that probably wouldn't have got[ten] play anywhere else five or six or seven years ago."

Overall the tone is snarky and skeptical, but it also invites fans to feel like insiders. The Provies more closely reflect the sort of conversation that two sports journalists might have in a bar together rather than the sort of work those journalists are likely to produce for public consumption. There's a take-no-prisoners approach to Botchford's work that occasionally rubs everyone—including Canucks management, posters on Reddit, and the players themselves—the wrong way.

"Some players love it, some players don't. I always say all of them either know about it or read it," Botchford said. "One particular player was always angry about the coverage he would get in the Provies, and there was one time that I was walking out of the rink and he was hitting pucks over the upper net so they could get over the glass and potentially drop on my head as I was walking by and out of the rink."

On the other hand, there are the occasional positive reactions too. The mother of one Canucks player thought so much of Botchford's take on her son that she asked to meet him. And for fans, it's a completely unique view into some of the day-to-day weirdness that characterizes the experience of covering an NHL team from a beat writer's perspective.

Though there's often a good deal of hard news gathering and reporting in the Provies, the Provies are also interactive. Some Canucks fans on Twitter—including a combative fan named Seen, or a sardonic media skeptic with his own rebuilding plans named PA Islander—have become recurring characters in the Provies drama, as have some local media members, who are generally referred to by nicknames such as Drancer, Baby Dragon, or the Boat Captain.

"The more that people say [the jokes are too inside], the more committed I am to doing it," Botchford said. "I don't think I do it a lot. I'd probably like to do it more. I do want people who read regularly to get a big payoff."

While the interactive elements of the Provies may be confusing to wade through for the uninitiated, they're also an opportunity for lifelong Canucks fans. If you're looking to be part of the most widely read Canucks postgame article, all you have to do is tweet the right thing to Botchford or Arndt. "I would think that the best way to [make the Provies] is to [contact] me on a comment that I've made and have an authentic, different take," Botchford said. "A lot of snark usually gets you in. And if you somehow incorporate some theme or some subject that is often covered in the Provies, I think that's a pretty good way to do it."

82 Dave Nonis Wasn't Successful but Was a Conservative Steward

The West Coast Express era, which so captured the imagination of Vancouverites, seemed to arrive overnight. After Martin Gelinas and the Calgary Flames eliminated the Vancouver Canucks from the 2004 Stanley Cup playoffs, this fondly remembered era came to an end almost as quickly.

Behind the scenes, Canucks owner John McCaw was looking to sell the team to a local bidder. The Aquilini Investment Group would purchase a 50 percent share of the team from McCaw in November 2004, purchasing the remaining half a couple years later. The sale was controversial as some rival bidders, Ryan Beedie and Tom Gaglardi, contended Aquilini had been part of their rival bid for the club and had violated the terms of a legal partnership.

The dispute made it all the way to the Supreme Court of British Columbia, which means that a full blow-by-blow of the sale process is available in the public record. Essentially the Aquilini family was initially interested in being a minority partner in a joint bid with Beedie and Gaglardi, but the sides never formally consummated their joint bid status and parted ways amicably. A few months later, when Gaglardi's talks with Stan McCammon and John McCaw stalled—at one point Gaglardi told McCammon a poorly received joke about Mafia connections, and it generally appears the future Dallas Stars owner overplayed his hand as he mistakenly believed he was the only serious bidder—Francesco Aquilini and the Aquilini family reengaged, put up several lucrative properties as collateral, and enhanced the scope of their bid. The court found in favor of the Aquilinis in 2008.

Not only was the Canucks franchise on the market, there were also significant changes taking place internally. Brian Burke, the Canucks president and GM, had rejected an extension offer from McCaw and McCammon in the fall of 2003 and didn't have his contract renewed. He was replaced by his lieutenant, Dave Nonis, a hardworking executive with a reputation for innovation who had worked his way into Canucks hockey operations after getting his start as a sales rep during the Pat Quinn era.

And, of course, all this was taking place under the shadow of the NHL lockout, which would scuttle the entirety of the 2004–05 season. At one point during the year, Canucks players sought to unionize independently from the players association in the province of British Columbia. Trevor Linden, the Canucks' alternate captain, played a key role in collective-bargaining talks as the president of the NHLPA and was widely scrutinized for the part he played in deposing NHLPA head Bob Goodenow in the spring of 2005.

When the lockout ended, the two warring factions agreed to a hard salary cap that would fundamentally alter how NHL teams were constructed and maintained. The Canucks were a "have" team in the previous system, with a payroll that generally landed in the top half of the league and occasionally verged into the top 10. Even so, the NHL's new hard salary cap—set at $39 million for the 2005–06 campaign—would have major implications going forward for a club that had a payroll of more than $42 million the season preceding the lockout.

Almost immediately upon the opening of the free-agent market in early August, the Canucks were forced to make a cap-related move. To make room for Markus Naslund, an unrestricted free agent, and Mattias Ohlund, who was eligible for arbitration, Nonis dealt Brent Sopel to the New York Islanders.

The move was a necessary one, but it weakened the Canucks defensive corps significantly. Nolan Baumgartner, who replaced Sopel on a pair with Ohlund, played well, earned nearly $2 million less than Sopel, and led all Canucks defensemen in scoring that season. This was a new world.

Initially, it seemed, it was a new world that suited Nonis rather well. The Canucks general manager did extremely well with the Anson Carter signing, as the journeyman winger found instant chemistry with the twins on his way to scoring 33 goals at the low, low price of $1 million. That Vancouver lost Carter the subsequent off-season was just another testament to how much the industry had changed thanks to the hard cap.

Despite some savvy Dumpster diving on Nonis' part, the last West Coast Express era team felt a bit stale. Todd Bertuzzi was productive, but the counting stats don't really tell the whole story. The so-called "new NHL" was characterized by on-ice officials calling all manner of additional penalties that season, which temporarily inflated scoring, so despite the 25 goals and more than 70 points, Bertuzzi didn't seem to be his old, rambunctious self after the Moore incident. And of course goaltending was an issue, as Cloutier's hips betrayed him and Alex Auld proved to be below the level of a 1A starting goaltender.

The summer of 2006 came to define Nonis' Canucks tenure in a positive light. Following his first season at the helm, Nonis fired Marc Crawford and hired Alain Vigneault, who would go on to become the winningest coach in franchise history. He made a savvy move to sign Willie Mitchell as an unrestricted free agent. And in his pièce de résistance, Nonis dealt Bertuzzi, Bryan Allen, and Alex

Auld to the Florida Panthers for a package highlighted by future Hall of Fame goaltender Roberto Luongo.

It was highway robbery, made even sweeter because it was Mike Keenan who was then the Panthers general manager. Bertuzzi sustained a series of injuries in his one season in south Florida, ultimately appearing in fewer than 20 games in his Panthers tenure. Luongo, meanwhile, would go on to pad his Hall of Fame résumé in Vancouver, leading the Canucks to multiple playoff berths, earning multiple Vezina Trophy nominations and even a Hart Trophy nomination while cementing himself as the greatest goaltender in franchise history.

There's a lot to like about Nonis' overall body of work during his relatively brief tenure as Canucks general manager—particularly at the draft table in his first two seasons, when the Canucks selected players such as Alex Edler, Mason Raymond, and Jannik Hansen beyond the first round—but the team Nonis constructed was ultimately weighed down by a lack of offensive skill, some poor depth additions, and a variety of inefficient contracts.

Some of those contract inefficiencies were Nonis' own doing, but Brendan Morrison's lengthy deal was one Nonis inherited. Those relatively large tickets for players on the back end of their primes left Vancouver little wiggle room under the cap, particularly after giving the Sedin twins a well-deserved raise, to make necessary additions.

These flaws were exacerbated when Nonis' ability to find value on the scrap heap, as he did with Carter that first summer, seemed to abandon him. Byron Ritchie, Brad Isbister, and Marc Chouinard just never worked out.

It's also worth noting that Nonis' deadline-day deals to bolster the team proved inexpensive and inefficient in his first two seasons. Trading two second-round picks, a fourth-round pick, a third-round pick, and a pair of B-level prospects for Eric Weinrich, Sean Brown, Mika Noronen, and Keith Carney in 2006 just didn't move the needle as the team failed to make the postseason. The next season the club dealt two second-round picks and a fourth-round pick for Bryan Smolinski and Brent Sopel.

Considering Nonis' costly deadline moves in 2006 and 2007, that his Canucks tenure was finally sunk by his wholly justifiable conservatism at the 2008 deadline—according to reports from TSN's Darren Dreger—is perhaps ironic. Vancouver was reported to be one of two finalists for the services of Tampa Bay Lightning star Brad Richards, but Nonis quite rightly refused to keep up with the Stars when the auction got a bit overheated.

Nonis was the first Canucks general manager of the salary cap era, and in some ways his firing is inextricably linked to the tectonic shifts that were taking place across the league. Weighed down by millstone contracts to aging players, Nonis was unable—despite a promising start—to supplement his club's offensive depth.

If Nonis was a bit late in arriving to some concepts that have now become a mainstay in the salary cap era—being wary of signing non-star players to big terms and not unduly trading draft picks for rentals, for example—he was still responsible for completing a variety of moves that paid off in a major way during the peak years of the Gillis era. By acquiring Luongo for a song; drafting Edler, Hansen, Raymond, and Cory Schneider; and avoiding Brad Richards at the 2008 NHL trade deadline, Nonis left his successor with a solid foundation.

The Canucks still lacked offensive depth and had a slow, aging blueline, but all one had to do was squint, and the core of a team that might contend in the near future came into focus.

83 Gillis' New Approach to Winning in Vancouver

There is perhaps no single individual in the history of the Vancouver Canucks franchise with as complicated and controversial a legacy as Mike Gillis, the former president and GM. A powerful forward in his youth, Gillis was selected fifth overall in the 1958 NHL Entry Draft. Plagued by knee injuries, Gillis never delivered on his appreciable promise as a player. Instead, he went to law school and sharpened his intellect. He became a player agent, a modern thinker, and a hard-nosed negotiator with a keen sense of the details.

The combative, no-nonsense former player agent replaced Dave Nonis as general manager in the spring of 2008, amid whispers that he'd worked in a calculated fashion to undermine Nonis and become friendly with Canucks owner Francesco Aquilini. He took over a Canucks team that had a solid core in place but had missed the playoffs in two of the past three seasons, was constantly limited by salary cap constraints, and wholly lacked a quality supporting cast.

Controversy wasn't new to Gillis. As a player agent, Gillis had a Scott Boras–like reputation. He was Pavel Bure's agent during the famed Russian winger's legendary holdout, the deals he'd negotiated for clients such as Bobby Holik were often cited as precipitating factors explaining the 2005 NHL lockout and, as a younger man, Gillis had brought down former NHLPA head Alan Eagleson with a lawsuit that served to expose Eagleson's embezzlement and fraud.

Whether it was the way the Colorado Rockies team that drafted him mismanaged his injuries or the fact that the head of the players association defrauded Gillis out of a hefty portion of his disability insurance, Gillis came to nurse a certain disdain for hockey's "old boys." He often seemed skeptical of the media and the industry as a whole, and that skepticism was often perceived as arrogance.

That perceived arrogance is at the root of why Gillis' Canucks legacy is so unnecessarily controversial. There should be no doubt—or controversy—that the Gillis era was an unrivaled golden age for the franchise and the club. Because Gillis was disliked by so many in the media and in the wider hockey world, however, it's hard to find anyone willing to give him much credit for the success that he presided over.

It's said that Gillis inherited an elite core, which is true to some extent. Ryan Kesler, the Sedin twins, and Roberto Luongo were already in place. They were star players and formed the backbone of the 2010–11 Canucks—easily the greatest team in franchise history.

Three star forwards and an elite goaltender is enough to make the playoffs, perhaps, but for a team to finish with the best record, the best defense, the best power play, nearly the best penalty kill, and to make the Stanley Cup Finals, as the Canucks did in 2011, you also need a super-high-end supporting cast.

Gillis constructed one—and did so under the constraints of the salary cap. Pavol Demitra, Mats Sundin, Mikael Samuelsson, Manny Malhotra, Raffi Torres, and Dan Hamhuis were brought in as free agents on relatively conservative deals, and Vancouver stole Christian Ehrhoff from the San Jose Sharks for a song. It should also be noted that by the time the 2010–11 season rolled around, all of Henrik and Daniel Sedin, Kesler, and Luongo were on contracts negotiated by the Gillis regime, which enabled Vancouver to fill in the depth around their stars.

The trick in the salary cap era isn't just in amassing talent. It's in retaining and fitting all the pieces under the cap. Accumulating elite talent is crucial, but it's also an efficiency contest. It's crucial for contending teams to find a way to provide the top end of their roster with the depth pieces necessary to compete into June.

It's a too-popular notion that Gillis took over a team poised for greatness and just had to sit back and let it happen. But it's a notion that doesn't hold up under any sort of scrutiny. After all, the 2007–08 Canucks were a mess—a team that couldn't score, even with the Sedin twins nearing the height of their powers, and couldn't really defend, even if that particular defect was hidden by Luongo's greatness.

This was a team that apportioned far too much of its salary cap space to players such as Brendan Morrison and Markus Naslund, both of whom were on the wrong side of 30 and had little in the way of suitable depth pieces. Players such as Brad Isbister, Aaron Miller, Ryan Shannon, Byron Ritchie, Lukas Krajicek, and a 37-year-old Trevor Linden played regular minutes for the 2007–08 Canucks (and even some on the power play), and none were long for the NHL.

After Nonis—wisely, to his credit—didn't execute a deal for Brad Richards that would've upgraded the club's scoring at the 2008 NHL trade deadline, the Canucks were still in the race thanks almost solely to their otherworldly goaltending. When Luongo stopped playing like an immortal down the stretch—the Canucks lost six of his final seven starts, and Luongo's dip in performance was blamed on his being preoccupied by his wife's pregnancy rather than on fatigue, despite the fact that he started 73 games that season—the team sagged and missed the playoffs. Enter Gillis and company.

The task ahead was enormous, and Gillis set about building a new management team. He hired Laurence Gilman, promoted Lorne Henning, retained longtime Canucks front office hand Steve Tambellini, and set out to build a durable team that could contend for the Stanley Cup.

Right off the bat, Gillis had a handful of PR nightmares to deal with. He had no intention of re-signing team captain Markus Naslund, who was previously his client, even though Naslund was prepared to make major concessions in order to remain in Vancouver and had said so privately and publicly. "I always envisioned myself retiring a Canuck, and I told Mike that too," Naslund recalled. "I was willing to take a pay cut to stay, but [Mike] didn't feel at the time that he had a spot that made sense for me."

Gillis also made it clear to Linden that he had no intention of returning the storied Canucks captain, who eventually retired in mid-June. And Gillis permitted fan favorite Brendan Morrison to test free agency, making no real attempt to re-sign the long-tenured and locally reared Canucks center.

So when the free-agent frenzy hit, Vancouver's rookie general manager needed a public win. Gillis was still mostly unknown in the Vancouver market, and the dismissal of Nonis was met with widespread recrimination among local media.

As the day unfolded, though, the Canucks were striking out on their primary targets. With a lot of cap space to play with, Vancouver had prioritized adding two or three top-six forwards, ideally players with right-handed shots who might complement the Sedin twins. In particular, they wanted Michael Ryder.

The 27-year-old Newfoundlander was coming off a down year offensively, but he'd twice managed to score 30 goals. Ryder's agent was dragging the club along, though, upping his ask and ultimately insisting on a fourth year on a deal worth roughly $13 million.

With the deal on the table, the Canucks faced a decision. Gillis called everybody in Canucks management into his office and went around the room, asking for everyone's quick take on whether the club should sign the deal. When everyone had expressed their opinion, Gillis thought for a moment. "We're not doing business this way," the Canucks general manager said, according to multiple sources.

Gillis had been on the other side of the aisle for long enough to know Ryder was after a cash grab. (He'd ultimately sign for more than $1 million less in Boston and play a key role in defeating Gillis' 2011 Canucks in the Stanley Cup Finals.) Gillis had made up his mind: he wouldn't overpay for players who didn't really want to be in Vancouver.

Having struck out on Ryder, the Canucks very probably leaked their interest in Mats Sundin and the massive two-year, $20 million contract the club had offered him. They also signed promising St. Louis Blues restricted free agent David Backes, a physical young forward with a right-handed shot, to an offer sheet. The rookie general manager, after all, needed a public win or two.

In retrospect, Gillis' actions in his first few months were telling. The offer sheet to Backes indicated strongly that Gillis cared little for the mores of the old guard of hockey general managers—the Blues would match the deal and retaliate by signing Steve Bernier to an offer sheet of their own. Gillis would ultimately abandon the offer sheet as a realistic player acquisition tool.

The willingness to walk away from Ryder, meanwhile, was suggestive of the way the Gillis regime would prioritize signing players who wanted to be in Vancouver. And the decisions made in respect to Naslund, Morrison, and Linden revealed Gillis was comfortable flying in the face of public opinion, even if—as the likely Sundin leak suggests—he had an awareness of its importance.

Even more telling, there was a conservative, patient approach evident throughout. Gillis knew he needed to flesh out his club's depth, and he knew he needed to find a right-handed shot for the Sedin twins, but he was willing to pass on talent on July 1 and wait for the right deals to present themselves. He'd ultimately complete a trade for Bernier on July 4 and sign Pavol Demitra to a relative bargain contract on July 10.

There was luck involved, but that patient conservatism would serve the Gillis regime well during their stewardship of the

Canucks. This was a club that was always willing to be patient, even earning Gillis the nickname Stay Still Gill. When it came to the Sundin acquisition or the Ehrhoff trade, Gillis' patience served the team well. When the Luongo saga blew up in the club's face, it also ultimately proved to be a double-edged sword. Whatever one thinks of Gillis, there's no denying the record. Gillis earned ownership a lot of money and did a lot of winning during his five-year stint in Vancouver.

84 Vancouver Came Close to Losing the Sedins in Free Agency

It's hard to imagine the Canucks without the Sedin twins, and it's impossible to imagine them wearing any other NHL sweater. Henrik and Daniel Sedin are, without question, the greatest Canucks players of all time. And yet the five-year, $30.5 million contracts they signed in 2009 were agreed to at the buzzer, immediately prior to the opening of free agency. So how close were the Canucks to actually losing them? It depends on who you ask.

"It came really close," longtime Sedin agent J.P. Barry told Bruce Dowbiggin in his seminal work *Ice Storm*. "We had our final meetings at the weekend of the draft in June, and it didn't go well. We were feeling a lot of tension. I told Mike that weekend that we were done, and I was headed to Sweden to prepare for free agency. Negotiations had completely broken down that weekend."

Mike Gillis, however, later characterized the negotiations as hard but almost fated. "We understood the twins were essentially loyal, conservative people whose families liked the Vancouver community and the schools in which their children were registered," Gillis said in retrospect.

It's hard to imagine now, but Barry's recollection of the pessimism surrounding the negotiations at the 2009 NHL Entry Draft in Montreal matches the memory of many among Vancouver's management team at the time. It's true the Canucks wanted to keep the Sedins; it's also true the Sedins always preferred to remain in Vancouver...but it still almost fell apart.

As the hockey industry convened in Montreal in late June 2009, Barry took a meeting with key Gillis lieutenants at the Hotel Nelligan in downtown Montreal. The meeting was acrimonious, a disaster. Barry was left to report to his clients, and Laurence Gilman was left to report to Mike Gillis that it was over, that there would be no deal.

The draft unfolded and the Canucks began to plan for life without the Sedin twins. At that point in the negotiating process, Gillis still hadn't pushed all his chips into the center of the table. He hadn't met with Henrik and Daniel face-to-face. It's unlikely that this was a feint on his part, though.

Following the 2009 NHL draft, the Canucks had an organizational dinner at the now-shuttered Globe restaurant in Montreal, and Gillis was prepared to leave things be. Everyone knew—because Toronto Maple Leafs coach Ron Wilson had effectively said so—that Brian Burke and the Maple Leafs would be hot on the trail of the Sedins, and according to several people who attended that dinner, Gillis was prepared to leave his final offer on the table and otherwise leave it to fate.

At the organizational dinner, Stan Smyl and Gilman pushed for an alternative course of action. Smyl insisted the club needed the twins, that Henrik and Daniel were still on the upswing of their careers despite being in their late twenties. Gilman was bearish on the club's ability to get the twins under contract but suggested it was going to be crucial for the club to do everything in its power to get them signed, not just for hockey reasons but so Gillis could stand up at the podium in the Norm Jewison Media Room at

Rogers Arena on July 1, face the cameras, and tell Canucks fans in good faith that he'd done absolutely everything he could. Gillis was swayed. He would set off to Stockholm, along with Gilman, the club's chief negotiator. They would give these crucial contract talks one last kick at the can.

As fate would have it, Gillis and Gilman boarded the flight to Stockholm and encountered Barry in first class. Not only were the parties on the same flight, they were seated right near each other and passed the flight in conversation. As this particular poker hand came down to the turn, it seems probable that this shared travel arrangement—and the opportunity for a more convivial form of interaction—came as a relief to both sides.

Perhaps it took Gillis going to Sweden, looking the twins in the eye, and explaining his larger plan, but once the two sides finally met—Gillis and Gilman went to a dinner in Stockholm where they expected the twins to be but found only Barry, causing Gillis to exclaim, "We didn't fly all this way to see you, J.P."—a deal that had taken a full year to negotiate began to move quickly.

At a coffee shop in the Stockholm airport and with his boarding time approaching, Gillis explained to the twins his plan to construct the Canucks around them. He explained why their deals needed to be kept reasonable, to leave space to fill in the roster around them. The basis for the below-market deals signed by players such as Ryan Kesler, Roberto Luongo, Alex Edler, and Kevin Bieksa was set at that coffee shop. What Gilman would later refer to as "the covenant" was born.

"The Sedin contract allowed us to create a culture about the team, not individuals," Gillis later said. "We live in a salary cap world. My position with every player is we're going to pay you the most we can within this context. If it gets beyond a context that doesn't let us win, we may have to take a step sideways, but we're determined to have this plan."

Thirty minutes before Gillis and Gilman ran off to catch their flight, the basis for an agreement was done. It would be at least $30 million over five years, with the Canucks subsequently agreeing to move an additional $100,000 per season, which was mostly a good-faith gesture to Barry and the twins.

With Henrik and Daniel locked in and the basis for cooperation between Canucks stars and management now set, the team could turn their attention to Luongo.

85 A Doomed Extension: The Luongo Contract

Roberto Luongo is the greatest goaltender in Vancouver Canucks history. It's a fact, pure and simple. There was nothing simple about Luongo's Canucks tenure, though. In Vancouver, Luongo was perhaps a victim of his own success. He was so good and so reliable while holding down such a heavy workload in the regular season that expectations were always sky-high down the stretch and into the playoffs. When things went sideways—such as when a far superior Anaheim Ducks side eliminated the Canucks in 2007, or when the club sagged down the stretch while the media described Luongo as distracted by the impending birth of his child in 2008—the blame always fell disproportionately on Luongo's shoulders.

In the fall of 2009, not long after the Sedin twins had agreed to their five-year contract extensions with the Gillis regime, Luongo signed a lifetime pact with the Canucks organization. The deal ended years of speculation about whether Luongo would leave in free agency and the term and dollar amount were stunning: a 12-year contract worth $64 million that would take Luongo through age 42.

"We were [initially leery] of signing a lifetime pact," Luongo recalled. "It was a big commitment, and we know how pro sports work. Things change and things happen.... Even though we wanted to stay in Vancouver...you can never know what can happen in sports. There is always somebody younger and faster and better trying to take your job. At the end of the day we made the right decision for ourselves and we took it, but there's always that doubt in the back of your mind that you never know."

According to multiple sources, Luongo's side was most concerned about the annual average value of his deal at first. Both sides recognized that Luongo should be paid more on average than the twin $6.1 million cap hits possessed by both Henrik and Daniel Sedin, and the fateful 12-year deal Luongo signed was a compromise of sorts, a contract that permitted the club to pay Luongo more than $6.1 million over an extended period of time but without the negative salary cap ramifications.

The NHL wasn't pleased. The back-diving tail on Luongo's contract—he was only due to make $7 million over the last four seasons of the deal—was technically legal but circumvented what the league believed to be the spirit of the 2005 collective-bargaining agreement. Tense telephone calls between executives from the league office and the Canucks front office were exchanged. In fact, nearly a full year after the extension was announced, the league threatened to de-register the contract in the wake of their decision to reject Ilya Kovalchuk's initial "cheater" deal with the New Jersey Devils, though a settlement between the NHLPA and the league resulted in Luongo's contract being "grandfathered" in.

Ironically the league's reaction to the Luongo contract seems altogether quaint now. Nine years after agreeing to that controversial 12-year extension, Luongo remains a high-end starting goaltender, and his $5.33 million cap hit is a relative bargain considering the reliability of his performance.

Though Luongo was now a Canuck to stay, questions lingered in the Vancouver market as to his ability to win in the postseason. Losses to the Chicago Blackhawks—a burgeoning NHL dynasty—in the 2009 and 2010 postseason were pinned on Luongo, despite the fact that Vancouver iced an objectively inferior club in both series.

The notion of Luongo as a player who struggles in the post-season is central to this narrative, but the fictional element of this widespread belief should be noted (and debunked). In his career Luongo has posted a .919 save percentage in regular-season play and a .918 in the playoffs. His 2.49 goals-against average in the regular season matches his 2.49 goals-against average in the playoffs to the second decimal point.

In 2011 the Canucks, the best team in the league by a fair margin, drew the Blackhawks once again in the first round. It was a brutal draw, made possible only because the Dallas Stars had coughed up a third-period lead to the Minnesota Wild in the final game of the regular season. The 2011 Blackhawks had seen some of their high-end depth gutted by a series of off-season trades the previous summer, but their underlying numbers suggested they were the second- or third-best team in the West, a much stronger side than your typical eighth seed.

Despite Chicago's overall quality, Vancouver jumped out to a 3–0 series lead and seemed set to cruise by their tormenters of playoff series past. Then things began to fall apart. The Canucks were blown out in Game 4. Game 5 was over before it began. Suddenly, with Game 6 set to go in Chicago, the pressure was back on the Canucks. And when the teams took the ice for the warm-up skate in Game 6, it became apparent that backup Cory Schneider was getting the nod ahead of Vancouver's $64 million man.

"We had a meeting and I was told I wasn't starting," Luongo recalled. "It was tough. I'm a competitor, and I wanted to be in there, but the thing that calmed me down the most was talking to

[Canucks goalies coach Rollie Melanson] that evening, or the next morning at the skate, and he was just telling me that it was a one-game thing and that if we won I was going to start the next round and if we lost I'd be back for Game 7. That calmed me down and helped me refocus on just being ready."

Game 6 was a game for the ages. Vancouver outplayed the Blackhawks, but Chicago capitalized off two puck-handling errors by Schneider and tied the game at three when Michael Frolik beat Schneider with a dramatic penalty shot goal. The play left Schneider injured, and he later admitted the injury was, in part, a physiological reaction to the stress of the situation. Luongo, having been told he wouldn't start, entered a tied game with a chance to advance, but the Blackhawks managed to win in overtime when Ben Smith scored off a Marian Hossa rebound.

Game 7 against Chicago would come to represent the pinnacle of the Gillis era, and Luongo—for all the doubts about his big-game ability—turned in a performance for the ages. Luongo was pitching a shutout late into the third period when Jonathan Toews scored a backbreaking shorthanded goal with less than 90 seconds to play. For Luongo skeptics it was another dubious data point, but Luongo rallied in overtime, making a crucial stop off a Patrick Sharp one-timer from the slot. Luongo's timely save permitted Alexandre Burrows to play Dragon Slayer.

"Game 7 against Chicago for some reason—and I don't know if it was the history we had against that team—but that game, the way it ended, the excitement, you saw how we all went crazy after we won that," Luongo recalled. "There was more excitement after that game than after the gold medal win [in Vancouver], I think, based on how my teammates responded after the goal was scored. It built up to such a high level of intensity that once we scored, it was just madness."

With the Blackhawks in their rearview mirror, Vancouver stormed through the balance of the Western Conference on their way to the 2011 Stanley Cup Finals, and Luongo provided sturdy goaltending—a series of unlikely Nashville Predators bank shot goals aside. In the finals against Boston, though, Luongo struggled in his three road starts and gave up two early goals in Game 6 that Canucks fans won't soon forget.

Luongo, once again, shouldered a disproportionate share of the blame for the club's loss in the playoffs. That he recorded two shutouts in the series and received eight goals of total offensive support in seven games didn't seem to matter.

Though Vancouver's starter was assured Schneider's start in Game 6 in Chicago was a one-game thing, it turned out to be a taste of what was still to come. The next year, after the Canucks fell behind 3–0 to the eventual 2012 Stanley Cup champion Los Angeles Kings in their first round series, the Canucks once again swapped out Luongo and went with Schneider.

It was at this point that Luongo approached Canucks management and informed them that he'd be willing to waive the no-trade clause on his contract in order to facilitate a trade to either the Florida Panthers or the Tampa Bay Lightning. "I saw the writing on the wall after that series, and I don't blame them at all," Luongo said. "Schneider was younger and great, and he played unbelievably. He was cheaper also, so it made sense for them to go in that direction. Originally I asked Mike if he could see if either Florida team would be interested in [trading for me]. There's a lot of twists and turns, and there's a lot of different people with different sides to the story."

Indeed there are. Canucks management contends that in the summer of 2012 there were two real opportunities to trade Luongo—at the 2012 NHL Entry Draft in Pittsburgh, and in the hours before the expiry of the 2005 CBA in mid-September. On both occasions, according to myriad reports and sources, Luongo wasn't willing to waive his no-trade clause to go to the Toronto Maple Leafs.

Luongo's side of the story differs in some crucial respects. "I was asking Mike that before [doing a deal with another team] that [he] try and make sure there [was] nothing to be done with a Florida team first," Luongo explained.

"For some reason the draft came and went and nothing happened. I'm not sure exactly what happened on their side of it, because I don't know the whole story. I didn't say no to the other teams, but I said if [they] could look at whether or not something could be done with [the Florida teams] first and foremost, I'd appreciate it, then some lies were told, and that's how it went down through that draft." And so the situation dragged on. And on. And on.

"I thought it would happen that first summer," Luongo recalled. "I didn't think there was any way I would be back for the next training camp, let alone three more."

The decision not to deal Luongo during the summer of 2012 would prove disastrous for Canucks management. Though Gillis left the 2012 NHL Entry Draft talking about the likelihood of a late-summer trade market developing (which, in fairness, did come to pass with the Rick Nash trade and the apparent Maple Leafs offer in September), when the Canucks went into the 2012 NHL lockout with Luongo still on the books, they took a massive risk. They had no way of knowing what things would look like on the other side.

When the lockout was resolved and the 2013 NHL CBA rolled out, it included a retroactive device—the salary cap recapture clause—designed to punish teams such as the Canucks for signing deals like Luongo's. A contract that was already likely to prove difficult to move was now officially a toxic asset, and Vancouver's leverage was gone.

As the lockout-abbreviated 2013 season unfolded, Luongo was relegated to a backup role. To the credit of both goaltenders, they remained close, professional, and supportive of one another while constant drama unfolded around them. In an untenable situation, the two elite netminders combined to form a tandem that provided Vancouver with consistent blue-chip goaltending.

By the time the 2013 NHL trade deadline hit, Luongo's trade watch was in its 10th month. The salary cap recapture rules had dinged Luongo's value substantially, and as the saga dragged on inexorably, the list of teams Luongo was willing to accept a trade to expanded. By this point in the process, he was more than agreeable to pressing *send* on a deal that would send him to the center of the hockey universe. He never got another opportunity.

In the days following the NHL lockout, the Maple Leafs changed management. Brian Burke was fired and Dave Nonis, the man who brought Luongo to Vancouver originally, replaced his longtime associate. It was widely believed that Nonis might push harder for Luongo than his predecessor. In fact, it's likely the window for a possible Luongo deal to Toronto shut with Burke's dismissal.

At the 2013 NHL trade deadline, the Maple Leafs and Canucks were engaged in talks for Luongo, and a deal seemed close enough that Luongo was pulled off the ice at Vancouver's practice. Speculation ran wild, with multiple Canadian sports networks carrying the feed from Rogers Arena. And then the deadline passed, the alarm proved false, and as the dust settled, Luongo remained in Vancouver.

Frustrated and emotional, Luongo was left to give a press conference at the podium in the Norm Jewison Media Room. "My contract sucks—that's what's the problem," Luongo said, diagnosing the issue. "I'd scrap it if I could now."

And as sports editors across the hockey world got set to wood with "my contract sucks" headlines, intimate details of the trade talks between the Canucks and the Maple Leafs materialized. After months of posturing about their ask, it was revealed by TSN's

Darren Dreger that the Canucks were willing to deal Luongo to Toronto in exchange for Ben Scrivens and a pair of second-round picks (one of which would've been shipped instantly to Arizona for Raffi Torres).

Dreger had the entire back-and-forth. His reporting portrayed the Canucks as lowering their asking price for Luongo the closer the clock got to noon Pacific time. Jason Botchford, meanwhile, would later report that the Maple Leafs insisted the Canucks retain a portion of Luongo's contract but waited until the waning moments to do so.

Vancouver's goaltending controversy seemed played out by this point, but in fact it wasn't even entering its third act. Late in the 2013 season, the Canucks were pulverizing the Blackhawks on home ice when Brandon Saad deked past Alex Edler shorthanded and skated in all alone for a breakaway chance on Schneider. His deke caused Schneider to hyperextend from side to side, and Schneider sustained an injury with only a few games remaining before the playoffs.

Luongo got the start for the Canucks in Game 1 of the fateful series against the San Jose Sharks, but the club tapped Schneider—who still wasn't fully recovered—after losing the first two games at home. Luongo wasn't even surprised to get the hook by this point, even if the decision provoked endless second-guessing among the media and Canucks fans.

"By that point Schneider was the starter," Luongo said. "We lost the first couple games of that series even though I thought I played pretty well, so it was a desperate time for the team. Schneider was ready to go. I expected it more than the first time around. I knew that Schneider was back, [though] he wasn't quite 100 percent, and I just tried to be ready."

For a second consecutive NHL Entry Draft, Luongo's status was the talk of the draft floor. The "will they or won't they" had reached Ross and Rachel proportions. As Vancouver's management team convened in Manhattan to discuss their approach to the draft, they sifted through the offers on Luongo. There just wasn't much of value to be had in trading the star goaltender. Though Gillis would say that weekend that he knew he would be keeping Luongo from the moment he read the 2013 NHL CBA, it's likely something did materially change during organizational meetings that weekend in New York. The decision was made to hold an auction for Schneider.

The 2013 NHL Entry Draft was stacked, with many prospect analysts touting it as historic. If the Canucks were going to sell Schneider, they wanted a top 10 pick, and three teams in the top 10 had a need for a goaltender: Calgary, Edmonton, and the New Jersey Devils.

Loath to do a deal with an Alberta-based team, Vancouver completed a deal with Lou Lamoriello and the Devils the night before the draft, after Edmonton and Calgary balked at paying the "regional rival" premium the Canucks asked for. The deal would be announced on the draft floor, which the Devils were hosting at the Prudential Center in Newark, New Jersey.

On the morning of the draft, Luongo was set up in his Fort Lauderdale home, preparing to take it all in. He was hoping that finally, at long last, his 15-month stint on the trade market would come to an end. Then his phone rang. It was Canucks owner Francesco Aquilini.

"Francesco called me, and he might have been in New Jersey, but he called me to tell me that he was coming to Florida and he wanted to talk to me," Luongo recalled. "For some reason I didn't ask why. I thought he just wanted to talk about what was going to happen in the near future and what was going on with my situation and how we were going to handle it.

"So he arrived at my front door right as the draft was starting. He sits down in my living room and the draft was on TV, and he said, 'Hey, can you turn that off for a second there so we can talk?' At that point we were a few picks into the draft. So he starts talking, and as he's talking, all of a sudden he tells me that they've traded Schneider.

"I swear to God as he's telling me, my cell phone is in my pocket, and it starts vibrating every five seconds. It's blowing up. My jaw just dropped. I couldn't understand why that happened; it didn't make sense to me at all."

It didn't make sense to many in the hockey world, even though the trade for Schneider—which returned the ninth overall pick that became Bo Horvat—would work out decently well for the Canucks in time. In the moment, it was seen as a rough day for the organization, and Gillis gave a zoo of a press conference, his comments mostly inaudible, at the press railing on the draft floor.

A three-and-a-half-hour flight south, in Fort Lauderdale, Luongo and Aquilini talked for hours. Luongo couldn't believe it. He couldn't reconcile that after all that, after being replaced in three consecutive first rounds and then usurped outright as the starter, the Canucks had decided to trade Schneider instead.

"He was just trying to make me realize that they wanted me in Vancouver, and I just kept explaining my situation and the whole thing," Luongo recalled.

Months of radio silence followed. Luongo didn't comment on what had transpired to the media. His silence was well deserved. It also said everything that needed to be said.

86 Cap Management Was a Crucial Part of the Success of the 2010–11 Team

Entering the summer of 2010, the Gillis era Canucks had extended their core and were now entering their practical window to go all in. The Sedin twins were locked up at a reasonable clip—a preposterously reasonable clip, actually, considering how they performed during the first year of their new contracts—and lucrative new extensions for Roberto Luongo ($10 million in salary for 2010–11 with a $5.33 million cap hit) and Ryan Kesler ($5 million in both salary and cap hit) were about to kick in.

In the spring of 2010 the Canucks were still smarting from their second consecutive elimination at the hands of the Chicago Blackhawks, a team that would win the first of their three Stanley Cup championships that June. In that fateful 2010 series, a historically deep Blackhawks side laid waste to Vancouver's back-end depth. Sami Salo was hurt in that series when he took a Duncan Keith shot to the genitals, and when Alex Edler went down with an injury in Game 6, it was as good as over.

In typical Canucks fashion, the 2009–10 team used 12 defensemen and struggled to replace Willie Mitchell when he sustained a concussion on an Evgeni Malkin hit in midseason. The acquisition of Andrew Alberts at the trade deadline provided depth but didn't move the needle.

Entering the summer of 2010, Gillis and company were determined to build the deepest blueline possible within the parameters of the NHL's $59.4 million salary cap. With raises kicking in for Luongo and Kesler, and a raise due Mason Raymond, who'd put together a career year in 2009–10, and significant needs on the blueline—it would be an extraordinarily tight fit.

The Gillis regime, with Laurence Gilman and John Wall handling the bulk of the capologist duties, walked a tightrope all year. With luck and cunning, they threaded the needle. It remains perhaps the most stunning and sophisticated bit of hockey management in the history of the Canucks franchise.

And it began in June 2010. The apple of the Canucks' eye going into that off-season was free agent Dan Hamhuis, a hybrid-type shutdown defender capable of keying the rush. The club had discussed the possibility of acquiring Hamhuis in a trade at the 2010 NHL trade deadline, but when David Poile and the Nashville Predators insisted on Cody Hodgson, the Canucks balked. It was felt internally that the Canucks were Hamhuis' preferred destination anyway.

Signing Hamhuis was far from a guarantee, though, particularly as his rights were shopped around prior to free agency. The Predators dealt his negotiating rights to the Philadelphia Flyers in late June, and the Flyers recouped those picks by shipping Hamhuis' negotiating rights in-state to the Pittsburgh Penguins when Hamhuis wouldn't sign. Vancouver's gambit would pay off when Hamhuis, determined to play in his native province, spurned the Penguins and hit the open market.

As the 2010 NHL Entry Draft rolled around, the Canucks needed insurance and needed to replace the heavy minutes burden Mitchell seemed likely to vacate. And the Florida Panthers were conveniently shopping a tough, fast defenseman who seemed to fit the bill.

The 2010 Panthers were in the process of clearing salary cap space and accumulating future assets. Former Canucks defenseman Dale Tallon took over as Panthers general manager in May of that year, and he was about to embark on a scorched-earth rebuild that would see him jettison pricey veteran assets such as Keith Ballard, Nathan Horton, Gregory Campbell, David Booth, Michael Frolik, and Stephen Weiss in relatively short order.

Tallon's first order of business was accumulating draft picks and clearing salary cap space. At the 2010 NHL Entry Draft he sold Horton to Boston and Ballard to Vancouver. The Canucks aggressively bid for Ballard, sending Michael Grabner, Steve Bernier, and a first-round pick—conditional between 2010 or 2011, based on which players were still on the board—to the Panthers.

In Ballard the Canucks had solidified the left side of their blueline. Now no matter what Hamhuis did, they would go into the 2010–11 season with a projected top four of Alex Edler, Christian Ehrhoff, Kevin Bieksa, and Ballard, with Shane O'Brien, Aaron Rome, and Sami Salo as enviable depth pieces. When the club added Hamhuis on July 1 for $4.5 million, they looked to have the deepest defense corps in hockey—which was really the entire point. The club also signed defensive center Manny Malhotra, a necessity if they hoped to match up with teams such as Chicago.

Vancouver's blueline, center, and goaltending depth was now elite. This appreciable depth came at a cost, though, and the Canucks were already—as of July 1, 2010—over the upper limit of the NHL salary cap.

NHL teams are permitted to exceed the salary cap during the off-season, so Gillis and company had time. Time was always a resource you could expect them to use. It was widely believed the club would trade defenseman Kevin Bieksa that off-season, but throughout the draft and throughout the summer, the club waited. They held firm in negotiations with Jannik Hansen and Mason Raymond, the latter of whom filed for player-elected arbitration.

Then the Canucks got lucky. On July 22, while playing floor ball—a sport that's similar to but distinct from floor hockey—in his native Finland, defenseman Sami Salo ruptured his Achilles' tendon. It was an injury that would cost the veteran defender six months, and present the Canucks with a significant opportunity they wouldn't waste.

There is perhaps no more complicated a mechanism in the NHL's collective-bargaining agreement than long-term injured reserved (LTIR). The salary cap is calculated on a daily basis, and when a player is on injured reserve for at least 10 games, a team can place him on LTIR, which—in its simplest terms—permits the club to exceed the salary cap by the same amount as the value of that player's contract. Alex Burrows had shoulder surgery in June, which had provided the Canucks a little bit of wiggle room already, but with Salo and his $3.5 million salary hitting LTIR, the Canucks had a real solution to their cap issues.

It's almost certainly not a coincidence that the Salo injury coincided with the Canucks getting back to business in the summer of 2010. On July 22, the same day Salo got injured, the club announced a one-year agreement for $825,000 with Jannik Hansen. Four days later they avoided arbitration with winger Mason Raymond by agreeing to a two-year deal worth $5.1 million. The combined cap hits of Raymond's and Hansen's deals totaled $3.375 million, or nearly equal to Salo's $3.5 million.

The Canucks would make one more significant move prior to the opening of training camp, signing Raffi Torres to a one-year, $1 million deal. The reliable (if predatory) depth forward consistently scored goals at a top-six rate throughout his career and jumped at the opportunity to rebuild his value on a contending team.

Entering training camp, then, the Canucks were $3.6 million over the upper limit of the salary cap and in fact were carrying closer to $9 million in surplus salary above and beyond the $59.4 million cap.

As training camp unfolded, the Canucks were busy on the trade market. The deals were seemingly minor but were in fact crucial for a team with limited wiggle room under the salary cap. On October 5 the club swapped Shane O'Brien and Dan Gendur for Ryan Parent and Jonas Andersson in a trade that saved the club about $700,000 in cap space and permitted them to swap out an entry-level contract (which can add complications for teams in LTIR) for a standard one-way deal.

The very next day, October 6, the club dealt enforcer Darcy Hordichuk for enforcer Andrew Peters. The deal ultimately wouldn't save anything off the cap, because Peters never spent a single day on the 23-man roster, but it was still cap motivated. If the Canucks needed a tough in the lineup, Peters' deal counted for $250,000 less against the cap and would be easier to fit in.

October 6 was a key date for another reason too. It was the final day the Canucks could make moves before setting their opening day roster. The team made a baffling series of cuts that day, sending Cory Schneider, Alex Bolduc, and Jeff Tambellini—three players who had very clearly made the team—to the Manitoba Moose, while keeping three players who clearly weren't going to play on opening night in Eddie Lack, Cody Hodgson, and Lee Sweatt on the roster.

While Vancouver media covered the moves in a baffled sort of fashion, the logic of these moves was simple. A team is able to maximize their ability to spend LTIR space the closer they are to the upper limit of the NHL salary cap when LTIR is invoked. Sweatt, Hodgson, and Lack counted for $1 million more against the cap than Tambellini, Schneider, and Bolduc, which gave the Canucks even more precious room to maneuver.

Vancouver's actions in this case caused rival teams to complain of circumvention, and the rules were changed thereafter. Not for the last time the Gillis era Canucks had stretched the rules of the collective bargaining agreement to their breaking point, and going forward NHL teams would have to play at least one game with their opening night roster before engaging in such shenanigans.

With their roster pressed to the brim against the upper limit of the salary cap, the Canucks likely placed Salo and Burrows on LTIR (it's possible one was on LTIR during the summer). Burrows would, in eyebrow-raising fashion, return to the Canucks lineup precisely 10 games later.

Two days later the Canucks returned Lack, Sweatt, and Hodgson to Manitoba and recalled Tambellini, Schneider, and Bolduc. They also swapped out another entry-level deal (Sean Zimmerman) for an easier to manage and similarly priced contract (Nathan Paetsch). For the 2010–11 Canucks, the devil was in the details.

Once the season began, things became a little bit simpler, but only a bit. Until Salo's return the Canucks were likely to be fine, particularly because their depth pieces—Joel Perrault, Guillaume Desbiens, Rick Rypien, Tanner Glass, Peter Schaeffer, Andersson, Tambellini, and Aaron Volpatti—all had similar cap hits. The club had to be careful, as they were within spitting distance of the upper limit, but Gilman stayed on it.

In late November the NHL and the Canucks granted Rypien, who had laid hands on a Minnesota Wild fan, an indefinite leave of absence. Though Rypien remained on the Canucks payroll, the Canucks were given cap relief by the league—who were determined, to their credit, to do the right thing by a player struggling with significant mental health issues.

As Vancouver rolled to the top of the NHL standings, they sustained a smattering of injuries. Mason Raymond went down in December and went on LTIR for a stint, as did Kevin Bieksa and Andrew Alberts ahead of the NHL trade deadline. The big break for the Canucks was when Alex Edler left a game in late January and went under the knife to manage a herniated disc issue in his back.

Edler's injury and the necessity of placing him on LTIR permitted the Canucks to activate Sami Salo, who made his season debut on February 12. If they couldn't before, now Gilman and Wall could sleep at night.

There was a good deal of luck involved in the timing of Salo's injury and then Edler's, but Vancouver had also made their own luck by being disciplined and shrewd in the way they organized the roster. And not all their luck was good luck.

On February 5, 2011, the Canucks attempted to reassign Lee Sweatt to the American League, only to have the league void that attempt on February 7. Sweatt was due to be reassigned but had become popular thanks to a dramatic game-winning goal over the Nashville Predators during his recall. The club allowed him to practice one last time with the team, and at that practice, he took a shot off his foot and broke it. He was due his NHL salary for the rest of the season and couldn't be reassigned. Sweatt would hit LTIR by the trade deadline, but this bit of happenstance cost the Canucks somewhere in the neighborhood of $600,000 in cap space.

That $600,000 might not seem like much, but the Canucks were under the cap by the skin of their teeth, and every bit counted. By the 2011 NHL trade deadline, the Canucks were clearly the team to beat, and they wanted to bolster their fourth-line depth—the only nagging issue that management saw as holding the club back.

Early in the morning on February 28, 2011, the club agreed to a deal with the Anaheim Ducks that wasn't announced until much later in the day. The trade sent a third-round draft pick and Joel Perrault to Orange County in exchange for Maxim Lapierre and an AHL contract. Lapierre was on a $900,000 contract and was seen as an upgrade over the likes of Perrault, Bolduc, and Hodgson, though as fate would have it, he ended up playing key third-line minutes for the Canucks during the 2011 Stanley Cup playoffs.

In the waning minutes before the deadline, the Canucks were still looking to add fourth-line depth and were in talks with the Panthers for Chris Higgins. Higgins was injured at the time, but the medical staff suggested he'd be back in time for the playoffs, which was all the Canucks cared about. Florida, however, had roughly equal offers on the table from both Vancouver and the Flyers. Ultimately Florida agreed to ship Higgins and his $1.6 million salary to the Western Conference in exchange for Evan Oberg and draft picks.

Even with Alberts, Edler, Sweatt, and Bieksa on LTIR at the time of the deadline, the Canucks had more than $68 million in salary committed against a $59.4 million salary cap upper limit. Thanks to a year's worth of insanely complicated salary cap gymnastics, the team came out of the deadline with roughly $27,000 in total salary cap space, or less than $1,000 clear of the daily upper limit, according to the indispensable reporting work done by the late Matthew Wuest. This was despite the club having added more than $2.5 million worth of cap hits to the books on deadline day.

Because the salary cap doesn't count come the postseason, Vancouver could have played that tournament with a roster that cost nearly $9 million more than should have been permissible under a salary cap system. It took a cheater contract for Luongo, a smattering of no-trade clauses, and some immense management creativity, but the Canucks had set a new standard for maximizing roster value in a cap system during a contending team's competitive window.

Unfortunately, injuries to Malhotra and Mikael Samuelsson prevented the Canucks from ever icing their optimal roster during a 2011 Stanley Cup playoff run that fell just short. Acquired to bolster the club's fourth line, Higgins and Lapierre ended up playing top-nine minutes as Vancouver rolled through the Western Conference.

Move by move, Canucks management put together a master class throughout the 2010–11 season. Fate, Zdeno Chara, and Tim Thomas would intervene, but no contending team has ever gone into the postseason with as much surplus salary above and beyond the salary cap as the 2010–11 Canucks did.

87 How Newell Brown and the 2010–11 Canucks Changed the Way Teams Enter the Zone on the Power Play

At the height of the Mike Gillis era, expectations for the Vancouver Canucks were sky-high. After the team fell short in the second round of the Stanley Cup playoffs for a second consecutive season in 2009–10, the team decided to prioritize center depth, blueline depth, and improving their special teams play.

The first two areas were of genuine concern. Vancouver's lack of blueline depth was fatal against the Blackhawks, with Shane O'Brien playing top-four minutes after Alex Edler and Sami Salo were injured. The Canucks' lack of quality center depth was similarly exposed in games against the Blackhawks when Kyle Wellwood occasionally logged more ice time than Henrik Sedin.

Vancouver's special teams, though...well...they were pretty good. The penalty kill finished the 2009–10 season as a below-average unit overall, but the club was above average in shot prevention and finished in the top five in shot-attempt prevention. The power play, meanwhile, converted on better than 21 percent of their opportunities with two balanced units manufacturing a good deal of offense with the man advantage.

For Alain Vigneault and Canucks management, though, a great power play and a solid penalty kill simply wasn't good enough. Canucks higher-ups believed the travel demands placed on the team were unique and that without icing an elite special team side, a Vancouver-based club didn't have a chance at performing like an elite club on the road. It was resolved that the club would rethink their approach to special teams.

Enter Newell Brown. Brown was actually an eighth-round draft pick of the Canucks organization back in 1982, but he never made it to the NHL as a player and hung up his skates in the late 1980s to try his hand at coaching. After stints at two Michigan-based universities, Brown coached Detroit's AHL affiliate in the early 1990s before catching on with the Chicago Blackhawks as an assistant. He picked up a few more things during stints in Columbus and Anaheim, where he was an assistant coach to Randy Carlyle when Anaheim won the Stanley Cup.

When the Ducks' fortunes—and their penalty kill—sagged during the 2009–10 season, the club opted against renewing Brown's contract. That meant he was available when the Canucks went searching for an assistant coach to replace Ryan Walter, who they fired in the spring of 2010.

"The speed of the game and their style really appealed to me," Brown recalled. "It was in my wheelhouse. I was really excited. They were one team that I thought would be a good fit for my style.

"I knew that it was going to be a big challenge and that the bar was going to be set high," Brown continued. "The power play was fourth in the league the year before I arrived, and nobody was happy with it."

Brown's task was significant, but he had two tricks up his sleeve. The 2009–10 Canucks were an offensive juggernaut and managed to outscore every team in the Western Conference despite missing Daniel Sedin for 14 games. Their fourth-ranked power play was a big part of that, and attacked teams with two potent units.

The first unit included the Sedin twins with Alex Burrows (though Steve Bernier and Mikael Samuelsson got some looks as well) up front and were most often deployed with Alex Edler and Christian Ehrhoff on the blueline. The second unit was most frequently composed of Mikael Samuelsson, Ryan Kesler, and Mason Raymond up front, with Kevin Bieksa and Sami Salo on the back end (though Pavol Demitra would occasionally operate from the point as well). Oddly enough, the Kesler, Samuelsson, Raymond group outscored the Sedin, Sedin, Burrows group by 11 goals on the power play that season.

While the ideal of "balance" is often pursued in a team sport such as hockey, the power play is a different beast. The man advantage is a timed exercise, and efficiency is everything. Brown decided he'd be best served by loading up on his first unit and playing Kesler with the Sedin twins.

"I felt that if you could do that and really get good chemistry… then that's the way to go because it's way more potent," Brown explained. "You may not get two balanced units, but if you have the five best players on your team finding some chemistry, then the end result will be a more productive power play overall."

Replacing Burrows with Kesler on the first power play unit also had the advantage of giving the Sedin twins a right-handed shot to work with, even if Kesler was to be the designated net-front guy. The Sedin-led 2009–10 unit was most frequently composed of five left-handed shooters, which dramatically limits a team's ability to make forehand-to-forehand passes on the breakout and to create one-timer opportunities on in-zone play.

Even so, with Ehrhoff and Edler—two left-handed shooters—manning the point on the first unit, Brown needed his loaded first power-play unit to be a bit flexible and creative in order to create better shooting opportunities. In Henrik and Daniel Sedin, he had the perfect pieces to install such a system. "What we tried to do is that we had Henrik and Daniel play both sides of the ice, which created a different dynamic," Brown said. "We felt that good hockey players could make good plays, even if they might make slightly better plays on their strong side. We felt it made us difficult to pre-scout and created a lot of confusion. We were able to set up plays from both sides of the ice and work behind the net, on the half wall on both sides, and that created a lot of confusion for penalty killers."

In contrast with the relatively stationary 1-3-1, or overload, setups that are so common these days, Vancouver's 2010–11 power play was built on a more fluid system that required players to rotate and read the Sedin twins' cycle game more instinctively. Ehrhoff, Edler, and Kesler became masters at moving around to find soft areas in coverage, and the Sedin twins found them repeatedly.

Even so, Brown always believed the power play needed another right-handed shooter, and when Edler went down to have surgery on a bulging disc in his back, he promoted Samuelsson to the first unit. The four-forward look with the twins, Kesler, and Samuelsson, and Ehrhoff on the points, formed perhaps the most potent power-play group in Canucks history. "When Edler went down and Samuelsson joined the first unit, our power-play percentage went up because of the two right-handed shots," Brown recalled.

While the loaded first-unit approach paid dividends for the Canucks in 2010–11, one of Brown's other ideas came to fundamentally change the way NHL teams get set up on the power play. From Brown's time in Columbus, he recalled Dave King using a set breakout in five-on-four situations that called for a forward (or two) to trail the puck-carrying defenseman through the neutral zone. The defenseman would read the penalty killer's coverage and could, if he elected to, drop the puck back to a forward following closely (and with speed) behind him.

"It became our staple breakout," Brown recalled. "The guys, whenever we talked about it, they'd say, 'If we do this right, they can't stop us.' It suited the twins well because they're really good at skating the puck in and not so good at dumping it in and chasing it. But we conserved a lot of energy because they found a smart way to skate it in."

The neutral-zone drop pass became a whipping boy among some Canucks fans, partly because when the opposing team managed to break it up, it made the offensive players look pretty foolish. When it worked, though—and it worked most notably on Ryan Kesler's "beast mode" goal during the club's second-round playoff series against the Nashville Predators—Brown and the Canucks' power-play personnel looked brilliant.

If the set neutral-zone drop bothered Canucks fans incessantly, the rest of the league took notice. As the Sedins embraced and found clever new ways to utilize the play—eventually Vancouver would start to drop both Henrik and Kesler behind the puck-carrying defenseman, forcing teams to cheat to such an extent that the initiating blueliner could simply pass the puck to Daniel, open on the left-side blueline, where he'd step over the line uncovered and gain the zone—the rest of the league caught up and started to copy Brown's set entry.

"I learned as much from the twins [as they learned from me], I assure you," Brown said. "It was more about all of us working together. They love to talk about hockey, they have a great passion, especially when it comes to the power play. We took the drop-pass breakout to the next level because they had some great ideas about how to use it, and I think it kind of became a template for other teams to copy thereafter."

The results speak for themselves. Over the past 10 seasons only four teams have managed to generate goals at a higher rate over the course of a full 82 games than the 2010–11 Canucks did at five-on-four. And those four teams all share a common trait: they all employed Alexander Ovechkin, who is hockey's version of the atom bomb.

88 Slaying the Dragon

The Mike Gillis era Canucks had their fair share of tough opponents, but there was one team that thoroughly and consistently tormented them unlike any other: the Chicago Blackhawks.

This torment largely hinged on results, but it went far beyond wins and losses. Did the Blackhawks beat up on the Canucks? Yes. Did the Blackhawks often do it in dramatic fashion? Yes. Did the Blackhawks emerge as the team to beat? Yes.

But Vancouver's issues with Chicago went deeper. They cut to the core of the team and the city, putting their collective psyche in a box labeled *fragile*. Essentially, the Blackhawks owned a large chunk of real estate in Vancouver's head for the better part of three years, thanks in no small part to the following:

- In 2009 the Canucks blew a 2–1 series lead and were bounced out of round two. In the deciding Game 6, Patrick Kane erupted for three of Chicago's seven goals, all of which came against a bewildered and beleaguered Roberto Luongo. Afterward, with reporters gathered and television cameras rolling, Luongo pulled his baseball cap low to his eyes and muttered, "I let my teammates down. It's going to take a while to get over." Then he broke down and cried.
- In 2010 the two teams met in the second round (again), and Chicago wiped out Vancouver in six games (again). Luongo was ventilated in the elimination tilt (again), but this time, instead of crying, he opted to go the sarcastic route. "I'm going to leave tonight with my head up," he said. "Not like last year. I battled for 60 minutes and kept it under seven goals, so improvement was made."

- Chicago's goal song at the United Center, "Chelsea Dagger" became a rather unpleasant earworm for the Canucks. Global BC, a local TV station, went so far as to queue up "Chelsea Dagger" on an iPod, make the Canucks listen to it, and film their responses.

  "Worst song in hockey," said D-man Kevin Bieksa. "I don't even want to listen to it anymore. I was in the press box last game in Chicago, and I heard it six times—and I was cringing every time. So we all know about that song in this room—and we all hate it."
- In 2011 super-pest Dave Bolland went on a local Chicago radio show and mocked the Sedins. "Well, they'll never become Hawks," Bolland said. "I don't think we'd let them on our team. That'd probably be one thing. We'd be sure not to let them on our team.

  "And yeah, they probably still would be sisters. I think they might sleep in, like, bunk beds. The older one has the bottom one, the younger one's got the top."

  The Canucks almost immediately replied to Bolland… or stooped to his level, depending on how you look at it. "When you have comments like Bolland's, he's obviously an individual whose IQ is probably the size of a bird seed," Alain Vigneault said. "And he has a face that only a mother could look at." Mom jokes!
- There was also that time Alex Burrows got lambasted for pulling Duncan Keith's hair during a fight. There was also that time Dustin Byfuglien scored a hat trick. There was also that time Jonathan Toews scored a hat trick. There was also…ah, you get the point. There were lots of times.

The catharsis for all this appeared to have arrived in the spring of 2011, when the top-seeded Canucks drew a weakened Chicago team—visibly tired from the previous year's Cup run and minus several key players due to a salary cap crunch—in the opening playoff round. There were two specific trains of thought on this. One saw the Hawks as the perfect opponent, a mental hurdle the Canucks could and would overcome en route to the first Stanley Cup in franchise history. It would be perfect, really.

The second school of thought was in direct contrast. These folks were straight-up terrified at the prospect of facing Chicago in round one.

Those adhering to the first school of thought were loving life early in the series. Vancouver jumped out to command a 3–0 lead in the series, and the demon was all but exorcised. Just one problem: Vancouver didn't finish the job in Game 4. Didn't finish in Game 5, either. Or Game 6.

The Hawks stormed back to win three straight by doing what they'd always done—rattling the Canucks, getting in their heads, and convincing several Vancouverites that maybe, just maybe, the Hawks couldn't be beat. What's more, Chicago's usual suspects were up to their old tricks, making the pending collapse all the more painful. Bolland, just months removed from his remarks about the Sedins, made his series debut in Game 4 and promptly scored four points. Marian Hossa caught fire. So did Keith. And just like they had so many times in the past, Chicago got after Luongo—to the point where, following an ugly 5–0 home loss in Game 5, Vigneault benched his longtime No. 1 in favor of Cory Schneider.

Schneider, as if cognizant of the drama, proceeded to cramp up in Game 6, forcing Luongo *back* into action, where he lost in overtime. Which set up Game 7.

Vancouver's nerves going into the final contest were beyond frayed. Three straight losses, the Luongo-Schneider drama, and Chicago's confidence—now sky-high—set the stage for a game in which everything was on the line. Win, and the Canucks would exorcise their biggest demon. Lose...well, most didn't want to think about that.

Game 7 was, as expected, an incredibly tight and hard-fought affair. Burrows staked his claim for hero status by scoring less than three minutes into the opening frame, but that was it for goals for the majority of the evening.

In the third, some of Burrows' luster was knocked off when he failed to convert on a penalty shot, which would have all but salted the game away.

Then the Hawks decided they had one more dramatic turn. With less than two minutes remaining, and while shorthanded—Keith had taken a late hooking penalty—the Hawks evened things up when Toews converted on a scramble in front of Luongo. To call it a gut punch would be unjust to guts…and punches for that matter. It felt like a catastrophic blow. The Canucks were 1:56 away from finally beating Chicago. And now they were off to overtime.

Just 24 seconds into the extra frame, Burrows nearly became the goat. He took a holding penalty on Keith, and the Hawks responded to the ensuing power play like there was blood in the water, and nearly ended it when Toews' cross-crease pass found Patrick Sharp all alone, staring at an open net.

Sharp, a right-handed shot on his off wing, fired quickly…only to see the puck batted away by Luongo, who slid across to make arguably the biggest save of his career. It was a nice bit of redemption for Luongo, who'd had a nightmarish series. And redemption would soon become a prevalent theme.

Having avoided the ignominy of being "the guy who took the penalty that lost us the series," Burrows came back out for a shift a short while later. Circling the offensive zone, he intercepted a Chris Campoli clearance with his right hand, batted it down to his stick, and found himself alone against Hawks goalie Corey Crawford.

Burrows wound up and fired a slapper high on Crawford's blocker side. Crawford waved at the puck and missed. It went in. Bedlam ensued.

"They've slayed the dragon!" cried Canucks play-by-play man John Shorthouse. "Alex Burrows, 5:22 into overtime! Game 7 goes to Vancouver, and the Canucks are off to the second round!"

Burrows' teammates poured off the bench for a ceremonial mobbing, while the GM Place faithful roared not just in approval but in relief as well. This was the game their team needed to win, and win they did—regardless of how it got done.

"It's great, a great feeling," Burrows said following the game. "It felt almost like it was a dream, but guys jumped on me and I couldn't breathe, so I knew it was right."

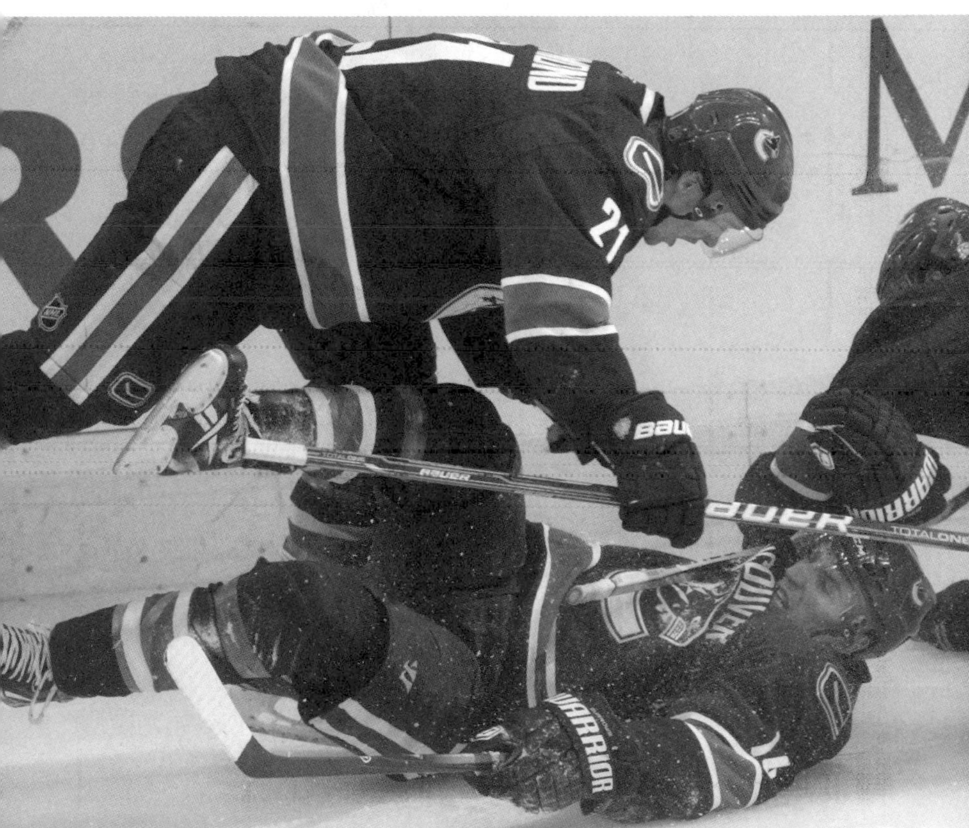

Burrows (bottom) and teammate Mason Raymond celebrate slaying the dragon.

89 How Did "Slay the Dragon" Come to Be?

In the aftermath of the Burrows goal, much was made of John Shorthouse's now-famous Slay the Dragon call. It has taken on a life of its own. When Rogers Arena celebrated its 20th anniversary, the goal was named the top moment of all time, and the call has become an unforgettable catchphrase among Canucks fans. Which begs the question: how did Slay the Dragon come to be?

"On the last day of the season, there were...myriad...possibilities of who the Canucks might play in the first round," Shorthouse explained. "They were coming off second-round losses to the Blackhawks in 2009 and 2010, and Chicago was only one of the possible teams they could've faced in the first round. And I think there were mixed emotions among the fan base. There was a faction of it that said, 'Bring on the Hawks, let's do this right, let's exorcise some demons and roll our way through the playoffs by getting that first dose of momentum by beating the team that's beaten us two years in a row.'

> Then there was a faction of people that were petrified of having to play Chicago again, and wary of the emotions that would come with bowing out of the playoffs to the same team in the same manner. So the season ended, and the final game scores were in, and the standings were decided, and the Canucks were playing Chicago in the first round.
>
> Among the messages I had and e-mails I got was one from a buddy in L.A. The subject line in his e-mail was 'Time to Slay the Dragon.' But I hadn't really thought of it. I hadn't made it something that I was definitely going to work in.

> But when the series ended—and the way the series went, with the Canucks going up three games to none, the feeling that the series was home and cooled, Chicago with its lineup tweaks and big goals and comeback, forcing Game 7—when the final puck finally went in, that e-mail just kind of popped into my head. It summed up the emotion of the entire fan base and the organization.
>
> Finally, they could exhale and know that they had vanquished this team that had ended their seasons two years in a row. So it just felt like they had exorcised a demon—and that was the line [CBC's play-by-play man] Jim Hughson used on TV, 'It's a wonderful day for an exorcism'—and I wound up going with 'They slayed the dragon.'

Though he's never actually spoken to Burrows about that particular call, Shorthouse has talked to numerous others about it. It's become one of the defining moments of his play-by-play career, which has stretched over the course of two decades in both radio and television.

For Vancouver supporters, it's one they'll never forget.

Shorthouse continued, "I remember going to L.A. the next year, and there were some Canucks fans standing outside [the] Staples Center. They'd made up T-shirts with a depiction of Burrows with a sword in his hand, taking the head off a dragon.

"It wasn't anything that I knew was going to grow into something, but it just seemed like something that captured the mood of the community—that finally they had been able to do away with Chicago, which had caused them so much misery for two years running."

Sure, exorcising demons might've been the flavor du jour. But Canucks fans will always remember it as the day they slayed the dragon.

90 Beast Mode

Hockey, by nature, isn't a game that lends itself to the individual. To play the game and be successful requires teamwork—this according to, well, basically everybody and anybody involved with it. Coaches will tell you the whole has to be greater than the sum of its parts. Players will tell you they've got to play together. GMs will tell you nobody can whistle a symphony—it takes a whole orchestra to play it (well, the more verbose GMs will tell you this, anyway).

Yet on occasion hockey does become a one-man show. Like in 2011, when Ryan Kesler carried the Canucks to a second-round victory over the Nashville Predators.

First, an overview. Vancouver beat Nashville four games to two to advance to the Western Conference Finals, and despite not going the full seven games, the entire series was remarkably tight. Five of the six contests were decided by a single goal, two went to overtime, and one went to double OT. The Canucks scored 14 goals in the series. The Predators scored 11. There was very, very little difference between the two.

But there was one key difference: Vancouver had Kesler. Nashville didn't. "[Kesler played] six of the most incredible games you will ever see," Predators head coach Barry Trotz said, following his club's ouster. "He just had one of those series that is absolutely remarkable for one player."

Trotz's words spoke volumes. Nashville was the prototypical lunch-bucket team, one that relied on stout defense and sound goal-tending to grind out results. They'd dispatched the 2007 Stanley Cup champion Anaheim Ducks in the opening round—the first playoff series win in Preds history—and often embodied Trotz's personality;

he was a tough, no-nonsense guy who had been the club's first and only head coach since its inception 14 years earlier.

So what exactly did Kesler to do elicit such praise? He finished with 5 goals and 11 points in just 6 games. That means Kesler was in on 11 of Vancouver's 14 markers over the course of the series (for you mathletes out there, that's 78 percent of Vancouver's *entire offense*).

He averaged just fewer than 25 minutes per night over the six games, which included a whopping 33:43 in a double OT loss in Game 2. That night, Kesler played more than all but two of Nashville's 18 skaters (only minute-munching blueliners Shea Weber and Ryan Suter were out there more). Two of Kesler's five goals were of the game-winning variety. He won more than 100 faceoffs (a 59 percent success rate), fired 24 shots on goal, dished out 16 hits, and recorded 12 takeaways.

"I think it created a legend that was impossible to live up to," longtime *Vancouver Province* scribe Tony Gallagher recalled. "He was so good in that series."

In short, Kesler went Beast Mode.

At this time, it's probably prudent to explain that roughly one year before Kesler's heroics, the city of Vancouver became somewhat enamored with the exploits of another one-man wrecking crew—Marshawn Lynch, the powerhouse Seahawks running back who plied his trade for Seattle, Vancouver's I-5 neighbor just a couple hours south.

There are hordes of Seahawks fans up north, to the point where, in 2014, the *New York Times* dispatched a reporter to investigate "Seahawks mania" in Vancouver. (The big takeaway? That there was, in fact, Seahawks mania in Vancouver.) Lynch may have resonated more with Vancouver's hockey-crazed denizens than any other Seahawk. And that's because of Beast Mode.

The term became synonymous with an individual athlete—in this case, Lynch—taking things over, often through sheer physical force. Lynch's signature moment was an unforgettable 67-yard playoff TD run in 2010, in which he essentially ran through the entire New Orleans defense, aptly referred to as the Beast Quake. It was thusly named because during the play Seahawks fans celebrated so loudly it registered on a nearby seismograph. The response to Kesler's effort against Nashville didn't register on the Richter scale, but it certainly made waves across the NHL.

The Stanley Cup playoffs are largely a war of attrition. The whole thing is a grind. Battles become fiercer, checking becomes tighter, and when one guy heats up, there's often an immediate effort to cool him off—be it through physically shadowing him, taking liberties after the whistle, increased stick work...or a combination of the three. It's a violent time.

The way Kesler fought through all this was, well, Beast Mode–ish. Tales of him gritting through pain against the Preds, and into subsequent series throughout those playoffs, were often bandied about, and there was a certain awe that Kesler didn't just fight through the pain—he almost thrived on it, taking on more ice time, a bigger role, and raising his game as things became more difficult.

"I thought as I said as I was going by him [in the handshake line], *If he doesn't play that way, we're probably going to Game 7 and we might win the series,*" Trotz lamented after the series loss. "He played to a level that few people can reach."

91 Bieksa, the Stanchion, and the Guy Who Saw It All

Given the Canucks have never won the Stanley Cup—a fairly focal narrative in this book, as you might have noticed—it's can safely be said that three of the biggest goals in franchise history were the ones that *got* them to the finals: Lars Molin against Chicago in 1982, Greg Adams against Toronto in 1994, and Kevin Bieksa against San Jose in 2011.

Now, let's clarify. Molin's goal was historic but hardly dramatic—the third in a 6–2 win. For some, Adams' marker is still the greatest ever, because of the opponent (the hated Leafs) and the call (as outlined in our earlier chapter).

Ah yes, the call. A crucial element of any famous goal. And that's certainly the case with Bieksa, because with his tally comes a very unique distinction—nobody saw it coming. Quite literally. Nobody. Saw. It. Coming.

The short version is that, in double overtime of Game 5 with the scored tied 2–2, Vancouver was one goal away from beating San Jose and moving on to its third-ever Cup Finals. Midway through the OT session, Alex Edler, trying to keep play in at the blueline, fired the puck off the glass—a routine move except for the fact that, rather than rim around the back of the net, the puck hit a stanchion and bounced *backward* out to Bieksa, who was standing at the blueline.

With nobody looking—including Sharks goalie Antti Niemi—Bieksa quickly knuckled the puck on goal and past Niemi, sending the GM Place faithful into hysterics. Niemi wasn't the only one caught off guard by the sequence. Nearly everyone calling the game on radio and television—had no idea what they had just seen, and they were left grasping, trying to explain the situation. But one guy caught it: John Shorthouse, the Canucks' longtime play-by-play man.

"Deflects back to Bieksa. He scores! Kevin Bieksa! 10:18 into overtime, the double overtime goal! And the Canucks, for the third time in their history, will play for the Stanley Cup!"

Here's his recollection of that unforgettable marker:

> There are times when a game ends and you know a certain call was a tough one, and you can feel good or bad about getting it right or wrong. Like, say, if a shot hits the crossbar but it really hit the back bar, and the red light doesn't come on and the referee doesn't motion, but you know it was in, and you call it that way—*that* feels good. Because you know that was a tough call.
>
> In terms of Bieksa, when the game ended, I had no clue that it had been a difficult call. I don't know if that's because of where I was situated—in the [broadcast] gondola—but I never lost sight of the puck. Which I realized afterward, pretty well everyone else did, and didn't understand what had happened.
>
> I saw [the puck] come clearly back to the blueline, but I thought it had been hit with a high stick. I didn't realize it had hit a stanchion. And I saw Henrik Sedin kind of tapping his head, which usually means the puck went out of play. So he thought the puck had gone over the glass, but from my angle I saw it come clearly back to Bieksa, and I knew in the moment—out of the corner of my eye—that among the people that had no clue where the puck was... was Antti Niemi.
>
> I knew as the rolling puck came back to Bieksa that if he got it on goal, it was likely going to go in, because Niemi was looking the completely wrong way. And lo and behold, that's what happened. The puck wobbled back off the glass to Bieksa, and he just hammered it on net, and before

> anyone knew what had happened—and most importantly, before Antti Niemi knew what had happened—the puck was in, the comeback was complete, the double OT win was final, and the Canucks were on to the Stanley Cup Final.

Shorthouse said he didn't have anything planned or premeditated for the moment—"I've never really worked that way," he explained—but soon realized his call was going to forever stand out because, y'know, he actually got it right.

"If you go into a game thinking *Here's what I'm going to say*, it's a whole lot different than, say, if the team you're covering is up 6–1 and you've got a solid minute to weave a fabulous tale about what this means to the community and to the organization. You have a chance to unleash some soliloquy, because the result of the game is decided.

"A lot of the time it's not. It might be in overtime, like [Bieksa]. I've always been the sort to say whatever pops into my head. Whether or not I'm any good at it or have a gift for it, that's for others to decide, but I've never really worked with the thought of, *Oh, here's what I'm going to say if such-and-such happens.*

"Once people got home and were able to sample the two national broadcast calls—both in Canada and the US—and the local San Jose radio call, I got few messages of 'Good job' and 'Way to pick it up.' I guess the coolest thing is that NBC didn't have a lot to choose from, so I wound up being the voice of their Stanley Cup Final promo."

92 Everybody Hates Vancouver

Heading into the 2011 Cup Finals, there were questions, all legitimate, about how much animosity there was between Boston and Vancouver. Some asked if there was any at all. The history of Vancouver-Boston relations could have been printed on a single-sided pamphlet, with plenty of white space. There was no rivalry, sporting or otherwise, between the two. Geographically, they were pretty far apart. And their lone meeting that season came and went without incident—a forgettable late-February affair featuring just five minor penalties.

Then the series started. And three important things happened.

1. In Game 1, Alex Burrows was accused of biting Patrice Bergeron but wasn't suspended.
2. In Game 3, Aaron Rome knocked out Nathan Horton with a devastating body check, and was suspended for the remainder of the series.
3. After posting a shutout in Game 5, Roberto Luongo complained that his goaltending counterpart, Tim Thomas, didn't talk him up to the media. "I've been pumping his tires ever since the series has started," Luongo said. "I haven't heard one nice thing he has to say about me."

By the time all this happened, two things were abundantly clear: One, Boston and Vancouver didn't like each other. Two, a whole lot of people *really* didn't like Vancouver.

Boston, expectedly, was quick to show disdain. Which made sense—the Canucks were standing in the way of the city's first Stanley Cup in more than 40 years, and the Burrows and Rome incidents were like gas to a campfire. The more this series resembled an alley fight, the better suited the Bruins were to win it. Boston was ready to embrace the hate and did exactly that.

But a funny thing happened as the series progressed. Those feelings of hatred extended well beyond Boston. Canucks loathing was everywhere, and coming from all directions.

NHL on NBC analyst Mike Milbury called the Canucks "smug, arrogant," and referred to Daniel and Henrik Sedin as "Thelma and Louise." Cathal Kelly, a sports columnist from the *Toronto Star*, said the Canucks would be "the least deserving champions in NHL history." The *National Post*'s Joe O'Connor put together a seven-point list of why Canada shouldn't jump on the Canucks bandwagon, which included "The two dudes in the green bodysuits who hang out near the penalty box in Rogers Arena." (More on them later!)

It didn't stop there. Players *watching* the Cup Finals teed off on the Canucks too. From veteran NHLer Ryan Whitney, appearing on a Boston radio show: "[Vancouver] is so easy to hate it is unbelievable.... I'd say that 90 percent of the guys in the league want nothing to do with seeing them win." And longtime Canucks enemy Dave Bolland said, "It sucks seeing them there. Typical, pulling hair and biting people. Sort of like a little girl...stuff like that isn't meant for hockey."

Now, look. The cases of Burrows v. Bergeron, Rome v. Horton, and Luongo v. Thomas didn't create the "I hate Vancouver" narrative. The team had plenty of enemies prior to that. But these incidents certainly provided a framework for the hate, and simplified things for those new to watching (or hating) the Canucks. Burrows was dirty, Rome was a cheap-shot artist, and Luongo was a whiner. They embodied three chief characteristics the Canucks were being pilloried for.

And to be fair, the Canucks certainly had their share of unlikable players. Burrows was considered one of the biggest pests in the league, and if he wasn't, it could have easily been his Vancouver teammate Maxim "Yappy Lappy" Lapierre. Ryan Kesler had a nasty disposition and surly personality. Raffi Torres was known as one of the NHL's worst headhunters. But all teams have their antagonists. Boston certainly did. And this is where things got interesting.

People weren't slotting Vancouver and Boston into the "bad guys vs. good guys" dichotomy—in fact, many fans and media didn't even like the Bruins. In that same piece where he said Vancouver would be the least deserving champion in NHL history, Kelly added, "That's not to say Boston deserves it any more." Folks weren't necessarily cheering for the Bruins. But they were cheering *against* the Canucks.

It was a weird development, to say the least. Throughout their history, the Canucks were known mostly for losing, and when the occasional good team surfaced, it was of the Cinderella variety—like that plucky 1982 team or that scrappy 1994 club. Nobody hated Vancouver, because there wasn't much to hate.

The 2011 Finals were different. That team developed a reputation that was impossible to shake, and the media played a huge role in that. One of the most fascinating facets was how players—such as the aforementioned Whitney and Bolland—began bad-mouthing the Canucks to anyone with a microphone, recorder, or paper and pen.

Even long after the series was done, players weren't done hating those 2011 Canucks. Following his retirement, Bruins forward Mark Recchi—who hailed from British Columbia!—had one final parting shot. "In 22 years they are the most arrogant team I played against," he said. "And the most hated team I've ever played against."

93 The Best-Laid Plans: Mitchell, Ballard, Baumgartner, and the Decimation of the Canucks Blueline

The hockey gods work in mysterious ways, and have a nasty habit of ironic cruelty. In constructing a 2010–11 Canucks team that was arguably as dominant from poll to poll (at least until Game 7) as any team we've seen in the salary cap era, Mike Gillis and Canucks management prioritized defensive depth. They believed the rigors of playing on the far West Coast of North America was particularly difficult on defensemen, and they went shopping with durability in mind.

"If you want to build a team that has a chance, you've got to have depth on the blueline," Canucks assistant general manager Laurence Gilman said in 2013, though the quote is instructive as to the overall approach of the Gillis-led management team. "When we set out to build the team, we built our model with eight defensemen on the NHL side, but we also sought out players who were going to be 9th, 10th, 11th guys who had the ability to play in the NHL."

In the summer of 2010, Vancouver bolstered their blueline with the acquisition of Keith Ballard from the Florida Panthers and Dan Hamhuis, a free agent who wanted nothing more than to sign in Vancouver and spurned more lucrative offers in the Eastern Conference to get to July 1. Ballard and Hamhuis were both mobile, left-handed defenders with "shutdown" reputations, but they shared another crucial trait: they were among the most durable big-minutes defensemen in hockey.

From 2005 until 2010, Hamhuis averaged 81 games per season. He was an everyday kind of defenseman. Ballard averaged 79 games per season, giving him a similar profile. Meanwhile the Canucks allowed veteran defender and fan favorite Willie Mitchell to walk in free agency. Mitchell sustained a significant concussion on a brutal Evgeni Malkin hit the previous season, a concussion so serious it kept him away from the bright lights of the hockey rink into the off-season. Factoring that concerning injury in with myriad other nicks, cuts, sprains, and bruises a hard-hat player such as Mitchell inevitably sustains over the course of an 82-game season and he'd averaged fewer than 69 games per season between 2005 and 2010.

Perceived durability was a key reason the Canucks opted to sign Hamhuis and trade for Ballard rather than returning Mitchell. And for most of the 2010–11 season, Vancouver's blueline depth held. The team won the Presidents' Trophy despite using 13 different defensemen. When the 2010–11 playoffs began, Vancouver had the likes of Ballard, Sami Salo, Aaron Rome, and Andrew Alberts—credible NHL defensemen all—occupying "depth roles."

The best-laid plans of the Vancouver front office paid off in the 2010–11 season right up until the moment it unraveled. And it unraveled at the worst moment, in the most painful possible way.

It began in the Western Conference Finals, when Christian Ehrhoff sustained an injury on a big hit by San Jose Sharks forward Jamie McGinn. McGinn's injury forced the Canucks to use Chris Tanev in a high-profile situation, and fortunately, the unsigned draft pick proved up to the task.

In Game 1 of the Stanley Cup Finals, Hamhuis—one of hockey's most consistently durable defensemen—threw an ill-advised hip check at Boston Bruins apex predator Milan Lucic and tore his groin. It was clear immediately that he'd miss the balance of the series.

No matter, the Canucks managed to win Game 1 with a late Raffi Torres goal, and in Edler, Ehrhoff (hurting but still effective), Salo, Rome, and Bieksa, the Canucks still employed five defensemen Alain Vigneault trusted to log big minutes. Andrew Alberts was inserted into the lineup for Game 2 and fared poorly, but not disastrously, in limited run.

Game 3 was the fateful contest during which things really began to get dire for Vancouver. Early in the game, Aaron Rome checked Nathan Horton with a high, late hit as the big Bruins winger crossed the blueline. Rome was assessed a misconduct, and the Bruins took over the game in the second period, on their way to a decisive 8–1 romp that fundamentally altered the series.

Rome was just a depth guy, but when the league decided to levy an unprecedented penalty and suspend him for the rest of the Stanley Cup Finals, that proved catastrophic for Vancouver. Ehrhoff was still playing hurt, Bieksa and Salo were right-handed shooters, Andrew Alberts couldn't be trusted in more than short bursts, and Vigneault had lost all trust in Keith Ballard. Vancouver was down to three healthy defenders who Vigneault trusted.

It was at this point that Vancouver got a bit desperate. The team had used 13 defensemen during the 2010–11 season, but most of their defensive depth was extremely green. With Hamhuis and Rome out and Ehrhoff playing well below 100 percent, the Canucks needed additional insurance. They needed a veteran farmhand who they hadn't called up once—despite using players such as Ryan Parent, Yann Sauve, Lee Sweatt, and Evan Oberg—all season. They needed Nolan Baumgartner.

Baumgartner was 35 years old at the time. Though he was only six years removed from a season in which he'd led all Canucks defensemen in scoring, he'd played only 63 NHL games in the intervening years. It was to be his last NHL call-up.

"I was down in California with my wife and family," Baumgartner recalled. "We rented a house down there for a month, just to have vacation in Laguna Beach, and I remember getting a call and the name wasn't coming up on my phone, but it had a California area code. So I just ignored it and never answered it.

"Well, it was Lorne Henning trying to call me, and I knew that some of our trainers with the Moose were up in Vancouver. I got a text from one of them saying to check my phone messages. So

I check, and it's Lorne Henning telling me, "Hey, we're going to call you up, so you have to call me right away.' You can imagine my shock."

The journeyman defender didn't have much time to pick his jaw up off the ground. He had to get to Vancouver so he might be ready for Game 5 if it came to that. And it was beginning to look like it might.

A dedicated athlete, Baumgartner had never taken more than a week to 10 days off following a season. But now at 35 years old and a family man, Baumgartner had taken off about a month. He wasn't remotely in game shape.

"Now I'm getting called up into the Stanley Cup Final, going into Game 4.... The next day I went onto the ice and skated for the first time in [a] month, and from not doing anything, well, you can imagine how that felt. I was nervous thinking about, *What's going to happen here?*"

As Baumgartner watched from a Vancouver hotel room, things went from bad to worse for the Canucks in Game 4. The club lost 4–0, and Ballard, a perpetual resident of Alain Vigneault's doghouse, was personally victimized on two Boston goals. A giveaway behind Vancouver's net on a second-period Brad Marchand goal all but sealed Ballard's fate. The Canucks coach declared to management after the game that he simply couldn't justify using Ballard again in the series.

The dam held for the Canucks in Game 5, as Salo, Bieksa, Ehrhoff, and Edler logged big minutes and held the fort in a gutty 1–0 win at Rogers Arena. Game 6, however, was a different story. In a vicious game best remembered for the incident in which Marchand "speed-bagged" Daniel Sedin, Edler broke two fingers in a slashing incident and Andrew Alberts left the bench for a stretch during the game. Watching in the Boston press box, Baumgartner began to entertain the idea that he might actually play in Game 7.

"[Canucks management] came to me and said, 'Look, you're going to practice with us tomorrow, and we'll see what unfolds on game day,' Baumgartner recalled. "At that point I was in shock, thinking, *Man, this actually might happen.*

"It would've been crazy if that had happened and we would have won. You have all these crazy things going through your head like, *There's a chance I'll get my name on the Stanley Cup*. I told my wife that if I played and scored, I'd retire right then and there, because I couldn't have topped it."

At practice prior to Game 7, Baumgartner took rushes on a pair with Kevin Bieksa. If Edler couldn't go, Baumgartner would be in. A team built with blueline depth in mind had been reduced in bodies to the point where this was a genuine possibility. Ultimately Edler played through two broken fingers in a 4–0 Game 7 loss that no Canucks fan, player, or executive will ever forget.

As the conflagrations began in downtown Vancouver, Canucks management was left with a million what-ifs. The one that loomed largest was the way the club's defensive depth had been torn asunder by a confluence of factors, including the playoff grind, an unprecedented suspension, and the head coach's steadfast refusal to use the club's prized trade acquisition from the summer previous with immortality on the line.

Which brings us back to Willie Mitchell. Less than one year following Vancouver's Game 7 loss to the Bruins, the veteran stay-at-home defenseman who was not unreasonably deemed expendable in the summer of 2010 because of concerns about his durability would hoist the Stanley Cup. Logging top-four minutes for the champion Los Angeles Kings, Mitchell would appear in 96 games, including every playoff game the Kings played.

If the hockey gods didn't have a cruel and ironic sense of humor, they'd have no sense of humor at all.

94 The Riot, Part Two

It all started in the Rogers Arena press area. In the aftermath of Vancouver's disheartening 4–0 loss in Game 7 of the 2011 Stanley Cup Finals, TVs in the media lounge were tuned to the podium, where a variety of Bruins discussed what they'd just accomplished.

For the uninitiated, this type of player availability is a fairly key cog in the postgame media machine. Reporters, often working on deadline, are either transcribing quotes from guys on the podium or, in certain cases, literally inserting quotes into their gamers while players are still speaking. Suffice it to say many folks are reliant upon those TVs.

So it seemed kind of odd when, seemingly out of nowhere, the TVs all cut away from the podium to a local news broadcast—to show what was transpiring outside.

Prior to Game 7, city organizers arranged a makeshift fan viewing zone stretching nearly two blocks in length. Buoyed largely by positive experiences during the 2010 Olympics—similar fan zones had been orchestrated with minimal issue—organizers propped up big screens and prepped for what they hoped would be a fun, historic gathering to watch the Canucks capture their first-ever Stanley Cup.

By game time, an estimated crowd of 100,000 flooded the streets of downtown Vancouver, many bypassing the (admittedly minimal) security checkpoints for alcohol and other prohibited items. Police were present, but the number of those patrolling the area was inadequate for a crowd of this size—especially if the crowd got unruly. And that's exactly what happened.

During the media TV cutaway, it was pretty obvious something had gone wrong outside. Though hardly earth-shattering,

Kiss Off

We'd be remiss if we didn't mention *the* enduring image of the riot—"the Kissing Couple."

Alex Thomas and boyfriend Scott Jones were the subjects of said picture, captured by Getty's Richard Lam. The photo depicts the pair on the ground, locking lips in a tender embrace, while the riot rages on around them.

Jones later explained that Thomas had been knocked to the ground by police and was "a bit hysterical" from all the commotion. He went to the ground to comfort her, which is when Lam snapped his unforgettable photo.

The image instantly went viral. *Sports Illustrated* called it the "most compelling sports image of the year," and it went on to win the 2011 National Newspaper Award for news photography. A year later, English rock band Placebo used the picture as the cover art for their album *A Place for Us to Dream.*

So in a weird, roundabout way, something good did come from the riot.

the first image on the media room televisions was symbolic—a Canucks jersey, set ablaze, lying on the edge of Georgia Street. Then cameras panned up and down Georgia. Vancouver was in the midst of a riot.

Having been in the GM Place media room and quickly exiting said room to retrieve a vehicle from the adjacent parking lot, here are some recollections of that disastrous night:

The initial scene outside was absolute chaos. It was one thing watching it on TV and another to be walking through it. You've got to remember, Georgia runs through the heart of the city, and there are all these grandiose, important buildings running adjacent: GM Place, BC Place, Vancouver Public Library, Canada Post headquarters, the CBC Building, the Queen Elizabeth Theatre, and the Hudson Bay building. It's really the epicenter of downtown Vancouver, and it was in total disarray. Just lit up, right in front of my eyes.

The crowd was really young. Lots of teenagers and twenty-somethings, many who'd been drinking for hours and had this pent-up anger coursing through their veins. Plus there was the looming specter of the 1994 riot, which a bunch of people were wearing like a stupid badge of honor. "This is what we do when we lose a Cup. We riot!" That sort of thing.

By the time I retrieved my car, so many were hell-bent on violence and destroying whatever they could. Rioters were quickly figuring out there weren't nearly enough police to stop them from doing whatever they wanted, and they kept upping the ante. There was a police cruiser parked next to us, and a pack of 5 to 10 kids—who looked like hyenas—were taking turns jumping on top, stomping out the lights, booting the windshield. The crazy part is none of them ran away afterward. One kid would lay the boots to the car, jump off, then stick around to see how much more damage the next kid could cause.

There were fights everywhere. One count had "at least" four people stabbed, so clearly some of the rioters showed up on the scene tooled up, ready to cause damage. This was when the mob mentality stuff really got scary. There were Good Samaritans trying to intervene in particular incidents who were soundly beaten by a group of rioters. And again, just not enough police to deal with it all.

Cops were, of course, trying everything they could to slow it down: tear gas, pepper spray, flash bombs. But they were so woefully outnumbered, and rioters were just powering through it all. Kids would be hacking on the fumes, gagging to the point of puking, then wipe their faces and throw rocks through a storefront window. Or try to set a police cruiser on fire.

In the end, the riot left a black mark that took years to erase, one many contend will never go away. National and international media coverage ripped the city and riot participants, while also expressing slight amusement that a city such as Vancouver—remember, one that successfully hosted *the Olympics* without incident—could become so completely unglued over the result of a hockey game.

Locally, embarrassed officials poured countless hours and resources into their investigation. Some of the findings were shocking: it was believed that as many as 155,000 people—far more than initial estimates—congregated downtown, and that the area was only adequately fit to contain roughly one-third of that.

Losses due to vandalism, theft, and damage to property were believed to be between $4 and $5 million, and after a four-year investigation, police announced there would be 887 charges laid against 301 people.

95 Become the Next Famous Superfan

In 2009 Ryan Sullivan and Adam Forsythe were a pair of twenty-something journalism students looking to break into the industry. Some way, somehow. Then fate intervened, in the form of *It's Always Sunny in Philadelphia.*

While binge-watching the FX cult comedy, the pair's interest was piqued by a character portrayed by *Always Sunny*'s Charlie Day—in which a not-so-sober Day dons a full-body, green, spandex suit and begins dancing outside the Philadelphia Eagles' practice facility. Not long after, Sullivan and Forsythe ordered their own green suits, with the goal of wearing them to a Seattle Seahawks game.

Just one problem—only one of the suits arrived in time. By the time the second showed up, Sullivan and Forsythe were left with green spandex suits, but nowhere to wear them. So hey, why not a Canucks game? The two were big fans, and Sullivan knew someone who could get seats next to the visitor's penalty box. Tickets secured and spandex donned, the pair made their way downtown for a late-December matchup against the Nashville Predators.

That's when fate intervened again. This time in the form of Dave Scatchard. Scatchard—a former Canuck, ironically enough—took a cross-checking minor in the first period, earning him a seat in the box next to Sullivan and Forsythe. And that's when the two began gyrating and gesticulating wildly, each movement pronounced by the tightness of their outfits. Fans went wild. Scatchard looked unamused, if not bewildered.

In the second period, Scatchard was back in the box, but this time he had a plan—he tossed a white towel over the penalty box camera, thereby denying an important shot of the dancing green spandex guys (and his reaction to said dancing).

With just seconds remaining in Scatchard's penalty, the Canucks scored. Sullivan and Forsyth celebrated. The crowd erupted. And with that, the Green Men—Sully and Force—were born.

"The first game was just ridiculous," Sullivan recalled. "Afterward we're seeing on Twitter and Facebook that people are going crazy, and then we went to the Roxy [a Vancouver nightclub institution]. We show up in these spandex suits, and the guy at the door goes, 'Oh, I saw you guys at the game! Get in here; that was hilarious.'

"We went home and the next morning woke up, and the phone was ringing off the hook. CBC wanted to interview us, Sportsnet wanted to do stuff. We did an interview with Global, then TSN, then ESPN. To this day I don't think we have any idea why it went as wild as it did, but it just started going nuts."

Forsythe said he recalls the Green Men shtick catching on immediately. "When we went down to the seats, security came down and said, 'If you act out, if you do anything out of sorts, we're kicking you out.' They were very hostile toward us," he said.

"But by the end of the game, they were coming up and asking for photos with us."

Part of the Green Men's allure was their anonymity. Sullivan and Forsythe kept their identities a secret. They were masked up, referring to themselves only as Sully and Force, and nobody knew exactly what they *were*. Some assumed it was a viral marketing campaign. Others suggested the Canucks hired them to antagonize the opposition. An alien invasion theory was floated.

Nobody knew who the Green Men were, or what their purpose was, but it quickly became apparent that whatever they were doing, they were good at it. They had choreographed bits, clever props, elaborate skits, and the physical dexterity to do handstands. Which, if you've never seen a grown man in a spandex suit do a handstand, it is quite the sight to behold.

Their antics kept people guessing. There was no way the Canucks were in on this, right? "The Canucks were kind of hesitant with it for a while, but we had an official-unofficial relationship with each other," Sullivan explained. "Official in the sense that we knew each other, we knew the marketing team, and we'd do the best we could to be ambassadors. But we were never officially with the team by any means.

"And it kind of worked out well—we couldn't say we were 'with' the team, but then the team really couldn't filter what we were doing, because if they made it G-rated, it would take away from it."

The Green Men certainly didn't mind taking risks. Their most notable stunts include:

- In (another) game against Nashville, Mike Fisher sat in the penalty box while the pair caressed a cardboard cutout of his wife, country music star Carrie Underwood.
- They put the face of Edmonton's Taylor Hall onto the body of a donkey.

- They superimposed a Canucks jersey onto a life-sized picture of actor Vince Vaughn, a huge Chicago Blackhawks fan.
- They wore Burger King masks for a game against the Kings.

Through their first two years, the Green Men became synonymous with the Canucks. And when the club went on its run to the 2011 Stanley Cup Finals, Sully and Force were there as well, crisscrossing North America to make guest appearances in *visiting* rinks, not just GM Place.

The pair met Keith Urban and Nicole Kidman in Nashville, and had a press conference in downtown Vancouver announcing they were being shipped off to Boston for the Cup Finals.

"It was wild; 2011 was super cool for two guys in college that didn't have a dime to their name. It was pretty awesome," Sullivan said.

Much like the team they rooted for, the run didn't end well for the Green Men. At TD Garden for Game 3 of the series against Boston, the pair weren't in their usual penalty box seats—they were about 20 rows up, and unable to get a good vantage point when Canucks D-man Aaron Rome knocked Bruins forward Nathan Horton out cold with a thunderous check. Horton was unconscious, lying prone on the ice. The Green Men were unaware, and thought it was a good check. They cheered. Whoops.

"People just turned on us," Forsythe said. "Throwing stuff at us. For the rest of that game, they had three in-uniform police officers standing in our row, protecting us. With about three to four minutes left in the game, they turned to us and said, 'Hey, boys, we gotta get you outta here safely. Let's go.'

"We followed them, and they took us into the first-aid room, then let us out a back corridor exit. It was terrifying."

The Green Men survived their trip to Boston, and continued to make regular appearances at Rogers Arena. In 2012 they were named to ESPN's Hall of Fans—along with two other inaugural inductees—and three years after that they decided it was time to hang up the spandex and retire.

"I'm glad that we embraced it, and that Ryan and I had the creativity and 'go for it' to embrace the suit and keep wearing it," Forsythe said. "We didn't want to be the voice of the fans, but we wanted them to give us their thoughts, and we had the platform to push those out.

"I hope someone else comes along and does something similar to what we did. We had a good run, and I hope someone takes our idea and becomes the next superfan."

96 Play Fantasy Football with Roberto Luongo

Roberto Luongo is a surefire Hall of Famer, the greatest goaltender in franchise history, and one of the best follows on Twitter. He's also a fantasy football geek. Luongo plays in multiple leagues every year. He plays with teammates, with former teammates, with team support staff, and with a group of Canucks superfans on Twitter in what is popularly referred as the Shap Football League. And if you're lucky, he'll play with you too.

"[Every year] I set up my Twitter fantasy football account and send a tweet out," Luongo explained. "I look for the most random responses. It's not anything in particular, it's whatever catches my eye that isn't just a typical response that you see, and then I'll select you [for the league]."

The fans in the league change annually. One year a prominent former Maple Leafs blogger named Jason Orachs, who goes by the Twitter handle @FelixPotvin, commissioned a bunch of his followers to pressure Luongo to admit him into the league. His efforts were ultimately rewarded.

In an age when social media has effectively flattened interactions between fans and the professional hockey players they see play in person and on TV, no major player is as accessible and as weird as Luongo is on Twitter. His unverified account @Strombone1 fundamentally altered the way players and fans interact, particularly during his lengthy trade saga, when Luongo

Legendary Canucks goalie Roberto Luongo wants to talk Shap with NHL and NFL fans.

would poke fun at himself (and his own team) with the occasional pointed jab. His tweets regularly made news and served as rallying cries for fans who declared their allegiance to #TeamLuongo.

Luongo's open-to-anyone fantasy football league is the natural evolution of that changing relationship. Not only can you tell Luongo what you think of his latest tweet—his hockey tweets are mostly self-deprecating, often including screen shots of him flubbing a save attempt in a shootout—but you can now tell him a funny joke and find yourself competing against him in the fantasy football playoffs.

This concept is taken to its most radical extreme with the Shap Football League, an annual league composed entirely of Luongo's Vancouver Twitter friends. The league includes Twitter luminaries such as the always controversial @taj1944 and a few select media members too, including *Vancouver Province* beat writer Jason Botchford. "Last year was the first year of the B pool, and Botchford came up to the A pool now, and he's been sniffing around in the short A-league life span that he's had," Luongo said.

That's right: over the years the Shap Football League has grown to include an A league and a B league. "Yeah, there's relegation," Luongo laughed. "The bottom three go down and the top three come up every year. It's pretty cool."

So who, amongst current or former Canucks players, are the sharps to be aware of? Luongo said it's mostly the team support staff that seem to have the time and effort to be annual contenders. "A lot of guys, they think they're good but they're not very good," Luongo said. "Usually it's more the PR guys, like Ben Brown and his brother have a team, Derek Jory puts in a lot of time. As far as players are concerned, Burr and the twins and those guys, they aren't very effective. [Alex] Burrows thinks he's good, but he's decent at best."

97 Boo Ryan Kesler

First, it must be said: Kesler is one of the best centers ever to play in Vancouver. His 10 seasons were dotted with significant accomplishments: a 40-goal campaign; back-to-back 70-point seasons; a stellar, unforgettable run during the 2011 playoffs—as outlined earlier—and his subsequent Selke Trophy win, snapping Pavel Datsyuk's reign as the NHL's best defensive forward. To put that last bit in perspective, consider that Kesler beat out Datysuk and *another* future Hall of Famer, Jonathan Toews, for the award.

So how, then, did Kesler become the target of boos from the Canucks faithful? Well...there's a lot to unpack. Like those halcyon days when Facebook let you describe relationships as "complicated," Kesler's relationship with Vancouver was basically that. Complicated. Very, very complicated.

It began in 2006, when the 22-year-old Kesler—coming off a modest 10-goal, 23-point sophomore campaign—signed a $1.9 million offer sheet with the Philadelphia Flyers. The move made a couple significant waves. One, signing elsewhere meant, quite obviously, that Kesler was willing to leave the city. Two, if he was to stay, the money required was more than three times Vancouver's qualifying offer, and matching it would put the team in a precarious financial situation. It was roughly $1 million more than the Canucks projected to pay Kesler, and they were already pressed up against the salary cap ceiling.

Kesler was a third-liner at the time. While high on talent and pedigree—he was a first-round pick at the 2003 draft—the pay bump was seen by many as too much too soon for a youngster who had yet to earn it. It was also the first offer sheet signed by a player since 1999, and the practice was viewed skeptically by some managerial types. One who didn't view it with such skepticism? Then–Flyers GM Bobby Clarke.

"Everyone says it's causing salaries to go up. That's crap," Clarke said at the time, per the *Globe and Mail.* "We've all got salary caps. A lot of guys in this league like rules when it suits them and they don't like them when it doesn't. Too bad for them. I'm just playing by the rules that are there."

Though clearly displeased—Clarke's brashness didn't help the matter—the Canucks ultimately matched. But it was an acrimonious incident, and it left a mark.

Four years later, Kesler was back in the spotlight. Representing the US at the Winter Olympics in Vancouver—yes, Vancouver!—the fiercely patriotic Kesler said he hated Team Canada, who the Americans beat in the group stage but ultimately fell to in the gold medal finale. The words were an albatross around Kesler's neck for the duration of his time as a Canuck, as fans took the remarks to mean he hated Canada and Canadians. Kesler, in turn, spent considerable time afterward explaining he actually didn't hate Canada or Canadians, but rather his comments merely reflected the mutual dislike between two fierce international hockey rivals.

That might've been fine, if he hadn't attempted to bolt from Vancouver four years earlier. And it might've been fine if Kesler had a less cranky disposition. And it probably would've been fine if his tenure in Vancouver didn't end like it did.

Following a disastrous 2013–14 campaign in which Vancouver missed the playoffs for the first time in five years, Kesler—then 29 years old—clearly wanted out. Reports claimed he'd requested a trade, which Kesler and agent Kurt Overhardt initially denied, but with the amount of smoke pluming, it wasn't as if the local fire department had to investigate. Everybody knew something was up.

Kesler was ready to move on, and to be honest, it was hard to blame him. The team was clearly regressing. He'd been a loyal soldier for a decade, playing his guts out for Vancouver, often grinding through nagging injuries that were a by-product of his physical, demanding style of play. He gave everything he had. Didn't he deserve a shot at joining a contender? Sure. It's just exceptionally tough—impossibly, really—for fans to appreciate.

As a result, Kesler's trade request became one of Vancouver's most engaging soap operas, at times surpassing the local housing crisis. (No small feat; I mean have you seen the real estate prices in this city?)

Eventually, the truth came out. Jim Benning, in his first significant move as Canucks GM, flipped Kesler to Anaheim, then proceeded to tell all in the aftermath, explaining that:

- Right after he took the GM gig, Kesler came to him and asked to be traded.
- Because Kesler had a no-trade clause, he controlled the process. The choices? One was Anaheim. The other, in what was a terrific heel turn, the Blackhawks—one of Vancouver's fiercest rivals at the time.
- How did Benning sum up the trade? "We don't want somebody that doesn't want to be here."

The result was Kesler being portrayed as a foil to the ultra-loyal Daniel and Henrik Sedin. The Sedins were the guys who loved Vancouver and loved being Canucks. They were the community staples who were going to stick through thick and thin. Kesler, conversely, was the guy who got going when the going got tough. Fair or not, it's how he's remembered in this city. And at no time was that more evident than on November 20, 2014, when Kesler played his first game back in Vancouver as a Duck.

Things started ominously when the organization paid him a flat, muted tribute in a short pregame ceremony. During the game, Kesler was booed throughout, cementing his status as one of the most polarizing players in franchise history.

Fittingly, it was Kesler himself who best summed up how he'd be remembered in Canucks lore. "My personality," he said. "You love me or you hate me."

98 Torts Reform

The date was June 21, 2013. The location? Vancouver International Airport. The situation? An uncomfortable one, which proved to be an uncanny bit of foreshadowing.

That day, a few local pundits and fans learned a flight containing John Tortorella—the fiery, controversial, and recently dismissed head coach of the New York Rangers—would be landing at YVR. Those same fans and pundits were there, on location, as Torts walked through the international arrivals area.

Given the major rumblings that he was in the running for Vancouver's coaching gig—vacant since Alain Vigneault was fired after eight years on the job—everybody quite rightly assumed this flight wasn't part of Tortorella's summer vacation.

But Torts wasn't about to indulge the crowd. He said nothing, answered no questions, and was quickly whisked away by a security guard who doubled as the driver of a waiting SUV. Four days later, Tortorella was named the 17th head coach in Canucks history.

It's fair to suggest the Tortorella era is worthy of a book itself—which, given it only lasted 11 months, is fairly impressive. There's a tremendous amount of material so, in order to get through it all, we will now identify and discuss *Three Things Canucks Fans Need to Know About the John Tortorella Era Before They Die.*

1. The hire in itself was wildly unconventional.

It began like an episode of *Trading Spaces*. Vancouver fired Vigneault in late May, and New York hired him 30 days later. Know what else happened in late May? The Rangers turfed Tortorella. And Vancouver hired him…27 days later.

So the Canucks and Rangers essentially made a coaching swap, which was odd in its own right. But the parallels didn't stop there. Vigneault received a lucrative deal from the Blueshirts: $10 million over five years. Tortorella got the *exact same contract* from the Canucks.

There were more weird instances to come. Right from the moment Tortorella was hired, there was widespread speculation he wasn't the first (or second…or third) choice of then-GM Gillis. That speculation boiled over late in the season, when the *Globe and Mail* penned a piece suggesting Tortorella was, rather, the No. 1 choice of the Aquilini ownership group, who felt Tortorella's brash demeanor would jump-start their underperforming hockey club, and essentially went over Gillis' head to hire him.

Chief owner Francesco Aquilini responded to these claims by texting the author of the *Globe and Mail* piece, David Ebner, calling him a prick.

That was followed by a legal letter to the *Globe and Mail* from Aquilini family counsel, alleging defamation while seeking a retraction and an apology.

So yeah, just your average, run-of-the-mill coaching hire.

2. Torts received one of the longest coaching suspensions in NHL history.

If there's a signature moment of Tortorella's time in Vancouver, it happened on January 18, 2014. That night, the Canucks hosted the Calgary Flames, who were coached by longtime Tortorella nemesis Bob Hartley. Hartley wasted little time renewing the rivalry, sending out his two toughest enforcers—Brian McGrattan and

Kevin Westgarth—for the opening faceoff. Tortorella responded by sending out his tough guys, including noted pugilist Tom Sestito.

The players responded with a massive line brawl, which resulted in 150 penalty minutes and a boatload of ejections. But that hardly put the issue to bed. An incensed Tortorella spent the remainder of the opening frame yelling obscenities at Hartley. And he wasn't done there. During the first intermission, Tortorella made his way over to the opposing dressing room and attempted to physically attack the Flames coach. Calgary players and team staff managed to keep it from happening—many with bemused smirks on their faces—but the fact Tortorella went after Hartley at all was stunning. It was a throwback to hockey's reckless past, like a scene out of *Slapshot*. It was the kind of unhinged, kneejerk, reactionary violence popularized by the Broad Street Bullies of the 1970s.

Unsurprisingly, the NHL came down hard on him. Torts was suspended for 15 days for his actions—six games in total—in which he wasn't permitted to have any interaction with his team prior to, during, or after games.

And even though Tortorella was remorseful—"I'm not proud of it," he said of the incident—that didn't prevent the NHL's VP of hockey ops, Colin Campbell, from laying down the hammer. "Mr. Tortorella's actions in attempting to enter the Calgary Flames locker room after the first period were both dangerous and an embarrassment to the league," Campbell said. "Coaches in the NHL bear the responsibility of providing leadership, even when emotions run high, and Mr. Tortorella failed in his responsibility to the game."

3. He played an integral role in the Luongo trade.

In March 2014, Vancouver played Ottawa in the Heritage Classic outdoor game at BC Place. Though the game had little effect on the standings—the Canucks were well on their way to missing the playoffs for the first time in five seasons—the event still had prestige. It was the first outdoor game in franchise history, and more than 54,000 fans were in attendance.

Explaining that rookie Eddie Lack gave the team a better chance to win, Tortorella made the controversial decision to bench starting netminder Roberto Luongo, who days earlier had expressed excitement about playing in his first-ever outdoor game.

Torts' decision bombed on all fronts. Lack was thrown into an impossible situation and struggled in the 4–2 loss, possibly due to the fact that fans began chanting "We want Lu!" midway through the second period. The bizarre goaltending decision overshadowed the entire event and, eventually, the weeks to come.

The Heritage Classic was the last time Luongo ever wore a Canucks uniform. For all he'd been through in Vancouver—the botched captaincy, the meltdown in the 2011 Cup Finals, all the complaints about his monstrous contract—getting benched by Tortorella finally sent him over the edge.

Luongo immediately demanded a trade out of Vancouver, and two days later, he got his wish. He was sent to Florida, to the same team from whom the Canucks acquired him eight years earlier.

In the aftermath, Luongo explained his side of things. "When I got back from Sochi [the 2014 Winter Olympics, where Luongo sat as a backup to Team Canada starter Carey Price], they started Eddie and I'd just got back from Russia and the time change, and they wanted to give me a rest. His first game back I think he got a shutout against the Blues, if I'm not mistaken, so the next game we're playing Minnesota and Torts goes back to Eddie.

"It wasn't my favorite decision, but I understood. He got a shutout and he wanted to give him another try. That game I think we lost in a shootout, but Eddie played really well again.

"Going into the Heritage Classic—I know going into Sochi, right before, I wasn't playing my best hockey. I was struggling a little bit. But coming back from Sochi, I was in a different mind-set. I felt fresh, I felt excited to play. I knew that I was in a good spot mentally to come back. It's a game that I've always wanted to play in. A Winter Classic or Heritage Classic. I'd never played in one. And I felt I deserved to be starting in that game. I was really surprised when I didn't get the nod."

Later, Luongo admitted Torts' decision played a crucial role in him asking out. "There's no hiding it. I did want to play that game," Luongo told CBC. "That goes without saying, and if I would have played, I probably would maybe still be here."

99 Linden's Web

Twice Linden has returned to the Canucks, and both times, the reunion was pegged as a seminal moment in franchise history. The first, as outlined in Chapter 80, returned Linden in a familiar role—as a player. The second came 13 years later, in a position far removed from the ice yet infinitely more important with regard to the direction of the franchise. On April 9, 2014, Linden became Vancouver's president of hockey operations.

Linden was introduced in his new managerial role just 24 hours after the organization fired longtime GM Mike Gillis. The Canucks were in a tailspin, to put it mildly. Though they were just three seasons removed from their Stanley Cup Finals appearance, they'd missed the playoffs for the first time in six years under head coach John Tortorella and were viewed as one of the most dysfunctional teams in the league.

Optically, the Linden hire made plenty of sense. He was arguably the most popular player in franchise history, had a lengthy stint as team captain and, following his retirement, remained in Vancouver and ran a chain of eponymous health clubs. His No. 16 hung from the rafters—the second jersey retired in franchise history—and on many nights long after his playing days were over, Linden jerseys were still being worn by the Rogers Arena faithful. In announcing the hire, owner Francesco Aquilini said Linden was "back where he belongs."

"We believe in Trevor. We believe he's the perfect person to lead this hockey club, and we're confident in his ability as a leader," Aquilini said. "He has our full trust and confidence.

"Trevor has proven over 25 years in our community that he's committed to this organization. We all remember 1994, his last game, and the leadership he showed through his role as NHLPA president. He has provided many memorable moments, and we're excited to work together to deliver even more."

The move was in lockstep with others around the NHL. There was a growing trend among owners to return popular players in high-profile executive roles: Colorado hired two-time Cup winner Joe Sakic and, after a few years, promoted him to GM; Boston brought on legendary power forward Cam Neely, eventually elevating him to team president. Ron Hextall became GM in Philly. Same with Ron Francis in Carolina.

But there was one key difference between Linden and the others. Sakic, Neely, Hextall, and Francis were groomed for their positions, and worked their way up the ranks. Linden, meanwhile, had zero NHL front-office experience prior to taking his gig (which was why, some believed, Aquilini trumpeted Linden's role as NHLPA prez in his welcome address).

Following retirement, Linden—a renowned fitness fanatic—spent plenty of time on his bike and tending to his budding fitness empire. But as far as hockey work went, there wasn't much on the résumé. By any measure, he was inexperienced in the ways of front office work and, undeniably, had a huge task ahead of him. So it didn't come as much surprise when many of his initial moves as president were predicated on a singular theme: familiarity.

Just one month after taking his post, Linden made his first major hire, bringing in Jim Benning as general manager. The ex-Bruins AGM had major ties to the Canucks and Linden—Benning spent four years as a player in Vancouver, and spent two of them skating alongside Linden.

"Trevor was a teammate 25 years ago, but when I interviewed with Trevor, I thought we shared the same values and principles," Benning said upon getting hired. "He's cut from the same cloth I am. He's going to work hard, he's going to do everything that he can to make the organization successful, so I wanted to tie myself to somebody that had the same thoughts and beliefs that I did."

The next order of business for Linden and Benning was to find a replacement for Tortorella, who had been axed weeks prior to Benning coming aboard. There were several candidates floated, but one soon emerged as the guy—57-year-old Willie Desjardins, who'd never been an NHL head coach.

Desjardins had spent years behind the bench in junior, the American League, and as an assistant in Dallas. He'd achieved a ton of success at each level, including capturing the 2004 Memorial Cup as the bench boss for WHL Medicine Hat.

Ah yes, Medicine Hat. Linden's hometown. Oh, have we not mentioned Linden was born and raised there, and helped the Tigers capture two Memorial Cups in the 1980s? It's probably also worth noting, then, that Linden met Desjardins in 2004, and spoke to his team before they won junior hockey's biggest crown.

"My mother is a big fan and a big Medicine Hat Tigers supporter and our scout in the Western Hockey League, or one of them," Linden later joked. "So we talk about hockey a lot, and she kept talking about how much she loved watching the Tigers play in [Desjardins'] years."

The web weaving didn't end there. The Canucks quickly hired an alumnus and another ex-Linden teammate, Doug Lidster, as assistant coach. Scott Walker, another of Linden's old Vancouver mates, was brought on as a player-development consultant. Jason King, who played with Linden during his second stint as a Canuck, was hired as an assistant coach for the club's AHL affiliate. In 2016 *yet another* of Linden's old teammates was brought aboard, as former Vancouver netminder Dan Cloutier—yes, the same Dan Cloutier you've read about in this very book—took over from Rollie Melanson as the team's goalies coach.

100 How Rollie the Goalie Dug Up the Graveyard

For the better part of its existence, Vancouver was the place where goalies went to die. Oh, sure, there were some good ones: Smith and Richard Brodeur, Kirk McLean and John Garrett—who, as you might've heard, played in the 1983 All-Star Game—but those few were largely overshadowed by the many netminders who came, tried, and failed. To put it succinctly, Vancouver was a goalie graveyard.

How this came to be unfolds in two parts. At first, Vancouver was just a bad place for goalies to play, period. The teams were lousy, the defense was especially lousy, and the organization lost far more often than it won. For a position in which success and failure is so often measured by statistics, the Canucks didn't exactly help goalies pad their numbers. If anything, they did the opposite.

Later on, a new wrinkle emerged in the graveyard aesthetic. As the on-ice product began to improve and Canucks teams steadily became more competitive, the goaltending was expected to follow suit. Expectations rose. Only the goaltending didn't get much better. And there wasn't just an intense amount of pressure on the goalies but also the management groups in charge of acquiring them. And acquire them they did!

If there's a "golden era" for the goalie graveyard, it's probably the decade-long stretch between 1996 and 2006. It began with the ushering out of McLean—in 1996 he and Corey Hirsch basically split duties—and soon devolved into a revolving door of prospects, veterans, trade targets, and free agents who didn't have anything in common except for one thing: none of 'em could get the job done.

Arturs Irbe, Garth Snow, Sean Burke, Kevin Weekes, Felix Potvin, Bob Essensa, Dan Cloutier, Peter Skudra, Johan Hedberg, and Alex Auld were—at one point or another—entrusted with the Canucks' crease. It is not surprising that during this 10-year span, the club only made the playoffs four times, and won just a single round.

By then, the running joke was that Vancouver had more starting goalies than days of sunshine. A new guy would show up full of promise, only to struggle and face the inevitable fan/media backlash. And with each passing goalie, the graveyard got worse.

Then two things happened. The Canucks traded for Roberto Luongo. And they hired Rollie Melanson. "He is so far and away the best goalie coach they've ever had that it was laughable," Tony Gallagher said of Melanson. "[Former GM Mike] Gillis brought him in and thought it was a tremendous upgrade, right away, and Melanson just set about making everybody a better goaltender. No question he's been the best they've ever had."

Melanson's a cultish figure in NHL circles. His playing career began like a cannon shot—he won three Stanley Cups with the Islanders before he was 23 years old—and got to work in tandem with one of the greats, Hockey Hall of Famer Billy Smith. After his time on Long Island, he bounced to four different teams before retiring in 1994, and then transitioned to the coaching side of things. That's when his reputation as "the goalie whisperer" really took off.

As an assistant with the Canadiens, he was largely credited with developing and maintaining Montreal's constant stream of talent between the pipes, specifically Jose Theodore, Jocelyn Thibault, Jaroslav Halak, Cristobal Huet, and Carey Price. (To wit: Theodore and Price are the last two goalies to capture the Hart Trophy as league MVP.)

After more than a decade in Montreal, Melanson made the move out west in 2010 to become Vancouver's full-time goaltending coach. His primary objective upon taking the gig was to work with Luongo, the organization's biggest investment. Management thought so highly of Luongo that it tried to make him captain—bending NHL rules that prevented goalies from wearing a *C* on their jerseys in the process—then inked him to a monster 12-year, $64 million deal.

But Luongo wasn't Melanson's only project. He was also tasked with the development of Cory Schneider, Vancouver's first-round pick in the 2004 draft. Schneider, who starred for Boston College and the US World Junior team, was considered one of the top young netminding prospects in all of hockey.

One year into the job, Melanson showed his worth. As far as Canucks goaltending went, the 2010–11 campaign was a historic one. Luongo won an NHL-high 38 games and finished as a Vezina finalist for the third time in his career. Schneider, meanwhile, got his first significant look as an NHL regular—starting in 22 games, going 16–4–2 with a .929 save percentage and 2.23 GAA—and combined, the pair captured the Jennings Trophy, given annually to the team with the fewest goals allowed during the regular season.

"You want to believe in what someone is teaching you for it to work," Luongo said of that first year under Melanson, per the *Hockey News*. "I believe in what Rollie is trying to teach me. The good thing about it is I'm seeing the results. That's what makes the whole thing really fun."

"He's pretty consistent on what he wants you do to, and his philosophy," Schneider added. "He drills it into your head and makes sure you execute it over and over again. Just having that consistency and that base to work from has been really important for me."

Melanson continued to work with Luongo and Schneider through the ill-fated 2011 Cup Finals—in which Schneider twice came on in relief of Luongo—and a couple more years, during which time Vancouver's strength in goal became something of a detriment. Everybody knew the club had two top-flight, bona fide No. 1 netminders—"everybody" included Luongo and Schneider—and the debate between #TeamLuongo and #TeamSchneider raged on.

Eventually one of them would have to go. Yet, amazingly, the answer to "Luongo or Schneider?" would eventually be...neither. Schneider was dealt to New Jersey in a stunner at the 2013 draft. Months later, Luongo would be traded to the Panthers in another stunner.

And that's when Melanson really went to work. One of the pieces acquired in the Luongo trade was Jacob Markstrom, a former prospect who'd fallen on hard times. He hadn't been able to establish himself as an NHL-caliber netminder with the Panthers, who opted to cut bait with Markstrom six years after making him one of the first goalies taken at the 2008 draft.

Under Melanson, Markstrom remade his game, and in his first full campaign with the Canucks, won 13 games and posted a .915 save percentage. Both career highs.

Melanson also developed a lanky, undrafted Swede in Eddie Lack. Lack arrived in Vancouver high on potential but low on experience and know-how, with little certainty he'd make it in the bigs. Yet Melanson groomed him into a capable starter, and Lack impressively backstopped the Canucks to a surprise playoff appearance in 2015 after Ryan Miller—the veteran signed by new GM Jim Benning that previous summer—went down to injury.

Miller, too, enjoyed the fruits of Melanson's labor. Arriving in Vancouver in the twilight of his career, the former Vezina winner benefitted from Melanson tweaking and adjusting his game, as well as trying to modernize his technique.

Melanson took a significant step back when, in the summer of 2016, he turned over duties to become a part-time goaltending consultant. But his work in Vancouver won't soon be forgotten. In his six years on the job, Canucks goaltenders combined to stop 91.7 percent of all shots faced, the third-best mark in the league over that span. "Melanson just did his thing," Gallagher explained. "And the goaltending has been solid ever since."

Acknowledgments

The authors wish to thank the following people for agreeing to be interviewed for this work: Nolan Baumgartner, Newell Brown, Jason Botchford, George McPhee, Roberto Luongo, Arthur Griffiths, Mike Penny, Trevor Linden, John Shorthouse, John Garrett, Tony Gallagher, Stan McCammon, Markus Naslund, Ryan Sullivan, and Adam Forsyth.

Thank you to the following individuals and organizations for their guidance and assistance on this project:

Kimber Auerbach
Miragh Bitove
Ben Brown
Rod Braithwaite
Jonatan Lindquist
Arthur Griffiths
Joe Pelletier
The Hockey Hall of Fame Archives

Sources

Books:

Banks, Kerry. *Pavel Bure: The Riddle of the Russian Rocket.* Vancouver: Greystone Books, 2001.

Beddal, Justin. *Vancouver Canucks: Heartstopping Stories from Canada's Most Exciting Team.* Victoria, BC: Altitude Publishing, 2004.

Boyd, Denny. *The Vancouver Canucks Story.* Whitby, Ontario: McGraw-Hill Ryerson Limited, 1973.

Dowbiggin, Bruce. *Ice Storm: The Rise and Fall of the Greatest Vancouver Canucks Team Ever.* Vancouver: Greystone Books, 2014.

Farris, Jason. *Behind the Moves: NHL General Managers Tell How Winners Are Built.* Vancouver: Ciranow Productions, 2011.

Gallagher, Tony and Mike Gasher. *Towels, Triumph and Tears: The Vancouver Canucks' Amazing Drive to the Stanley Cup Finals.* Pender Harbour, BC: Harbour Publishing Co. Ltd., 1982.

Kerr, Grant. *A Season to Remember: The Vancouver Canucks' Incredible 40th Year.* Pender Harbour, BC: Harbour Publishing Co. Ltd., 2011.

Robson, Dan. *Quinn: The Life of a Hockey Legend.* Toronto: Penguin Canada, 2015.

Williams, Tiger with James Lawton. *Tiger: A Hockey Story.* Vancouver: Douglas & McIntyre, 1984.

Newspapers/Magazines/Agencies:

Associated Press

Buffalo News

Canadian Press

Globe and Mail

Hockey News
Miami Herald
National Post
New York Times
Sports Illustrated
Times Colonist
Toronto Star
Toronto Sun
Vancouver Province
Vancouver Sun
UPI

Websites:

buffalosabres.com
canucks.com
canucksarmy.com
cbc.ca
espn.com
greatesthockeylegends.com
hhof.com
hockeydb.com
hockey-reference.com
nhl.com
nytimes.com
passittobulis.com
SI.com
twitter.com
upi.com

Personal Interviews:

Nolan Baumgartner, Jason Botchford, Newell Brown, Adam Forsyth, Tony Gallagher, John Garrett, Arthur Griffiths, Trevor Linden, Roberto Luongo, Stan McCammon, George McPhee, Markus Naslund, Mike Penny, John Shorthouse, and Ryan Sullivan.